Marine Insurance Law of Canada

Marine Insurance Law of Canada

Rui M. Fernandes, B.Sc., LL.B., LL.M.,
Member of the Ontario Bar
Partner with the firm Beard, Winter
(Toronto)

Butterworths
Toronto and Vancouver

Marine Insurance Law of Canada

© 1987 Butterworths, A division of Reed Inc.,

Printed and bound in Canada

The Butterworth Group of Companies
Canada
Butterworths, Toronto and Vancouver
United Kingdom
Butterworth & Co. (Publishers) Ltd., London and Edinburgh
Australia
Butterworth Pty Ltd., Sydney, Melbourne, Brisbane, Adelaide and Perth
New Zealand
Butterworths (New Zealand) Ltd., Wellington and Auckland
Singapore
Butterworth & Co. (Asia) Pte. Ltd., Singapore
South Africa
Butterworth Publishers (SA) (Pty) Ltd., Durban and Pretoria
United States
Butterworth Legal Publishers, Boston, Seattle, Austin and St. Paul
D&S Publishers, Clearwater

Canadian Cataloguing in Publication Data

Fernandes, Rui M.
  Marine insurance law of Canada

Includes index.
ISBN 0-409-80531-9

1. Insurance, Marine — Canada.   2. Insurance law — Canada.
3. Maritime law — Canada.
I. Title.

KE1135.F47 1987   346.71'0862   C87-093805-3

Executive Editor (P. & A.): Lebby Hines
Sponsoring Editor: Derek Lundy
Managing Editor: Linda Kee
Supervisory Editor: Marie Graham
Freelance Projects Coordinator/Cover Design: Joan Chaplin
Production: Jill Thomson

Preface

This book arose out of the desire to provide students and practitioners with a text dealing strictly with the law of marine insurance as it exists in Canada.

The provincial statutes dealing with marine insurance have their roots in the United Kingdom's *Marine Insurance Act, 1906*. In fact, provincial statutes such as Ontario's *Marine Insurance Act*, R.S.O. 1980, c. 255, are word for word duplications of the English *Marine Insurance Act* of 1906.

There exist excellent texts for the English Act but there has not been any text written in the last fifty years that deals with Canadian case law on this subject. I have endeavoured in this text to start to fill this gap. As this is a new text, I welcome any comments and suggestions from the reader. These may be sent to my publishers who will forward them to me.

The book deals with Canadian judicial decisions in marine insurance. The *Marine Insurance Act*, R.S.O. 1980, c. 255, is used as the basis for the structure of the text. There is a table of statute concordance which is included to assist readers in other jurisdictions.

I wish to express my thanks to my publishers, Butterworths, especially Derek Lundy, and Linda Kee. I also wish to thank my family and my firm for their support during the preparation of the manuscript.

Table of Contents

Marine Insurance Act

R.S.O. 1980, c. 255

Compilation

Insurable Value

Disclosure and Representations

The Policy

Double Insurance

Warranties, Etc.

The Voyage

Assignment of Policy

Premium

Loss and Abandonment

Partial Losses
(Including Salvage and General Average and Particular Charges)

Measure of Indemnity

Rights of Insurer on Payment

Table of Cases

A

C

D

E

F

G

H

I

J

N

O

P

Q

R

S

T

V

W

X

Y

Z

Table of Statutes

Concordance

	Ont.	U.K.	B.C.	Man.	N.B.	N.S
Interpretation	1	90	1	2	1	184
Marine Insurance defined	2	1	2	3	2	185
Mixed sea, land and air risks	3	2	3	4	3	186
Marine adventure subject of contract	4	3	4	5	4	187
Wagering or gaming contracts void	5	4	5	6	5	188
Insurable interest	6	5	6	7	6	189
When interest must attach	7	6	7	8	7	190
Defeasible or contingent interests	8	7	8	9	8	191
Partial interest	9	8	9	10	9	192
Reinsurance	10	9	10	11	10	193
Bottomry	11	10	11	12	11	194
Master's and seaman's wages	12	11	12	13	12	195
Advance Freight	13	12	13	14	13	196
Charges of Insurance	14	13	14	15	14	197
Quantum of interest	15	14	15	16	15	198
Assignment of interest	16	15	16	17	16	199
Measure of insurable value	17	16	17	18	17	200
Insurance is uberrimae fidei	18	17	18	19	18	201
Disclosure by assured	19	18	19	20	19	202
Disclosure by agent affecting insurance	20	19	20	21	20	203
Representations pending negotiation of contract	21	20	21	22	21	204
When contract is deemed to be concluded	22	21	22	23	22	205
Contract must be embodied in policy	23	22	23	24	23	206
What policy must specify	24	23	24	25	24	207
Signature of insurer	25	24	25	26	25	208
Voyage and time policies	26	25	26	27	26	209
Designation of subject matter	27	26	27	28	27	210
Valued policy or unvalued	28	27	28	29	28	211
Unvalued policy	29	28	29	30	29	212

Table of Abbreviations

A.C. — Law Reports, Appeal Cases
A.C.W.S. — All Canada Weekly Summaries
All E.R. Rep. — All England Law Reports Reprint
B. & S. — Best and Smith's Reports, Queen's Bench
B.C.C.A. — British Columbia Court of Appeal
B.C.L.R. — British Columbia Law Reports
B.C.S.C. — British Columbia Supreme Court
B.R. — Cour du Banc de la Reine/Roi
C.A. — Court of Appeal
Cass. S.C. — Cassels' Supreme Court Decisions
C.C.L.I. — Canadian Cases on the Law of Insurance
C.C.L.T. — Canadian Cases on the Law of Torts
C.P. — Upper Canada Common Pleas
C.R.C. — Consolidated Regulations of Canada
C.R.T.C. — Canadian Railway and Transport Cases
C.S. — Quebec Official Reports, Superior Court
D.L.R. — Dominion Law Reports
E. & B. — Ellis and Blackburn's Reports, Queen's Bench
E.L.R. — Eastern Law Reporter
Ex. C.R. — Canadian Exchequer Court Reports
F.C. — Canada Federal Court Reports
F.C.A. — Federal Court of Appeal
F.C.T.D. — Federal Court Trial Division
G.R. — Upper Canada Chancery (Grant)
H.L. — House of Lords
I.L.R. — Insurance Law Reporter
J.C.P.C. — Judicial Committee of the Privy Council
K.B. — Law Reports, King's Bench Division
K.B.D. — King's Bench Division
L.C.J. — Lower Canada Jurist
L.C. Jur. — Lower Canada Jurist
L.C.R. — Lower Canada Reports
Lloyd's L.L.R. — Lloyd's Law List Reports
Lloyd's Rep. — Lloyd's Law Reports
L.R.P.C. — Law Reports Privy Council Appeals
Moo. P.C. — Moore, Privy Council
Moo. P.C. N.S. — Moore, (N.S.) Privy Council
N.B.C.A. — New Brunswick Court of Appeal
N.B.R. — New Brunswick Reports
N.B.S.C. — New Brunswick Supreme Court

Nfld. C.A. — Newfoundland Court of Appeal
Nfld. S.C. — Newfoundland Supreme Court
N.R. — National Reporter
N.S.C.A. — Nova Scotia Court of Appeal
N.S.R. — Nova Scotia Reports
N.S.S.C. — Nova Scotia Supreme Court
O.A.R. — Ontario Appeal Reports
O.L.R. — Ontario Law Reports, 1901-1930
Ont. C.A. — Ontario Court of Appeal
Ont. Co. Ct. — Ontario County Court
Ont. H.C.J. — Ontario High Court of Justice
O.R. — Ontario Reports
O.S. — Upper Canada, Queen's Bench Old Series
P.C. — Privy Council
P.E.I. — Prince Edward Island Reports
Q.B.D. — Queen's Bench Division
Q.L.R. — Quebec Law Reports
Q.K.B. — Quebec Official Reports (King's Bench)
Q.R. — Rapports Judiciaries de Quebec
Q.S.C. — Quebec Official Reports, Superior Court
(Q.S.C.) — Quebec Superior Court
R.E.D. — Russell's Equity Decisions
R.S.B.C. — Revised Statutes of British Columbia
R.S.C. — Revised Statutes of Canada
R.S.M. — Revised Statutes of Manitoba
R.S.N.B. — Revised Statutes of New Brunswick
R.S.N.S. — Revised Statutes of Nova Scotia
R.S.O. — Revised Statutes of Ontario
S.C.C. — Supreme Court of Ontario
S.C.R — Reports of the Supreme Court of Canada; Canada Law
          Reports, Supreme Court of Canada
U.C.C.P. — Upper Canada Common Pleas
U.C.Q.B. — Upper Canada Queen's Bench
W.W.R. — Western Weekly Reports

1

Introduction

In Canada marine insurance falls within the realm of power of the provincial legislature. Six provinces have legislation dealing specifically with marine insurance. They are as follows:

Ontario: *Marine Insurance Act*, R.S.O. 1980, c. 255.
Quebec: *Civil Code*, arts. 2606 to 2692.
Nova Scotia: *Insurance Act*, R.S.N.S. 1967, c. 148 (Part IX).
British Columbia: *Insurance (Marine) Act*, R.S.B.C. 1979, c. 203.
New Brunswick: *Marine Insurance Act*, R.S.N.B. 1973, c. M-1.
Manitoba: *Marine Insurance Act*, R.S.M. 1970, c. M40.

In Saskatchewan, Alberta and Prince Edward Island, marine insurance contracts fall under legislation dealing with insurance generally.

The legislation in Ontario, Manitoba, New Brunswick, Nova Scotia and British Columbia is essentially a duplication of the marine insurance legislation which originated and still exists in the United Kingdom today; that is, *An Act to Codify the Law Relating to Marine Insurance*,[1] or the *Marine Insurance Act, 1906*, as it is commonly known. The *Marine Insurance Act, 1906*, is largely a codification of the common law existing at that date. Justice Lambert of the British Columbia Court of Appeal has warned:[2]

> [I]n considering the cases it is important to bear in mind whether they were decided before or after the passage of the *Marine Insurance Act*. The 19th century cases reveal why the particular wording of the codification was chosen and the 20th century cases explain the way it should be applied.

In considering Canadian decisions it should also be noted that the provinces adopted the English codification at different times.

In the provinces that have specific legislation dealing with marine insurance, marine insurance is generally excluded from the legislation pertaining to other types of insurance. For example, s. 120(1) of the *Insurance Act*,[3] specifically excludes the application

---

1. 6 Edw. 7, c. 41 (U.K.).
2. *Case Existological Laboratories Ltd. v. Foremost Insurance Co. et al.*, 133 D.L.R. (3d) 727, at 733, [1982] I.L.R. 1-156 (B.C. C.A.), affd [1983] 2 S.C.R. 47 (*sub nom. Century Insurance Co. of Canada v. Case Existological Laboratories*), 150 D.L.R. (3d) 9.
3. R.S.O. 1980, c. 218.

of the fire provisions of the *Insurance Act* to marine insurance. Marine insurance is defined in s. 1, par. 38[4] of the *Insurance Act*. In *James Staples v. Great American Insurance Co., New York*[5] a motor yacht was insured against perils of the seas and waters as well as fire. The boat was lost by fire on an inland Ontario lake. The insurer contended that the contract was a policy of fire insurance and subject to the statutory conditions of the Ontario *Insurance Act*.[6] However, the Supreme Court of Canada found that the policy was not subject to the provisions of the Ontario *Insurance Act*[7] that dealt with fire insurance. Justice Kerwin, speaking for the court, stated:[8]

> Loss by fire was a risk insured against but the mere reading of the policy demonstrates that this was insurance incidental to some other class of insurance... The contract was one of insurance against losses incident to marine adventure... [T]he insurance against loss by fire was incidental to marine insurance and, therefore, not within the definition of "fire insurance" in subsection 23 of section 1. The statutory conditions do not apply and need not be considered.

---

4. See s. 1, par. 38:

    38. "marine insurance" means insurance against,

    (a) liability arising out of,

    (i) bodily injury to or death of a person, or
    (ii) the loss of or damage to properties; or

    (b) the loss of or damage to property,

    occurring during a voyage or marine adventure at sea or on an inland waterway or during delay incidental thereto, or during transit otherwise than by water incidental to such a voyage or marine adventure.
5. [1941] S.C.R. 213, [1941] 2 D.L.R. 1, 8 I.L.R. 98.
6. R.S.O. 1927, c. 222.
7. *Ibid.*
8. *Supra*, note 5 at 218-19, S.C.R.

Interpretation and Jurisdiction of Courts

Marine Insurance Act, R.S.O 1980, c. 255, s. 1: In this Act, unless the context otherwise requires,
(*a*) [rep. 1984, c. 11, s. 192]
(*b*) "freight" includes the profit derivable by a shipowner from the employment of his ship to carry his own goods or movables, as well as freight payable by a third party, but does not include passage-money;
(*c*) "movables" means any movable tangible property, other than the ship, and includes money, valuable securities and other documents;
(*d*) "policy" means a marine policy.

s. 2: A contract of marine insurance is a contract whereby the insurer undertakes to indemnify the assured, in manner and to the extent thereby agreed, against marine losses, that is to say, the losses incident to marine adventure.

A marine insurance contract is substantially a contract of indemnity. Ideally an assured is entitled to be compensated to the precise extent of his pecuniary loss. Thus, where a shipper was unable to sell wheat due to its excessive moisture content as a result of rain during a voyage, the insurer was liable for the depreciation.[1]

There are occasions when there is a departure from the principle of indemnity: that is to say, one may sometimes recover less than the loss and sometimes one may recover more than the loss. It depends on the contract entered into by the parties.[2] Where the parties are *ad item* as to all the essential terms of an agreement and there is an offer and an unequivocal acceptance, a court will accept that a complete contract of insurance has been created.[3]

A policy of marine insurance is a "maritime contract" and therefore an action on such a contract is within the jurisdiction of the Federal Court of Canada. This was the result arrived at in *Intermunicipal Realty & Development Corp. v. Gore Mutual Insurance Co.*[4] Justice Gibson of the Federal Court, Trial Division reviewed

---

1. See *James Richardson & Sons, Ltd. v. Standard Marine Ins. Co.*, [1936] S.C.R. 573, [1936] 3 D.L.R. 513, 3 I.L.R. 494.
2. See the comments of Justice MacKinnon in the English decision of *Goole and Hull Steam Towing Co., Ltd. v. Ocean Marine Insurance Co., Ltd.*, [1928] 1 K.B. 589, [1927] All E.R. Rep. 621.
3. *Osborne v. The Queen, in right of Canada*, [1984] I.L.R. 1-1724 (F.C. T.D.).
4. [1978] 2 F.C. 691, 108 D.L.R. (3d) 494, [1979] I.L.R. 1-1114 (T.D.). An action against an insurance agent for breach of duty, however, is not within the jurisdiction of the Federal Court.

the jurisprudence and concluded that: "As to whether these policies are 'maritime contracts', apparently there is practically universal agreement".[5]

The jurisdiction of the Federal Court in marine insurance matters has been confirmed by the Supreme Court of Canada in *Zavarovalna Skupnost Triglav (Insurance Community Triglav Ltd.) v. Terrasses Jewellers Inc. et al.*[6] The respondent, Terrasses Jewellers Inc., was the consignee of jewellery imported from Yugoslavia. The respondent insured the shipment with the appellant insurer, a Yugoslavian company. The appellant challenged the constitutionality of s. 22(2)(r) of the *Federal Court Act*[7] and the jurisdiction of Federal Court over the appellant. In holding that s. 22(2)(r) is valid federal legislation Justice Chouinard, speaking for the court, stated:[8]

> In my opinion, the Attorney General of Canada is correct in regarding marine insurance as a matter falling within property and civil rights, strictly speaking, but one which has nonetheless been assigned to Parliament as a part of navigation and shipping. The same is true, for example, of bills of exchange and promissory notes, which form part of property and civil rights, but jurisdiction over which was assigned to Parliament by subs. 18 of s. 91 of the *Constitution Act, 1867.*

The court found that "marine insurance, which proceeded other forms of insurance by several centuries, originated as an integral part of maritime law."[9]

Justice Chouinard reviewed briefly the history of marine insurance and distinguished it from other types of insurance.[10]

> It is wrong in my opinion to treat marine insurance in the same way as the other forms of insurance which are derived from it, and from which it would be distinguishable only by its object, a maritime venture. It is also incorrect to say that marine insurance does not form part of the activities of navigation and shipping, and that, although applied to activities of this nature, it remains a part of insurance.
>
> Marine insurance is first and foremost a contract of maritime law. It is not an application of insurance to the maritime area. Rather, it is the other forms of insurance which are applications to other areas of principles borrowed from marine insurance.
>
> I am of the opinion that marine insurance is part of the maritime law over which s. 22 of the *Federal Court Act* confers concurrent jurisdiction on that Court.... I am further of the opinion that marine insurance is contained within the power of Parliament over navigation and shipping.

---

5. *Ibid.*, at 694, F.C.
6. [1983] 1 S.C.R. 283, 54 N.R. 321, [1983] I.L.R. 1-1627.
7. R.S.C. 1970, c. 10 (2nd Supp.).
8. *Supra*, note 6 at 292.
9. *Supra*, at 293.
10. *Supra*, at 298.

In *Gould v. Cornhill Insurance Co. Ltd.*[11] the jurisdiction of the District Court to try claims arising under policies of marine insurance was challenged. The trial judge found that a vessel which filled with water and sank while at sea was lost by a peril of the sea. The insurer, on appeal, argued that the subject-matter of the action was maritime or admiralty law and the District Court was without jurisdiction to hear the matter. Justice Gushue of the Newfoundland Court of Appeal, rendering the judgment of the Court and dismissing the appeal, stated:[12]

> [I] am satisfied that, at the time of Confederation, the Supreme Court of Newfoundland in its common law jurisdiction was competent to try claims arising under policies of marine insurance and that jurisdiction has not been varied.
>
> A thorough research into the practice in England reveals that, invariably, actions on marine policies have been taken in King's Bench or Queen's Bench Division and not in the Admiralty Division. The same is true of actions in the provinces of Canada. Further, prior to Confederation, such actions in Newfoundland were not taken on the admiralty side, but were taken as any ordinary action in contract. . . . [I]t is sufficient to say that by the year 1720 the settlement of marine insurance claims had been assumed by the common law courts.

---

11. 1 D.L.R. (4th) 183, [1983] I.L.R. 1-1715, 2 C.C.L.I. 148 (Nfld. C.A.).
12. *Ibid.*, at 186, D.L.R.

3

What May Be Insured

s. 3: (1) A contract of marine insurance may, by it express terms or usage of the trade, be written so as to protect the assured against losses on inland waters, or may be extended so as to protect the assured against losses on any land or air risk that may be incidental to any sea or inland water voyage.

(2) Where a ship in course of building, or the launch of a ship, or any adventure analogous to a marine adventure, is covered by a policy in the form of a marine policy, the provisions of this Act, in so far as applicable, apply thereto; but, except as provided by this section, nothing in this Act alters or affects any rule of law applicable to any contract of insurance other than a contract of marine insurance as defined by this Act.

s. 4: (1) Subject to the provisions of this Act, every lawful marine adventure may be the subject of a contract of marine insurance.

(2) In particular there is a marine adventure where,

(a) any ship, goods, or other movables are exposed to maritime perils and such property is in this Act referred to as "insurable property";

(b) the earning or acquisition of any freight, passage money, commission, profit or other pecuniary benefit, or the security for any advances, loan, or disbursements, is endangered by the exposure of insurable property to maritime perils;

(c) any liability to a third party may be incurred by the owner of, or other person interested in or responsible for, insurable property by reason of maritime perils.

(3) "Maritime perils" means the perils consequent on or incidental to the navigation of the sea, that is to say, perils of the seas, fire, war perils, pirates, rovers, thieves, captures, seizures, restraints and detainments of princes and peoples, jettisons, barratry, and any other perils, either of the like kind or which may be designated by the policy.

A marine insurance contract may be made on ships, on goods, on freight, on liabilities to third parties, on bottomry and respondentia bonds, on master's and seamen's wages, on mortgage and loan monies, on premiums of insurance, on passage money, on commissions, on profits, and on disbursements which are exposed to the risk of navigation upon a lawful marine adventure.[1]

A marine policy may cover a risk on inland waters. Where a

---

1. See ss. 4, 11, 12, 13, 14, and 15 of the *Marine Insurance Act*, R.S.O. 1980, c. 255.

yacht was destroyed by fire on an Ontario inland lake the insurer was liable for the loss. The contract was not a policy of fire insurance as contended by the insurer but was one of insurance against losses incidental to a marine adventure and hence a policy of marine insurance.[2]

A marine policy may cover a risk on land or in the air during part of the voyage. Thus, where grain was unloaded from a vessel and stored in an elevator and was lost on the destruction of the elevator by fire the court treated the policy as marine.[3] Justice Britton of the Ontario Supreme Court stated:[4]

> It seems to me a very reasonable thing to treat this policy as marine, whatever liabilities might attach or whatever exemption from or limitation of liability may follow. In greater part it was marine....
>
> A marine policy may cover a risk on land during part of the voyage: *Rodocanachi v. Elliot* (1873), L.R. 8 C.P. 649.

---

2. *James Staples v. Great American Insurance Company, New York*, [1941] S.C.R. 213, [1941] 2 D.L.R. 1, 8 I.L.R. 98.
3. *Richardson v. Canadian Pacific R. Co.* (1914), 20 D.L.R. 580, 7 O.W.N 458 (S.C.) (on appeal, new trial ordered, 8 O.W.N. 221).
4. *Ibid.*, at 583, D.L.R.

4

Insurable Interest

s. 5: (1) Every contract of marine insurance by way of gaming or wagering is void.

(2) A contract of marine insurance is deemed to be a gaming or wagering contract,

(*a*) where the assured has not an insurable interest as defined by this Act, and the contract is entered into with no expectation of acquiring such an interest; or

(*b*) where the policy is made "interest or no interest", or "without further proof of interest than the policy itself", or "without benefit of salvage to the insurer", or subject to any other like term, provided that where there is no possibility of salvage, a policy may be effected without benefit of salvage to the insurer.

s. 6: (1) Subject to the provisions of this Act, every person has an insurable interest who is interested in a marine adventure.

(2) In particular a person is interested in a marine adventure where he stands in any legal or equitable relation to the adventure or to any insurable property at risk therein, in consequence of which he may benefit by the safety or due arrival of insurable property, or may be prejudiced by its loss or by damage thereto or by the detention thereof, or may incur liability in respect thereof.

s. 7: (1) The assured must be interested in the subject-matter insured at the time of the loss though he need not be interested when the insurance is effected; provided that, where the subject-matter is insured "lost or not lost", the assured may recover although he may not have acquired his interest until after the loss, unless at the time of effecting the contract of insurance the assured was aware of the loss and the insurer was not.

(2) Where the assured has no interest at the time of the loss, he cannot acquire interest by any act or election after he is aware of the loss.

s. 8: (1) A defeasible interest and a contingent interest are insurable.

(2) In particular, where the buyer of goods has insured them, he has an insurable interest, notwithstanding that he might, at his election, have rejected the goods, or have treated them as at the seller's risk, by reason of the latter's delay in making delivery or otherwise.

s. 9: A partial interest of any nature is insurable.

s. 10: (1) The insurer under a contract of marine insurance has an insurable interest in his risk and may reinsure in respect of it.

(2) Unless the policy otherwise provides, the original assured has no right or interest in respect of such reinsurance.

s. 11: The lender of money on bottomry or respondentia has an insurable interest in respect of the loan.

s. 12: The master or any member of the crew of a ship has an insurable interest in respect of his wages.

s. 13: In the case of advance freight, the person advancing the freight has an insurable interest, in so far as such freight is not repayable in case of loss.

s. 14: The assured has an insurable interest in the charges of any insurance that he may effect.

s. 15: (1) Where the subject-matter insured is mortgaged, the mortgagor has an insurable interest in the full value thereof, and the mortgagee has an insurable interest in respect of any sum due or to become due under the mortgage.
(2) A mortgagee, consignee, or other person having an interest in the subject-matter insured may insure on behalf and for the benefit of other persons interested as well as for his own benefit.
(3) The owner of insurable property has an insurable interest in respect of the full value thereof, notwithstanding that some third person may have agreed, or be liable, to indemnify him in case of loss.

s. 16: Where the assured assigns or otherwise parts with his interest in the subject-matter insured, he does not thereby transfer to the assignee his rights under the contract of insurance, unless there is an express or implied agreement with the assignee to that effect; but the provisions of this section do not affect a transmission of interest by operation of law.

In order to benefit from a contract of marine insurance an individual must have an insurable interest in the subject-matter insured. An insurable interest is any interest which would be recognized by a court of law or equity. Thus, in *Clark v. Scottish Imperial Insurance Co.*,[1] where an assured had advanced funds to a shipbuilder on a vessel still unfinished and in the possession of the shipbuilder, the assured was found to have an insurable interest in the vessel. Justice Henry stated:[2]

---

1. (1879), 4 S.C.R. 192.
2. *Ibid.*, at 212-13.

The doctrine, that under the circumstances of this case an equitable lien existed, is so firmly established and unequivocally recognized by so many authorities that it cannot now be questioned.

.....

It is equally well settled that a party has a right to insure property over which he has an equitable lien; and if a party goes to an insurance company, and offers to have such an interest insured and they take the risk, the contract is valid.... Neither the actual or constructive possession of the property is necessary to be in the insure[d], either at the time of issue of the policy or when the loss insured against takes place. It is sufficient if he have an equitable lien on specific chattel property covered by the policy.

(1) "For whom it may concern"

A party may insure property "for whom it may concern". In *McGhee v. Phoenix Insurance Co.*,[3] a vessel was owned by a firm consisting of three partners, but was registered in the name of one of them and was insured "for whom it might concern". The court found that any one of the three partners had a right to insure the interest of the partnership and any payment made to one would have been a good payment. One partner was held to be the agent of the other members of the partnership in obtaining the insurance.

Similarly, where a part owner of a vessel obtained coverage for himself and "for whom it may concern" the insurance contract was valid, and he did not need to disclose the interest really insured.[4]

It follows that an undisclosed principal may sue and be sued on a policy made by an agent in his own name.[5]

It has been held, however, that where the words "for whom it may concern" are omitted in a policy taken out by an individual for the benefit of another, the party for whose benefit the insurance was obtained will not be able to sue on the policy.[6]

On the other hand, it has been held that where in an application form the question "on whose account is the insurance to be made?" is left blank and the policy is issued it will be interpreted as issued "for whom it may concern".[7]

In interpreting the wording of a policy, to determine if there exists an insurable interest, the court will read the words in conjunction with the context and the rest of the policy in such a way,

---

3. (1889), 28 N.B.R. 45 (C.A.); appeal allowed, case remitted to court below 18 S.C.R. 61.
4. *Merchants' Marine Insurance Co. v. Barss* (1888), 15 S.C.R. 185.
5. *Browning v. Provincial Insurance Co. of Can.*, (1873), 5 L.R.P.C. 263.
6. *McCollum v. Aetna Insurance Co.* (1870), 20 U.C.C.P. 289 (C.A.).
7. *Cunard et al. v. N.S. Marine Insurance Co.* (1897), 29 N.S.R. 409 (C.A.). "The underwriters may require to know who the principles are, and, in some cases, they may not. In my opinion, speaking from experience, they waive the answer when they accept the risk without insisting upon the questions being answered." (*Per* Graham E. J., at 412).

if possible, as to be valid and effectual and not in such a way as to be void.[8]

A shipbuilding company which is owed money on the sale of a vessel has an insurable interest on the vessel and may take out a policy "for the account of concerned".[9]

In *West v. Seaman*[10] a ship's husband, who was also a mortgagee of the vessel, insured the vessel "for the benefit of all concerned" under the authority of the owners of the vessel. The court held that the ship's husband in these circumstances was under no obligation to disclose his individual interest to the underwriters.

(2) Mortgagees

A party who has a mortgage on a vessel has an insurable interest in the vessel to the amount of the mortgage.[11]

A mortgagee who had assigned his interest to a bank by endorsement on the mortgage as a collateral for a pre-existing debt with the bank insured his interest. The vessel struck a reef during a voyage and was damaged. The insurer argued that the mortgagee had no interest in the vessel. The Supreme Court of Canada found that the mortgagee did not know the vessel was already damaged when he placed the insurance and further held that the mortgagee's assignment did not divest him of all interest in the vessel so as to disentitle him to recover.[12]

(3) Shippers and Consignees of Goods

A supplier of goods on a trading voyage has an insurable interest in the property. In *Merchants' Marine Insurance Co. v. Rumsey*[13] an assured had an agreement with the charterers of a ship, a joint venture being contemplated, that they were to have control of all goods until the return of the ship. They were as well to have control of the goods exchanged. The Supreme Court of Canada held that the assured had an insurable interest in the property, including goods loaded at intermediate ports.

A consignee of cargo may have an insurable interest in the cargo.[14]

---

8. *British America Assurance Co. v. William Law & Co.* (1892), 21 S.C.R. 325.
9. *Queen Insurance Co. of America v. Hoffar-Beeching Shipyards Ltd.*, 46 B.C.R. 233, [1932] 3 W.W.R. 240 (S.C.).
10. (1885), Cass. S.C. 219.
11. *Crawford v. St. Lawrence Insurance Co.* (1851), 8 U.C.Q.B. 135 (C.A.).
12. *Anchor Marine Insurance Co. v. Keith* (1884), 9 S.C.R. 483.
13. (1884), 9 S.C.R. 577.
14. *Cusack v. Mutual Insurance Co.* (1862), 6 L.C. Jur. 97, 10 R.J.R.Q. 194.

A shipper of goods who has sold those goods to a buyer and has shipped them on board a vessel to the buyer may no longer have an insurable interest in those goods. The question for the court to determine is whether the property has vested in the buyer at the time of the loss.[15]

Justice Addy in *Green Forest Lumber Ltd. v. General Security Insurance Co. of Can.*[16] has tied the principle of insurable interest to the "passing of the risk". He states:[17]

> In my view, however, there might in certain circumstances be a distinction drawn between the case of a purchaser contracting for a shipment of goods or of a specific cargo on a c.i.f. basis and that of a purchaser contracting to buy quantity of goods c.i.f., which may be sent in as many loads or shipments as the vendor might decide. In the former case, the risk does not pass to the buyer until the ship is completely loaded and the cargo contracted for complete, while in the latter, the risk might very well be held to pass as each part of the total amount of goods purchased is loaded aboard a ship for shipment to the purchaser.
>
> . . . . .
>
> In the present case the contract . . . called for the quantity of wood purchased to be furnished . . . "in two shipments". The first shipment had already been sent and therefore the total quantity remaining to be shipped had to be loaded aboard the *Elarkadia*. Until the total amount of lumber remaining was loaded aboard the ship, the lumber loaded aboard did not constitute a shipment and the risk did not pass to the purchaser. There, therefore, remained in the plaintiff until the entire cargo was loaded, an insurable interest in the lumber which had been stowed aboard and which was no longer at the risk of the mill owners . . .

(4) Freight

A vessel owner has an insurable interest in freight.[18] Such freight however must be specifically insured.[19]

Where a policy of insurance on freight contains the following words "which insurance is hereby declared to be upon freight . . . at and from Pictou, to and at Aspinwall" such freight will be recoverable from underwriters if "the voyage commenced, and that the ship was ready to take in the cargo".[20]

Where a party has no interest in a vessel or in her cargo he cannot create an insurable interest in the freight by spontaneously

15. See *Outram v. Smith* (1876), 11 N.S.R. 187 (C.A.) and also *Pugh v. Wylde* (1876), 11 N.S.R. 177 (C.A.).
16. [1977] 2 F.C. 351, [1977] I.L.R. 1-849; affd [1978] 2 F.C. 773, [1978] I.L.R. 1-990 (C.A.); affd [1980] 1 S.C.R. 176, 34 N.R. 303, [1981] I.L.R. 1-1332.
17. *Ibid.*, at 361-62, [1977] 2 F.C.
18. *Driscoll v. Millville Marine Insurance Co.* (1883), 23 N.B.R. 160 (C.A.); revd 11 S.C.R. 183 and *Wylde v. Union Marine Insurance Co.* (1875), 10 N.S.R. 205 (C.A.).
19. *Heard and Hall v. Marine Insurance Co.* (1873), 1 P.E.I. 428.
20. *Lord v. Grant* (1875), 10 N.S.R. 120 at 125 (C.A.) (McDonald J.A.).

advancing such freight to the shipowner.[21] Chief Justice Macaulay in *Orchard v. Aetna Insurance Co.* outlines the difficulty of a party in such a position.[22]

> [H]e must shew that he is the person named in and by the policy, insured, or the person beneficially interested in the insurance in a way that entitles him to sue upon the policy.... Then, to sustain the action in respect of his interest in the subject matter, the plaintiff must shew that he had an insurable interest in the freight. He does not shew that he possessed such an interest as owner of the vessel; and the only other way by which he could have acquired an insurable interest therein would be by proving that as shipper or owner of the goods he had advanced the whole or a portion of the freight, as freight, to the owner or charterer of the vessel in anticipation of its being earned, but before it was earned; and that such advances were made strictly on account of and in part payment of the freight expected to be earned and to become due, and without recourse against the owner or charterer of the vessel personally. It must bear analogy to *bottomry* or *respondentia loans*, in which the advance is put in hazard and risked upon the success of the adventure or expected voyage. Here the plaintiff was not owner of either the vessel or goods; nor did he ship the goods as shipper or carrier.

---

21. *Orchard v. Aetna Insurance Co.* (1856), 5 U.C.C.P. 445 (C.A.).
22. *Ibid.*, at 449-50.

5

Insurable Value

s. 17: Subject to any express provision or valuation in the policy, the insurable value of the subject-matter insured must be ascertained as follows:

1. In insurance on ship, the insurable value is the value, at the commencement of the risk, of the ship, including her outfit, provisions and stores for the officers and crew, money advanced for seamen's wages, and other disbursements, if any, incurred to make the ship fit for the voyage or adventure contemplated by the policy, plus the charges of insurance upon the whole, and the insurable value, in the case of a steamship, includes also the machinery, boilers, and coals, oils, and engine stores if owned by the assured, and, in the case of a ship engaged in a special trade, the ordinary fittings requisite for that trade.

2. In insurance on freight, whether paid in advance or otherwise, the insurable value is the gross amount of the freight at the risk of the assured, plus the charges of insurance.

3. In insurance on goods or merchandise, the insurable value is the prime cost of the property insured, plus the expenses of and incidental to shipping and the charges of insurance upon the whole.

4. In insurance on any other subject-matter, the insurable value is the amount at the risk of the assured when the policy attaches plus the charges of insurance.

In practice, policies on ships are always valued policies and therefore the provisions of s. 17 are inapplicable. Goods and freight payable on arrival are sometimes the subject of unvalued policies.

As to the measure of indemnity, ss. 68 to 72 set out the extent of liability of the insurer for the loss.

6

Good Faith

s. 18: A contract of marine insurance is a contract based upon the utmost good faith, and if the utmost good faith is not observed by either party the contract may be avoided by the other party.

The principle of good faith is common to the entire law of contract but it is one of the cornerstones of the relationship between insurer and assured in a contract of marine insurance. The principle has been confirmed and strengthened by codification. Together with ss. 19 to 21, the principle laid down in s. 18 requires an even greater standard of honesty between the parties than in non-marine insurance contracts. Perfect good faith has been described as "the very essence of this contract."[1] Sections 19 through 21 outline the duties of the assured in his dealings with the insurer. The insurer, though, has the same obligation of good faith. This obligation formed part of the common law as it existed prior to codification.[2]

---

1. *Mahoney v. Prov. Insurance Co.* (1869), 12 N.B.R. 633 (C.A.).
2. *Beacon Life & Fire Assurance Co. v. Gibb,* [1862] 1 Moo. P.C. N.S. 73, 15 E.R. 630 (J.C. P.C.). "The law of insurance requires *uberrima fides* from the insured. The like is or should be imposed upon the insurer" (at 85).

7

Disclosure of Material Circumstances

s. 19: (1) Subject to the provisions of this section, the assured must disclose to the insurer before the contract is concluded every material circumstance that is known to the assured, and the assured is deemed to know every circumstance that in the ordinary course of business ought to be known by him and if the assured fails to make such disclosure the insurer may avoid the contract.
(2) Every circumstance is material that would influence the judgment of a prudent insurer in fixing the premium or determining whether he will take the risk.
(3) In the absence of inquiry the following circumstances need not be disclosed,
(*a*) any circumstance that diminishes the risk;
(*b*) any circumstance that is known or presumed to be known to the insurer and the insurer is presumed to know matters of common notoriety or knowledge and matters that an insurer in the ordinary course of his business, as such, ought to know;
(*c*) any circumstance as to which information is waived by the insurer;
(*d*) any circumstance that it is superfluous to disclose by reason of any express or implied warranty.
(4) Whether any particular circumstance that is not disclosed be material or not is in each case a question of fact.
(5) The term "circumstance" includes any communication made to or information received by the assured.

s. 20: Subject to the provisions of section 19 as to circumstances that need not be disclosed, where an insurance is effected for the assured by an agent, the agent must disclose to the insurer,
(*a*) every material circumstance that is known to himself, and an agent to insure is deemed to know every circumstance that in the ordinary course of business ought to be known by or to have been communicated to him; and
(*b*) every material circumstance that the assured is bound to disclose, unless it comes to his knowledge too late to communicate it to the agent.

In accordance with the principle of good faith the assured is required to disclose all that he knows or ought to know, to the insurer, that affects the placement of the risk.

(1) Onus of Proof

In order for an insurer to succeed with a defence of non-disclosure, he must prove on the balance of probabilities that the "circumstance" not so disclosed was a material circumstance, that is, it would influence the judgment of a prudent insurer in fixing the premium or determining whether he would take the risk. In addition, the circumstance must be one which does not fall within the exceptions of par. 3 of s. 19.

In *AMO Containers Ltd. v. Drake Insurance Co. Ltd.*[1] the assured claimed indemnity from the insurer under a policy covering loss of containers and cargo baskets used in connection with the supply and servicing of offshore rigs. The property was lost on a rig which sank during a storm off the coast of Newfoundland. In the negotiations leading up to the issuance of the policy of insurance, the assured had advised the insurer that the containers were leased to Mobile Oil for one year and that Mobile Oil would be responsible for damage to the containers while in their care. There was, in fact, no written lease with Mobile Oil. The insurer argued that this amounted to a material representation which was false and, in accordance with s. 21, it was entitled to avoid the contract. In his decision, Justice Goodridge reviewed ss. 18-21 and made comments about materiality and onus of proof. He adopted the reasoning of Lord Justice Kerr in the English case of *Container Tpt. Int. Inc. v. Oceanus Mutual Underwriting Assoc. (Bermuda) Ltd.*[2] wherein Justice Kerr stated:[3]

> To prove the materiality of an undisclosed circumstance, the insurer must satisfy the Court on a balance of probability — by evidence or from the nature of the undisclosed circumstance itself — that the judgment, in this sense, of a prudent insurer would have been influenced if the circumstance in question had been disclosed. The word "influenced" means that the disclosure is one which would have had an impact on the formation of his opinion and on his decision-making process.

Justice Goodridge concluded that:[4]

> The duty of proving the materiality of an undisclosed circumstance lies upon the insurer. In this respect Mr. Asnani completely failed to satisfy the Court that the failure to disclose the fact that the "lease" so-called was not in fact a written document, probably not an agreement at all, was a circumstance that would have influenced a prudent [insurer] in making a determination as to whether to provide the policy of insurance at the agreed premium, a larger premium or not at all.

Justice Goodridge added:[5]

> It is true as noted above that there was a misrepresentation. It was an innocent misrepresentation. That, of course, would not excuse Mr. Dalton [of

---

1. (1984), 8 C.C.L.I. 97 (Nfld. T.D.).
2. [1984] 1 Lloyd's Rep. 476 (C.A.).
3. *Ibid.*, at 492.
4. *Supra*, note 1, at 105.
5. *Ibid.*, at 106.

AMO] as he is deemed to know and ought to have disclosed every circumstance which in the ordinary course of business he ought to have known.

What he referred to as a lease was probably a combination of the rental terms and conditions appearing on the back of the invoice together with the informal arrangement which he had orally reached with Mr. Beattie.

In *Central Native Fishermen's Co-Operative v. Commonwealth Insurance Co. et al.,*[6] a wooden barge developed a list, lost her cargo and was seriously damaged. Prior to the loss a condition survey had been requested by the underwriters. Underwriters had also requested that a specific surveyor be used. The assured's agent obtained the survey as requested but did not submit it to the underwriters as it was not very positive. Instead, the agent submitted a second, and more positive, survey. The court was satisfied on the evidence submitted to it that the underwriter was aware that there was another survey report which was not as positive as the one submitted. As such, the underwriter was put on inquiry, an inquiry which was waived. In accordance with par. 3 of s. 19, no further disclosure was necessary. Justice Fawcus concluded that "Commonwealth has failed to satisfy the onus of proving, by a preponderance of evidence, that neither the plaintiff nor its agent met the duty to disclose as imposed upon them by the *Marine Insurance Act*."[7]

(2) Behaviour of Assured

In any action in which non disclosure is an issue the behaviour of the assured immediately before the loss will be of utmost importance. If the assured is perceived as being underhanded, deceitful or is perceived as attempting to take advantage of the insurer, the courts will not be eager to rely on the onus of proof to assist him. If he is perceived as an innocent or naive assured who has made mistakes, all sins will be forgiven.

In *James Yachts Ltd. v. Thames and Mersey Marine Insurance Co. Ltd. et al.,*[8] an assured was carrying on the business of boat building contrary to municipal by-laws. A building inspector had advised the assured that a fibreglass operation was a high-hazard combustible use for which the building was not designed. The assured retained an engineer who advised him that the cost of alterations to qualify the building for a permit would be $150,000. The assured dismissed the project as too expensive. A fire destroyed the assured's boats at the premises. The insurers gave evidence that, had they

---

6. [1979] I.L.R. 1-1091 (B.C. S.C.).

7. *Ibid.*, at 166.

8. [1976] I.L.R. 1-751 (B.C. S.C.).

known about the building inspector's conclusions, they would have turned down the risk. Justice Ruttan concluded:[9]

> The evidence of the witnesses called on behalf of the defendants is sufficient to satisfy me that the definition of the material circumstances . . . applies to the non-disclosures made respecting the right of use and occupation of the premises, and respecting [the] financial stability of the plaintiff. On these grounds of non-disclosure therefore the insurers are entitled to avoid the contract and the plaintiff's claim must be dismissed.

In *McFaul v. Montreal Inland Insurance Co.*,[10] a cargo of wheat was insured from Presqu'Isle in Lake Ontario to Gananoque. The assured had failed to advise the insurer that the wheat had in fact been loaded at an earlier port, that the vessel had encountered severe weather on its voyage to Presqu'Isle and had suffered damage, and that the cargo was at least partially wet. In disallowing the assured's claim Justice Robinson expressed the opinion that "any suppression of a fact, on which it may be important to the insu[r]er that he should be allowed to exercise his judgment, either as to taking or refusing the risk, or in fixing the rate of premium, invalidates the policy."[11]

In *Mahoney v. Provincial Insurance Co.*[12] the assured was aware of a hurricane in the area in which its vessel was located and failed to communicate this information to the insurers. In dismissing the assured's claim, Chief Justice Ritchie pointed out that:[13]

> [I]t is clear that if a party having given instructions for effecting a policy, receives intelligence material to the risk he must forthwith, or with due and reasonable diligence, communicate it or countermand his instructions. Many things may or may not be material, according as the circumstances of the case make them the one or the other, and then these same circumstances determine whether they must be disclosed. All facts material to the risk known to the one party and not to the other, must be fully and fairly declared for ... [I]n determining whether any fact, actual or rumored, is material, we must ascertain whether the fact would naturally and reasonably enter into the estimate of the risk or the reasons for or against entering into the contract of insurance.

In *Atlantic Freighting Co. Ltd. v. Provincial Insurance Co. Ltd.*[14] the court found that the following circumstances were in existence at the time the policy of insurance was entered into and were not disclosed to the insurers:[15]

---

9. *Ibid.*, at 147.
10. (1845), 2 U.C.Q.B. 59 (C.A.).
11. *Ibid.*, at 61.
12. (1869), 12 N.B.R. 633 (C.A.).
13. *Ibid.*, at 639.
14. 5 D.L.R. (2d) 164, [1956] I.L.R. 1-245 (N.S. S.C.).
15. *Ibid.*, at 174, D.L.R.

(a) That the vessel had no certificate on board and in force in accordance with the provisions of the *Canada Shipping Act, 1934*,[16] as amended.

(b) That the vessel had a "hog" of 7 or 8 inches at Tampa at the end of March 1948.

(c) That the vessel was generally weak.

(d) That the captain noticed the vessel's timbers moving under him.

(e) That the vessel was continually spewing oakum out of the seams.

(f) That it was recommended that stiffening plates be placed on the inside of the vessel alongside the keelsons.

The insurer was therefore able to avoid the contract.

(3) Uninsurability

The Supreme Court of Canada has stated that non-disclosure by an assured that a vessel was uninsurable, for other reasons other than unseaworthiness, does not vitiate a policy.[17]

(4) Waiver by Insurer

As has been pointed out in the *Central Native*[18] case, if the insurer is put on notice of inquiry and fails to request further information he will be deemed to have waived the need for further disclosure. This was also noted in the *AMO*[19] decision, wherein Justice Goodridge stated:[20]

> Apart from the foregoing jurisprudence it is quite impossible to conceive of circumstances where the existence or nonexistence of a lease without further data could possibly have influenced Drake one way or the other. Its failure to enquire supports this position. The existence of a lease is completely irrelevant to the underwriting of the risk; the terms of the letting may be material.
>
> Inasmuch as Drake made no enquiry as to the terms of the letting, it is a reasonable conclusion that that was not a matter that would influence its accepting the risk for it could scarcely be said to be influenced one way or the other by the existence of a one-year lease if it was unaware of the terms of the lease.

Similarly if an underwriter regards the existence of certain equipment on a vessel as important in considering a risk it should expressly ask in the application or survey regarding the said equipment.[21]

---

16. S.C. 1934, c. 44.
17. *Standard Marine Insurance Co. v. Whalen Pulp and Paper Co.*, 64 S.C.R. 90, [1922] 3 W.W.R. 211, 68 D.L.R. 269.
18. *Supra*, note 6.
19. *Supra*, note 1.
20. *Supra*, note 1, at 106.
21. *Berner and Bradley Finance Ltd. v. Sun Insurance Office Ltd.*, [1952] I.L.R. 1-069 (Ont. H.C.).

(5) Deemed Knowledge of Insurer

In many situations the insurer is deemed to know certain circumstances. In *MacDonald v. Liverpool and London and Globe Insurance Co. Ltd. et al.*,[22] a cabin cruiser was destroyed by fire on October 6th while moored and waiting to be hauled out of the water. Navigational lights and equipment had been removed from the boat, windows had been sealed and fresh water tanks had been filled with anti-freeze. There was a warranty in the policy of insurance that the boat would be "laid up and out of commission" from October 1st to April 1st. One of the defences raised by the insurer was non-disclosure of a material circumstance. The reported decision does not indicate what this circumstance was. Presumably it dealt with the knowledge that pleasure boats were not able to physically sail in the Northumberland Strait between October 1st and April 1st, for Justice Richard concludes that:[23]

> With regards to the second defence under section ... 19 ... of the *Marine Insurance Act*,[24] c. M-1, it is sufficient to say that on the facts of this case, I do not see where these provisions can possibly be invoked and successfully relied upon by the insurer or the agent....
>
> In this case, I find that the insurer and indeed the agent ought to have known that pleasure boats are not to be seen in the waters of Northumberland Strait, or for that matter, in the Bay of Shediac, in the month of April. Indeed April is the month where the ice melts or drifts away and furthermore, the weather at that time is still very cold and most unfavorable.

In *Case Existological Laboratories v. Foremost Insurance Co. et al.*,[25] a scow was converted to perform as a floating platform with a stern that could be submerged by the use of compressed air. The vessel sank when a member of her crew negligently permitted an air pressure control valve to remain open. One of the defences raised by the insurers was that the assured had failed to disclose to them material circumstances, that the vessel required a cushion of compressed air to keep it afloat. A marine surveyor, proposed by the underwriter, had been retained by the shipowner and his report was provided to the insurance underwriter. The Court of Appeal found that by describing the vessel accurately in the report of the marine surveyor, the assured had discharged the obligation of disclosure. Justice Lambert stated:[26]

---

22. (1978), 22 N.B.R. (2d) 172, 39 A.P.R. 172 (Q.B.).
23. *Ibid.*, at 179-80.
24. R.S.N.B. 1973, c. M-1.
25. 133 D.L.R. (3d) 727, [1982] I.L.R. 1-1567 (B.C. C.A.); affd [1983] 2 S.C.R. 47 *(sub nom. Century Insurance Co. of Canada v. Case Existological Laboratories Ltd.)*, 48 B.C.L.R. 273, [1984] 1 W.W.R. 97, 150 D.L.R. (3d) 9, 49 N.R. 19, [1983] I.L.R. 1-1698.
26. *Ibid.*, at 739, 133 D.L.R. (3d).

Every material circumstance was disclosed. It was not the obligation of the assured to speculate about the various possibilities for improper operation of the vessel which would cause it to sink, including leaving the deck valves open, thereby permitting too much sea water to enter the hull.

Following disclosure to him of every material circumstance, the underwriter is required to assess the risk. In his own admission, Mr. Barber, for the lead underwriter in this case, reached an incorrect assessment of the risk. But that does not mean that the material circumstances were not disclosed to him.

In *Riverside Landmark Corp. v. Northumberland General Insurance*,[27] an insurer of two barges which sank while being towed from Toronto to Mexico denied liability on the ground that the assured failed to disclose that the vessels would be lashed together and not in tandem tow. The insurer also argued that the assured had failed to disclose to it that the surveyor who approved the suitability of the vessels for tow had also recommended the purchase of the vessels to the assured. The court found on the evidence presented to it that the insurers knew or ought to have known that the surveyor had advised the plaintiff on the purchase of the vessels. On the question of disclosure that the vessels would be lashed together, Justice Anderson concluded that:[28]

> [O]n the evidence I would conclude that the practice of lashing the vessels together, or "marrying" the vessels as one of the witnesses said, is so prevalent that it would be known to any competent marine underwriter and there was, therefore, no need to make disclosure.
>
> In that connection I have reference, of course, to s. 19(3)(*b*) which relieves of the obligation to disclose that which is "known or presumed to be known", "matters of common notoriety or knowledge."
>
> In this connection, I have not disregarded the evidence of Mr. Fitzgerald that an insurer is not an expert in towage arrangements. However, I cannot avoid the conclusion that the term "tandem tow" from its use without further elaboration in the binder and in the contract of insurance was indicative of the knowledge on the part of the draftsman that those dealing with the document had knowledge of content of the words. In my view, the defendant must be taken to have known the meaning of the term from those circumstances and the elements of such a tow in its initial stages. Those elements, as I have already outlined, include the lashing of the vessels together.

---

27. (1984), 8 C.C.L.I. 119 (Ont. H.C.).
28. *Ibid.*, at 133.

8

Material Representations

s. 21: (1) Every material representation made by the assured or his agent to the insurer during the negotiations for the contract, and before the contract is concluded, must be true and if it be untrue the insurer may avoid the contract.

(2) A representation is material that would influence the judgment of a prudent insurer in fixing the premium or determining whether he will take the risk.

(3) A representation may be either a representation as to a matter of fact or as to a matter of expectation or belief.

(4) A representation as to a matter of fact is true if it is substantially correct, that is to say, if the difference between what is represented and what is actually correct would not be considered material by a prudent insurer.

(5) A representation as to a matter of expectation or belief is true if it is made in good faith.

(6) A representation may be withdrawn or corrected before the contract is concluded.

(7) Whether a particular representation be material or not is in each case a question of fact.

The principles contained in s. 19 (non-disclosure of a material circumstance) and in s. 20 (material misrepresentation of a circumstance) are very closely linked. Non-disclosure involves an act of omission; that is, the assured fails to bring to the attention of the insurer a circumstance that is material to the risk. In a material misrepresentation situation the assured has actively done or stated something which is not true and the representation involves a circumstance that is material to the risk. The two sections share the concepts of utmost good faith and materiality.

Thus, it is not surprising to see that in the *AMO*[1] decision, the distinction between the two concepts was somewhat blurred. The assured had positively stated that the containers were leased to Mobile Oil. This was not really true. The court then found that there was a non-disclosure by the assured of the fact that the so-called lease was not a written document. However, the court found this was not material and the defence by the insurer failed. It seems that a less complex route for the court to have taken would have been to simply

---

1. (1984), 8 C.C.L.I. 97 (N.S. T.D.).

hold that the representation made by AMO was not material. Whether there was a lease or not did not really matter to the underwriter. Non-disclosure was not in issue.

In the *Riverside Landmark Corporation*[2] case the insurer also alleged misrepresentation by the assured in that the vessels would not come into contact during the tow. There was a warranty in the policy that the vessels would be in tandem tow. As indicated earlier, the court found that any competent underwriter would have known that the vessels would be lashed together in the initial stages of the tow. The court, therefore, interpreted the representation that the vessels would not come into contact to "mean and apply to that portion of the voyage after the vessels were strung out and not to the initial stage when, on the evidence, they would be, if not in contact, at least in ju[x]taposition and separated only by fenders or buffers."[3]

Earlier courts have not been as lenient towards assured. In *Brooks-Scanlon O'Brien Co. Ltd. v. Boston Insurance Co.*,[4] an assured stated to an insurer that scows were to be towed singly and a policy was thereupon issued at a lower rate of insurance. The scows were not taken up singly and one was lost. In holding that there was a positive representation which was breached, allowing the insurer to avoid the contract, Chief Justice Macdonald of the British Columbia Court of Appeal stated:[5]

> In an ordinary transaction, that representation would amount to a warranty, but in marine insurance law it appears to be regarded as a promissory representation which may be relied upon notwithstanding that it was made by word of mouth and not included in the written contract.

In *H.B. Bailey & Co. v. Ocean Mutual Marine Insurance Co.*[6] an application for insurance asked for the vessel's location and destination. The answer contained the following: "was ... at Buenos Ayres or near port 3rd February bound up river; would tow up and back." The vessel was damaged in coming down the river not in tow. The court found that the words "would tow up and back" were a promissory representation material to the risk. The breach entitled the insurers to avoid the contract. It should be noted that s. 21 no longer speaks of promissory representations but rather of representations of matters of fact or of matters of expectation or belief. Today if an insurer wants to have the benefit of a promissory representation, he may include it as a warranty.

---

2. (1984), 8 C.C.L.I. 119 (Ont. H.C.).
3. *Ibid.*, at 134.
4. [1919] 2 W.W.R. 129, 47 D.L.R. 93 (B.C. C.A.).
5. *Ibid.*, at 95, D.L.R.
6. (1891), 19 S.C.R. 153.

In *Nova Scotia Marine Insurance Co. v. Stevenson*,[7] an application
for insurance on a vessel asked "when built?" The vessel was actually
built 20 years earlier than stated. In allowing the insurer to avoid
the policy, Justice King stated:[8]

> Then as to the effect of the misrepresentation. If made with intent to deceive
> the misrepresentation vitiates the policy however trivial or immaterial to the
> nature of the risk. If honestly made it vitiates only if material and if substantially
> incorrect. The test of materiality is the probable effect which the statement
> might naturally and reasonably be expected to produce on the mind of the
> underwriter in weighing the risk and considering the premium.
>
> The age of a vessel is a point material to the risk ...
>
> A question respecting the age of a vessel would *prima facie* be taken to
> imply that the underwriter considers the answer material, and in such case
> the answer may be presumed to have influenced his mind.

In *McDonald et al. v. Doull*,[9] the assured stated in the insurance
application form that insurance elsewhere would not exceed $2,000.
This prohibition did not appear on the policy issued. The vessel was
insured with other companies to the amount of $4,000. The court
found that the statement was a positive representation of a material
fact to the risk which was false and the insurer was allowed to avoid
the policy.

If an assured is expressly questioned by underwriters as to whether a vessel has sailed and the reply is positively that it has not sailed,
when she really has, the insurer is not liable on the policy.[10]

In *Eisenhauer et al. v. Providence Washington Insurance Co.*,[11]
an assured knew its vessel sailed on March 21st and that there was
heavy weather in the area. In reply to a question on the application
as to the location of the vessel and the date of sailing, the assured
replied that the vessel was loading. The court found that the assured's
knowledge of the actual date should have been communicated to
the underwriter. The information was material to the risk. The
answer that the vessel was loading was a material misrepresentation
which entitled the insurer to avoid the policy.

In *Ewart et al. v. Merchants' Marine Insurance Co.*,[12] a vessel
was described in the application for insurance as "A1". This description was understood by the insurer as a representation that the
vessel was so classed in *English Lloyds* when in fact she was classed
in the *American Lloyds Universal Standard Record*. The evidence

---

7. (1894), 23 S.C.R. 137.
8. *Ibid.*, at 141-42.
9. (1878), 12 N.S.R. 276 (C.A.); revd Cass. S.C. 384.
10. *Perry v. British America Fire and Life Assurance Co.* (1848), 4 U.C.Q.B. 330 (C.A.).
11. (1887), 20 N.S.R. 48 (C.A.).
12. (1879), 13 N.S.R. 168 (C.A.).

presented showed that there was no real difference between the two classification systems. The court found that there had been no misrepresentation.

Two "modern day" decisions have upheld the defence of material misrepresentation. As with the issue of non-disclosure, the behaviour of the assured appears to greatly influence the decision of the court. In *Intermunicipal Realty & Development Corp. v. Gore Mutual Insurance Co. et al.*,[13] the assured was asked who would be managing the vessel and if there was any connection between the new owners and the prior owners, the prior owners having failed to pay the premium on a prior policy. The assured advised the underwriters that March Shipping Ltd. would be managing the vessel and that there was no connection between the new owners and the prior owners. In fact, one of the shareholders of the prior owners was managing the vessel and not March Shipping Ltd. The court found that there had been a fraudulent misrepresentation of material facts. Justice Collier stated:[14]

> If a positive statement, or a non-disclosure, influenced the underwriter when the risk was undertaken, then the policy can be treated by the underwriter as void *ab initio*.
>
> . . . . .
>
> Josephson, as a business man, must have recognized that Ziff's name, in connection with this new enterprise, could lead to problems. There had been a bankruptcy of the Ziff company, the previous owner. There had been cancellation of the previous policy for non-payment of premium. I find that Josephson did not, for those reasons, disclose to Lachance that Ziff was going to be ship's manager. I accept Lachance's evidence that March Shipping Limited was designated as managing the vessel . . .
>
> All this was done knowingly, in my view, with the intention of inducing coverage from an underwriter.

In *DeGroot v. J.T. O'Bryan & Co. et al.*,[15] the assured had advised underwriters that the vessel had been surveyed prior to its departure from the Bahamas with the destination being Vancouver. The survey had in fact not been performed. As well, the underwriters argued that the owner had misled them as to the nature of the voyage. The voyage was to be a direct trip to Vancouver with experienced crew. In fact, it was not a direct trip to Vancouver and the crew were amateurs who were not fully experienced. The court found that there had been a misrepresentation as to facts and the insurers were entitled to avoid the policy.

---

13. [1981] 1 F.C. 151, 112 D.L.R. (3d) 432, [1981] I.L.R. 1-1350 (T.D.).
14. *Ibid.*, at 160-61, F.C.
15. 15 B.C.L.R. 271, [1979] I.L.R. 1-1152 (C.A.).

9

When Is the Contract Deemed to be Concluded?

s. 22: A contract of marine insurance is deemed to be concluded when the proposal of the assured is accepted by the insurer, whether the policy is then issued or not, and for the purpose of showing when the proposal was accepted, reference may be made to the slip or covering note or other customary memorandum of the contract.

Under s. 19, the assured has a duty to disclose all material circumstances to the insurer before the contract is concluded. Similarly, under s. 20 any material misrepresentations made during negotiations will vitiate the policy of insurance. Once the contract is concluded, however, no further disclosure is necessary. Likewise, representations made after the contract is concluded should not affect the position of the assured.

A contract of marine insurance will be concluded when the parties are *ad idem* as to all the essential terms of the contract.[1] As in any contract there must be an offer, an acceptance and consideration. Where an assured submits a written application to the insurer and receives in return a premium notice, a valid and binding contract exists. The written application constitutes the offer, the premium notice constitutes the acceptance and the consideration is the promise to pay.[2]

It is not necessary for a formal policy to be issued for a court to find that a contract of insurance has been concluded. In *Green Forest Lumber Ltd. v. General Security Insurance Co. of Canada*,[3] Justice Addy has made comments to this effect:[4]

> Although a formal policy bearing the seal of the company was not actually issued, the defendant was under an obligation to issue one and it could have been sued for specific performance. Equity looks upon that as done which ought to be done ... and the matter should be treated as if a policy had actually been issued.

It will also be open to a court on principles of equity to rectify a policy which has been issued so as to make it conform to the application.[5]

---

1. *Osborne v. The Queen in right of Canada*, [1984] I.L.R. 1-1724 (F.C. T.D.).
2. *Ibid.*
3. [1977] 2 F.C. 351 (T.D.); affd [1978] 2 F.C. 773 (C.A.); affd [1980] 1 S.C.R. 176.
4. *Ibid.*, at 356, [1977] 2 F.C.
5. *Wylde et al. v. Union Marine Insurance Co.* (1875), 10 N.S.R. 205 (C.A.).

There may exist situations where the duty to disclose continues beyond the conclusion of the contract. For example, this may present itself in a policy in which the underwriter has an option to cancel the policy on 30 days' notice and it comes to his attention that certain facts have changed since the issuance of the policy. If the underwriter makes inquiries of the assured regarding the circumstance, the assured has a duty to reply to the request truthfully. If the circumstance is material and if the assured has misled the underwriter and there is a loss at a time the policy could have been cancelled, the insurer should be able to avoid the policy.

10

The Policy

s. 23: A contract of marine insurance is inadmissible in evidence unless it is embodied in a marine policy in accordance with this Act and the policy may be executed and issued either at the time when the contract is concluded or afterwards.

s. 24: A marine policy must specify,
(a) the name of the assured or of some person who effects the insurance on his behalf;
(b) the subject-matter insured and the risk insured against;
(c) the voyage or period of time, or both, as the case may be, covered by the insurance;
(d) the sum or sums insured; and
(e) the name or names of the insurers.

s. 25: (1) A marine policy must be signed by or on behalf of the insurer; provided that in the case of a corporation the corporate seal may be sufficient, but nothing in this section shall be construed as requiring the subscription of a corporation to be under seal.
(2) Where a policy is subscribed by or on behalf of two or more insurers, each subscription, unless the contrary is expressed, constitutes a distinct contract with the assured.

s. 26: Where the contract is to insure the subject-matter at and from, or from one place to another or others, the policy is called a "voyage policy", and where the contract is to insure the subject-matter for a definite period of time the policy is called a "time policy" and a contract for both voyage and time may be included in the same policy.

s. 27: (1) The subject-matter insured must be designated in a marine policy with reasonable certainty.
(2) The nature and extent of the interest of the assured in the subject-matter insured need not be specified in the policy.
(3) Where the policy designates the subject-matter insured in general terms, it shall be construed to apply to the interest intended by the assured to be covered.
(4) In the application of this section regard shall be had to any usage regulating the designation of the subject-matter insured.

A court of equity will rectify a policy which has been issued so as to make it conform to the application.[1] It will also allow the

---

1. *Wylde et al. v. Union Marine Insurance Co.* (1875), 10 N.S.R. 205 (C.A.).

assured to rectify a policy which is incomplete.[2] However, it will not allow such rectification if the policy has been issued, accepted and acted upon by the assured.[3]

It is clear that any handwritten memorandum in a policy will prevail over the printed conditions left in the policy even if the conditions are inconsistent therewith.[4]

Where, however, there is ambiguity in the policy, the policy and the memorandum will be taken together and receive a reasonable construction according to the circumstances of the case.[5] In *British America Assurance Co. v. William Law & Co.*,[6] Justice Strong stated:[7]

> The well established rule of construction applicable to all deeds and written instruments, and especially to policies of marine insurance which are mercantile deeds not prepared by lawyers, is that they should be so interpreted, if possible, as to be valid and effectual and not in such a way as to be void.

Justice Patterson added:[8]

> "[I]t is to be construed according to its sense and meaning; that the terms of it are to be understood in their plain, ordinary and popular acceptation unless by known usage of trade they have acquired some peculiar and appropriate meaning, or unless the context evidently shows that they must, in the particular instance, and to effectuate the manifest intention of the parties, be understood in some other special and peculiar sense."

Any ambiguity will be construed against the party from whom the instruments emanated.[9] In *Dimock v. New Brunswick Marine Assurance Co.*,[10] a vessel was insured "for four months, beginning the 11th of June instant, on a fishing voyage." The insurers argued the policy was for one voyage which was to take place within the four months. Printed words in the margin of the policy stated "time risk". The vessel was lost on its second trip within the four months. The Court of Appeal for New Brunswick held that the policy was a time policy for four months absolutely. The words "a fishing voyage" merely denoted the nature of the business on which the vessel was to be employed.

The relationship between ss. 22-25 has been canvassed in the

---

2. *Cusack v. Mutual Insurance Co. of Buffalo* (1862), 6 L.C. Jur. 97, 10 R.J.R.Q. 194.
3. *Robertson v. Lovett et al.* (1874), 9 N.S.R. 424.
4. *Meagher v. Aetna Insurance Co.* (1861), 20 U.C.Q.B. 607 (C.A.), and *Meagher v. Home Insurance Co.* (1861), 11 U.C.C.P. 328 (C.A.).
5. *Creighton v. Union Marine Insurance Co.* (1854), 2 N.S.R. 195 (C.A.).
6. (1892), 21 S.C.R. 325.
7. *Ibid.*, 327-28.
8. *Ibid.*, at 333-34, quoting from *Arnould on Marine Insurance.*
9. *Mowat v. Boston Marine Insurance Co.* (1896), 26 S.C.R. 47.
10. (1848), 5 N.B.R. 654 (C.A.).

Green Forest Lumber[11] decision. The assured was an exporter of lumber and had ordered insurance through its broker. A certificate of insurance was issued but not a formal policy. The assured claimed that an oral undertaking had been given to it that its shipments would be covered under the Timber Trade Federation insurance clauses. These terms were not shown on the certificate. In describing the relationship between the relevant sections in the Act. Justice Addy stated:[12]

> Although section 23 of the *Marine Insurance Act* provides that a contract of marine insurance is inadmissible in evidence, unless it is embodied in a marine policy in accordance with that Act, section 23 must be read in the light of section 22 which states that a contract of marine insurance is deemed to be concluded when the proposal of the assured is accepted by the insurer whether a policy is issued or not and of section 24, which lays down the requirements of an insurance policy, and also of section 25 which states that, although the policy must be signed on behalf of the insurer, it need not bear the corporate seal of the insurer.
>
> In the case at bar, I find no difficulty in coming to the conclusion that the certificate of insurance issued contains all of the elements enumerated in section 24 and that it was duly executed on behalf of the insurer on the insurer's express authorization. It therefore constitutes a policy for the purpose of section 23 and is admissible in evidence as such.

Justice Addy then concluded that any oral agreement regarding the Timber Trade Federation clauses of insurance was not admissible in evidence by reason of s. 23 of the Act. He found that "section 23 is an absolute bar to the right of recovery of the plaintiff otherwise section 23 would be absolutely meaningless."[13]

---

11. [1977] 2 F.C. 351 (T.D.); affd [1978] 2 F.C. 773 (C.A.); affd [1980] 1 S.C.R. 176.
12. *Ibid.*, at 356-57, [1977] 2 F.C.
13. *Ibid.*, at 361.

11

Valued, Unvalued and Floating Policies

s. 28: (1) A policy may be either valued or unvalued.
(2) A valued policy is a policy that specifies the agreed value of the subject-matter insured.
(3) Subject to the provisions of this Act, and in the absence of fraud, the value fixed by the policy is, as between the insurer and assured, conclusive of the insurable value of the subject intended to be insured, whether the loss is total or partial.
(4) Unless the policy otherwise provides, the value fixed by the policy is not conclusive for the purpose of determining whether there has been a constructive total loss.

s. 29: An unvalued policy is a policy that does not specify the value of the subject-matter insured, but, subject to the limit of the sum insured, leaves the insurable value to be subsequently ascertained in the manner hereinbefore specified.

s. 30: (1) A floating policy is a policy that describes the insurance in general terms and leaves the name of the ship or ships and other particulars to be defined by subsequent declaration.
(2) The subsequent declaration or declarations may be made by endorsement on the policy or in other customary manner.
(3) Unless the policy otherwise provides, the declarations must be made in the order of dispatch or shipment and they must, in the case of goods, comprise all consignments within the terms of the policy, and the value of the goods or other property must be honestly stated, but an omission or erroneous declaration may be rectified even after loss or arrival, provided the omission or declaration was made in good faith.
(4) Unless the policy otherwise provides, where a declaration of value is not made until after notice of loss or arrival, the policy must be treated as an unvalued policy as regards the subject-matter of that declaration.

In a valued policy, in the absence of fraud, the value in the policy is conclusive as between assured and insurer. The Court of Appeal of Nova Scotia has found that:[1]

[W]here the value of the thing insured is stated in the policy in a manner to be conclusive between the insurer and the insured 'then in respect of all rights and obligations which arise upon the policy of insurance the parties

---

1. *Kenny v. Union Marine Insurance Co.* (1880), 13 N.S.R. 313, at 318 (C.A.).

are estopped between one and another from disputing the value of the thing insured, as stated in the policy.'

In practice, it is normal for the value in a policy to be higher than the actual market value of the subject-matter of insurance. This practice does not constitute fraud and in fact may be desirable. Lord Robson in *Thames and Mersey Marine Insurance Co. Ltd. v. Gunford Ship Co. Ltd. et al.*[2] explained why this may be so:[3]

> Although the contract of insurance is expressed to be a contract of indemnity, and the indemnity is properly based on market value at the time of the loss, yet the law allows the insured value to be agreed between the parties, and the agreed value, though frequently, and perhaps generally, in excess of the market value, is binding in the absence of fraud. There are often legitimate business reasons for this discrepancy between the selling value and the insured value, and it should not be assumed that it necessarily creates any actual conflict between duty and interest on the part of the shipowner in regard to the safety of the thing insured. The assured naturally aims at reinstatement rather than bare indemnity, and the insurer has also his own reasons for preferring that the values should be high so long as they do not constitute a temptation to loss. In order that he may be saved the trouble of small claims, which are often of a doubtful character, he stipulates that the ship shall be warranted free from average under 3 per cent, and where the total agreed value is high the insurer's protection under this clause is increased. Again, in claims for constructive total loss, the higher the value the more difficult it is for the assured to establish that the cost of repairs will exceed the repaired value, so as to entitle him to treat the vessel as lost and leave the wreck on the insurer's hands. The insurer is therefore willing to undertake the risk of a certain amount of over-valuation, relying no doubt on the character of the assured and also on the interest that the managing owners or managers have in preserving the ship as a source of business profit to themselves.

It is not common today to find unvalued policies on vessels. Occasionally, goods and freight are insured under unvalued policies. It is much more common today to find goods insured under floating policies. The particulars of the shipment, of the voyage and the value of the goods are set out in declarations filled out by the assured or his broker and submitted to the insurer. Premium is calculated according to the terms of the policy on the value of the declared goods. These floating policies are of great benefit to consignees who may have no knowledge of the value of the goods and of the ship by which they are carried until after the goods have been loaded but want the protection afforded by insurance. Similarly, sellers of goods with c.i.f. contracts to be performed over a period of time with a number of shipments also benefit from a floating policy.[4]

---

2. [1911] A.C. 529 (H.L.).
3. *Ibid.*, at 548.
4. E.R.H. Ivamy, *Marine Insurance*, 8th ed. (London: Butterworths & Co., (Publishers) Ltd., 1976), pp. 94-95.

Where no time is specified in a contract of marine insurance for the declaration of particulars of a shipment, and no local custom is alleged or proved, a reasonable time must be allowed. Thus, in *General Marine Assurance Co. v. Ocean Marine Insurance Co.*,[5] a delay of 15 days in submitting a declaration was held not to be unreasonable. The loss of the goods before the declaration of the particulars did not affect the contract of insurance.

---

5. (1899), 16 Que. S.C. 170.

12

Policy Form[1]

**s. 31: (1) A policy may be in the form in the Schedule.
(2) Subject to the provisions of this Act, and unless the context of the policy otherwise requires, the terms and expressions mentioned in the Schedule shall be construed as having the scope and meaning in the Schedule assigned to them.**

The Schedule is the *Lloyd's S.G. Policy* which has been used for over 100 years. The policy has been used world-wide by the marine insurance industry. Almost every word has been judicially considered and interpreted by the common law courts and has now acquired a special meaning. The policy is continually being required to adapt to changing time and changing conditions. One author has described the process as follows:[2]

> The main principles of marine insurance law are well settled. The difficulties that occur in practice arise chiefly out of the crabbed and obscure language of the time-honoured Lloyd's policy, which was framed with reference to the conditions of commerce in a by-gone era. New wine has continually to be put into the old bottle, often with inconvenient results.

In *Morrison Mill Co. v. Queen Insurance Co. of America*,[3] a raft of logs was insured. At issue was whether the raft was to be considered as cargo or goods under the contract (in which case the insurer was not liable) or whether it was to be considered as of the nature of a hull or ship, an entity apart from its component parts. On the face of the policy were the words "Cargo Policy, No. V3/438." In allowing the assured to recover for the loss of the raft, Justice Martin stated:[4]

> Too much attention should not, I think, be paid to the form of "cargo policy" which was being adapted in the quick endeavour to meet new conditions for which it was not really appropriate. The property insured was what is called a Davis raft, a recent, comparatively, invention in the construction of timber rafts for deep sea transportation requiring special construction and equipment to meet that class of navigation, and such a cylindrical self-contained raft is as far removed from an ordinary raft as it is from a scow or barge.

---

1. See Chapter 47.
2. E.R.H. Ivamy, *Chalmers' Marine Insurance Act, 1906*, 8th ed. (London: Butterworths & Co. (Publishers) Ltd., 1976), p. 3.
3. 34 B.C.R. 509, [1925] 1 W.W.R. 691, [1925] 1 D.L.R. 1159 (C.A.).
4. *Ibid.*, at 1160, D.L.R.

Justice McPhillips added:[5]

> It is to be observed that the form used was a cargo policy, with variations, notably the numerous provisoes that are usually found in a cargo policy as to loss arising from certain causes to cargo and as to exemption from liability, all indicating that the insurance really was not in its nature cargo insurance, were struck out. The policy issued was a somewhat clumsy effort to cover the particular risk undertaken, a risk no doubt somewhat unique in character, but analogous to the towing of a ship or boat. In these days of quick changes in trade and commerce and methods of transit, the attempt is always being made to meet the changing conditions and here, no doubt, the intention was to insure this raft of peculiar construction ...

In the United Kingdom, where the policy originated, "new clauses" have been introduced with the objective of bringing the wording in line with 20th century English.[6]

---

5. *Ibid.*, at 1164.
6. See chapter 50.

13

Additional Premium and Premium to be Arranged[1]

s. 32: (1) Where an insurance is effected at a premium to be arranged, and no arrangement is made, a reasonable premium is payable.
(2) Where an insurance is effected on the terms that an additional premium is to be arranged in a given event, and that event happens but no arrangement is made, then a reasonable additional premium is payable.

What is a reasonable premium is a question of fact.[2] Where the premium is to be arranged and no arrangement is made fixing the additional premium, the amount can be determined by a court.[3]

Where a cargo owner is required to pay an additional premium for insurance on his cargo as a result of a deviation in a voyage, the cargo owner may recover this amount from the shipowner as damages.[4]

Where a policy provides that a deviation in a voyage shall be held covered at a premium to be arranged, provided notice is given by the assured of the deviation, such notice may be given even after a ship is lost.[5]

---

1. See also ss. 53-55 and ss. 83-85.
2. See s. 89.
3. *Chartered Bank of India v. Pacific Marine Insurance Co.*, 33 B.C.R. 91, [1924] 1 W.W.R. 114, [1923] 4 D.L.R. 942 (C.A.).
4. *Peters v. Canada Sugar Refining Co.* (1886), 31 L.C. Jur. 72, M.L.R. 2 Q.B. 420 (C.A.).
5. *Supra*, note 2.

14

Double Insurance

s. 33: (1) Where two or more policies are effected by or on behalf of the assured on the same adventure and interest or any part thereof, and the sums insured exceed the indemnity allowed by this Act, the assured is said to be over-insured by double insurance.

(2) Where the assured is over-insured by double insurance,

(*a*) the assured, unless the policy otherwise provides, may claim payment from the insurers in such order as he may think fit, provided that he is not entitled to receive any sum in excess of the indemnity allowed by this Act;

(*b*) where the policy under which the assured claims is a valued policy, the assured must give credit as against the valuation for any sum received by him under any other policy without regard to the actual value of the subject-matter insured;

(*c*) where the policy under which the assured claims is an unvalued policy, he must give credit, as against the full insurable value, for any sum received by him under any other policy;

(*d*) where the assured receives any sum in excess of the indemnity allowed by this Act, he is deemed to hold such sum in trust for the insurers, according to their right of contribution among themselves.

In *Bank of British North America v. Western Assurance Co.*,[1] a consignee and a consignor each insured the same shipment of cattle from Boston to London. Justice Proudfoot, in holding that there was double insurance noted that "to constitute a double insurance there must be two or more insurances on the same subject, the same risk, and the same interest."[2] He also noted that "the law in Canada is the same as that in England, that in case of a double insurance, the insured may sue any of the insurers, leaving them to recover contribution from the others."[3]

---

1. (1884), 7 O.R. 166 (Ch.D.).
2. *Ibid.*, at 172.
3. *Ibid.*, at 169-70.

15

Warranties — Generally

s. 34: (1) A warranty, in the following sections relating to warranties, means a promissory warranty, that is to say, a warranty by which the assured undertakes that some particular thing shall or shall not be done, or that some condition shall be fulfilled, or whereby he affirms or negatives the existence of a particular state of facts.

(2) A warranty may be express or implied.

(3) A warranty as defined in subsection (1) is a condition that must be exactly complied with, whether it be material to the risk or not and if it is not so complied with, then, subject to any express provision in the policy, the insurer is discharged from liability as from the date of the breach of warranty, but without prejudice to any liability incurred by him before that date.

s. 35: (1) Non-compliance with a warranty is excused when, by reason of a change of circumstances, the warranty ceases to be applicable to the circumstances of the contract, or when compliance with the warranty is rendered unlawful by any subsequent law.

(2) Where a warranty is broken, the assured cannot avail himself of the defence that the breach has been remedied and the warranty complied with before loss.

(3) A breach of warranty may be waived by the insurer.

s. 36: (1) An express warranty may be in any form of words from which the intention to warrant is to be inferred.

(2) An express warranty must be included in or written upon the policy or must be contained in some document incorporated by reference into the policy.

(3) An express warranty does not exclude an implied warranty unless it is inconsistent therewith.

The Supreme Court of Canada had occasion recently to consider the use of warranties in policies of marine insurance. In *Century Insurance Co. of Canada et al. v. Case Existological Laboratories Ltd.*[1] (The *Bamcell II*) the policy in the case contained the following clause:[2]

> Warranted that a watchman is stationed on board the *Bamcell II* each night from 2200 hours to 0600 hours with instructions for shutting down all equipment in an emergency.

---

1. [1983] 2 S.C.R. 47, 48 B.C.L.R. 273, [1984] 1 W.W.R. 97.
2. *Ibid.*, at 55, [1983] 2 S.C.R.

There was no watchman stationed on board the vessel during the hours prescribed in the clause. The court held that this had absolutely no bearing whatever on the loss of the vessel which occurred in mid-afternoon. The issue then arose as to whether or not this clause constituted a warranty as defined in s. 34. If the clause constituted a true warranty, then, in accordance with s. 34 it must have been strictly complied with. A breach of the warranty at any time, even if the loss was unconnected with such breach, would entitle the insurer to be discharged from liability under the policy from the time of the breach. At the Court of Appeal level, Justice Lambert in the British Columbia Court of Appeal[3] concluded that the use of the word "warranted" in a policy of insurance is not conclusive of a warranty as defined in s. 34, the breach of which will discharge the insurer from liability. Justice Lambert said:[4]

> [T]he nature of the matter covered by the clause must be considered to determine whether the parties intended to create a warranty or whether they intended to create a "suspensive condition" or "warranty delimiting the risk" ... [T]he parties cannot have intended that if the watchman was late one night, or even missed a night, then the insurers should be discharged from liability for the remainder of the term of the policy ... [I]t is my opinion that the clause in this case under the heading of "Special Conditions" is a clause which limits the risk and not a true warranty which discharges the insurer. The limitation on the risk has no effect in this case.

Justice Ritchie in the Supreme Court of Canada concurred with the finding of Justice Lambert, stating:[5]

> The clause would only have been effective if the loss had occurred between 2200 hours and 0600 hours, and it was proved that there was no watchman stationed aboard during those hours. To this extent the condition contained in the clause constituted a limitation of the risk insured against but it was not a warranty.

It appears that if an insurer is able to demonstrate that a condition in a policy is a true warranty, then a breach thereof will invalidate the coverage. In *Norlympia Seafoods Ltd. v. Dale & Co. Ltd.*,[6] a decision handed down shortly after the *Bamcell II* case, it was a term of the policy that the assured must comply with all recommendations of the London Salvage Association. The London Salvage Association had required that a tug be in attendance on the barge

---

3. *Case Existological Laboratories Ltd. v. Foremost Insurance Co. et al.*, 133 D.L.R. (3d) 727, [1982] I.L.R. 1-1567 (B.C. C.A.); affd [1983] 2 S.C.R. 47 (*sub nom. Century Insurance Co. of Canada v. Case Existological Laboratories Ltd.*), 48 B.C.L.R. 273, [1984] 1 W.W.R. 97, 150 D.L.R. (3d) 9, 49 N.R. 19, [1983] I.L.R. 1-1698.

4. *Ibid.*, at 740-41, 133 D.L.R. (3d).

5. *Supra*, note 1 at 55-56, [1983] 2 S.C.R.

6. [1983] I.L.R. 1-1688 (B.C. S.C.).

in question whilst it was at anchor. The assured released the tug prior to the loss. Justice McLachlin did not make reference to the *Bamcell II* decision nor to the difference between suspensive conditions and warranties under s. 34. He simply held that the requirement was a warranty and stated:[7]

> It is now established that apart from cases where it is impossible or manifestly absurd to require compliance, warranties in policies must be strictly or literally fulfilled.

In *Federal Business Development Bank v. Commonwealth Insurance Co. Ltd., (The Good Hope)*,[8] a decision of the Supreme Court of British Columbia (also after *Bamcell II*), a clause warranted the vessel would be laid up at the foot of Columbia Street in Vancouver. The vessel, had for a short period of time, breached this condition. The court found that the parties never intended the warranty to be a condition that must be exactly complied with.

In *Riverside Landmark Corp. v. Northumberland General Insurance*,[9] a policy of insurance contained the words "covering whilst being towed in tandem by Irving Tug T.B.A. from Quebec City to Tampico, Mexico." The two vessels in question were not towed in tandem. The insurer argued that there had been a breach of warranty and that it was entitled to avoid the policy. It was the court's view that the words were descriptive of the risk rather than constituting a warranty.[10]

For 100 years, in Canadian decisions prior to the *Bamcell II*, the courts have essentially applied, in different ways, the same principle that Justice Lambert in the British Columbia Court of Appeal and Justice Ritchie in the Supreme Court of Canada applied in the *Bamcell II* case: that is, what was the intention of the parties when entering into the contract of insurance. The courts have examined the particular wordings of the policy, the purpose of the insurance, the customs and usage of the place and time the insurance was effected, and the effect of interpretation, in arriving at what the intention of the parties was.

(1) "Laid Up and Out of Commission" Warranties

In *Dolbec v. United States Fire Insurance Co.*,[11] a vessel was securely moored at a dock in Montreal with her engine removed

---

7. *Ibid.*, at 6483.
8. (1983), 2 C.C.L.I. 200 (B.C. S.C.).
9. (1984), 8 C.C.L.I. 118 (Ont. H.C.).
10. *Ibid.*, at 128.
11. [1963] B.R. 153 (C.A.).

when she was destroyed by fire. The policy of insurance stipulated that during the winter months, the yacht was to be "laid up and out of commission." The assured argued that the yacht was laid up and out of commission as she was securely moored with her engine removed. The court held that at the time of the fire, the yacht was not laid up and out of commission. The words "laid up and out of commission" had to be interpreted in accordance with the usual practice followed in laying up boats in the area where the loss occurred. The court found that the practice in the Montreal region was to remove boats from the water during the winter months.

In *Daneau v. Laurent Gendron, Ltée*,[12] a scow was beached and secured for the winter at Pointe Noire, Seven Islands. The vessel was insured under a policy which provided that the vessel was to be laid up and out of commission between the 16th day of November and the 30th of April. The vessel was damaged and the insurers appointed surveyors to investigate the loss. The court found that the location and manner of lay-up adopted was in accordance with the generally accepted practice at that place and allowed the assured's claim. The court also found that if there had been a breach of the lay-up warranty, the insurers had waived compliance with it. Justice Smith said:[13]

> [D]efendant's representative [the surveyor], generally without reservation, actively participated in, and in some respects actually directed and approved the arrangements made for the attempted repairs of the scow. It is not necessary that a waiver should be express or be based upon either a new agreement or estoppel. It is deemed to result when the insurer, after hearing of a breach of the contract which might give rise to forfeiture or right of cancellation, either expressly or tacitly recognizes the validity of the policy.

In *MacDonald v. Liverpool and London and Globe Insurance Co. Ltd. et al.*,[14] a policy of insurance warranted that the yacht insured was to be laid up and out of commission from October 1st, at noon until April 1st, at noon. The assured had removed all of the navigational lights and equipment, unplugged the stove and fridge, sealed some windows, and filled the fresh water tanks with antifreeze. The vessel was destroyed by fire on October 6th while moored awaiting to be hauled out of the water for the winter. In finding for the assured, Justice Richard said:[15]

> In large measure, the defence is a technical one. It is the equivalent of saying that if the boat had burnt one minute past 12:00 noon of the 1st day of October, 1976, that it would not have been covered by the insurance.

---

12. [1964] 1 Lloyd's L.R. 220 (Ex. Ct.).
13. *Ibid.*, at 224.
14. (1978), 22 N.B.R. (2d) 172, 39 A.P.R. 172 (Q.B.).
15. *Ibid.*, at 177-79.

Upon a consideration of all the evidence before me, I would find it most reasonable to interpret the warranty clause as meaning that sailing of the boat must terminate on the specified day and that retrieval from the water must be carried out within a reasonable time thereafter.

(2) "Towing" Warranties

A vessel was insured "from Quebec to Greenock, vessel to go out in tow."[16] The insurers denied liability on the basis that the vessel had not gone out in tow. The Supreme Court of Canada agreed that the vessel had not gone out in tow and that the warranty had been breached. The appeal by the assured was dismissed. The assured had unsuccessfully tried to introduce evidence of the custom of the port of Quebec that vessels were not towed beyond a certain point. Justice Ritchie commented that if the vessel had been partially towed and if the issue had been how far did the vessel have to be towed to comply with the warranty, then the usage and custom of the port of Quebec at that time of year would have been relevant. The vessel, however, had not been towed at all. Justice Henry (in dissent) said that in order to interpret the meaning of the words in question, one would have to admit evidence as to whether those words had any special meaning to the individuals in the area. He stated:[17]

Usages of trade are local as well as general, and are known, or presumed to be known, in any locality, to or by every one engaged in any particular trade or business to which they are applicable. So, particular terms, or provisions employed or made, have authoritative and prescribed application, and, when used in contracts, are as well understood as if specially recited or explained. That is why evidence of them is admitted. The well known and fully accepted technical meaning of such terms is properly assumed to have been in the minds of contracting parties when using them, and their presence in a contract manifests their intentions as fully as if stated at length, embracing, as it does, the principle that that is certain which can legitimately be made certain.

In *Brooks-Scanlon O'Brien Co. Ltd. v. Boston Insurance Co.,*[18] an insurer charged a lower rate of insurance on the basis that scows were to be towed singly. The scows were not towed singly and the insurers were allowed to avoid the contract.

An insurance policy permitted a dredge and a scow to travel "in tow of two approved tugs to Halifax" from Little Narrows.[19] The issue was whether the dredge and scow were to be towed separately by the two approved tugs or to be towed together by the two approved

---

16. *Provincial Insurance Co. of Canada v. Connolly* (1879), 5 S.C.R. 258.
17. *Ibid.,* at 269.
18. [1919] 2 W.W.R. 129, 47 D.L.R. 93 (B.C. C.A.).
19. *Porter (J.P.) & Son Ltd. v. Western Assurance Co.,* [1938] 1 D.L.R. 619, 12 M.P.R. 469, 5 I.L.R. 142 (N.S. C.A.).

tugs. Justice Archibald, speaking for the majority of the court, stated:[20]

> [I]t does seem to me to be just as reasonable to construe the endorsement as permitting "separate towing" of the dredge and scow as to construe it as permitting the trip to be made in "double tow" only. I think the words used are ambiguous and therefore must be construed against the insurer.

(3) "Navigation" Warranties

A steamship was described in a policy as "now lying in Tait's Dock, Montreal, and intended to navigate the St. Lawrence and Lakes from Hamilton to Quebec, principally as a freight boat, and to be laid up for the winter in a place approved by the Company."[21] The ship never left the dock and, approximately 11 months later, was destroyed by fire. Lord Kingsdown, of the Privy Council, gave the opinion of the court:[22]

> Their Lordships are of opinion that the question depends entirely on the meaning to be attached to these words. If they import an agreement that the ship shall navigate in the manner described in the Policy, there being an engagement contained in the Policy, they must be considered as a warranty; and, the engagement not having been performed, whether the engagement was material or not material, the insurers are discharged. But their Lordships think that this is not the true meaning of the words used. They consider that the clause in question amounts only to this: the assured says, My ship is now lying in Tait's Dock; I mean to remove her for the purpose of navigation in the manner described, and if I do, the Policy shall still be in force; but in that case I engage to lay her up in winter in a place to be approved by the Company.
>
> This construction, which implies no contract to navigate, seems to their Lordships the natural meaning of the words used, and imputes a reasonable intention to the parties to the Policy.

In *Grant v. Equitable Fire Insurance Co.*,[23] a policy covered a steamer "navigating the river St. Lawrence, between Quebec and Hamilton, stopping at intermediate ports." The vessel was laid up and not so engaged. The court found that the words used constituted a warranty and it having been breached, the insurer was not liable. The court stated that:[24]

> [I]t is sufficient to say that a warranty by the assured in relation to the existence of a particular fact must be strictly true or the policy will not take effect: this is so whether the thing warranted be material to the risk or not; it would

---

20. *Ibid.*, at 625, [1938] 1 D.L.R.
21. *Grant v. Aetna Insurance Co.* (1862), 15 Moo. P.C. 516, 15 E.R. 589.
22. *Ibid.*, at 594, E.R.
23. (1863), 8 L.C. Jur. 13.
24. *Ibid.*, at 17.

perhaps be more proper to say that the parties have agreed on the materiality of the thing warranted, and that the agreement precludes all inquiry on the subject.

A policy on a vessel contained a condition that the vessel was to sail not later than the 15th of December.[25] The vessel sailed on the 17th and was lost. The court found that time was of the essence of the contract and the assured could not recover. It reasoned that:[26]

> Every mercantile man understands the words "to sail by a certain day," or "not later than a certain day," to be an express agreement that such stipulation shall be performed, and to throw doubt on a rule so well understood would be attended with most mischievous consequences, as it would render the exact limits of an underwriter's liability, as well as the assured's rights, in many cases doubtful, and thus introduce uncertainty on a point of mercantile law where it is most important that none should exist.

If an insurer accepts a notice of abandonment after a constructive total loss, he cannot thereafter rely on a breach of a warranty that the vessel was within certain waters at a prohibited time.[27] By accepting the notice of abandonment he waives the breach of the warranty.

Under a policy of insurance, a vessel was "not allowed ... to enter the Gulf of St. Lawrence ... without payment of additional premium, or leave first obtained."[28] The vessel was sailing toward the prohibited area when she was lost. No additional payment was made, nor leave obtained. The court found that there was an unequivocal overt act showing that, but for disaster occurring, the vessel would have entered prohibited waters. The assured was denied recovery.

In *Campbell v. Canada Insurance Union*,[29] a policy contained a condition that the plaintiff was not to use the ports of Big Glace Bay, Schooner Pond, *etc.* The vessel was lost in a port in Big Glace Bay. The court interpreted the word "of" as "in" in finding against the assured and stated that that interpretation was needed to "effectuate the immediate intention of the parties."[30]

A policy containing a condition prohibiting the use of the Gulf of St. Lawrence was vitiated when the vessel sailed in the waters of the St. Lawrence.[31]

A policy on a vessel contained a condition that stated "warranted

---

25. *James Duncan & Co. v. British America Insurance Co.* (1871), 1 P.E.I. 370, Peters 243 *(sub nom. Duncan, Hodgson & Robertson v. Montreal Assurance Co.)*.

26. *Ibid.*, at 377, 1 P.E.I.

27. *Provincial Insurance Co. of Canada v. Leduc* (1874), 6 L.R. P.C. 224, 19 L.C. Jur. 281 (J.C.P.C.).

28. *Robertson et al. v. Stairs* (1875), 10 N.S.R. 345 (C.A.).

29. *Campbell v. Canada Insurance Union* (1877), 12 N.S.R. 21 (C.A.).

30. *Ibid.*, at 22.

31. *Royal Canadian Insurance Co. v. Pugh et al.* (1887), 20 N.S.R. 133 (C.A.).

to sail not later than 3rd of December, 1882". A policy on freight contained a condition that stated "warranted to sail from Charlotte-town not later than 3rd of December, 1882".[32] The vessel left the wharf at Charlottetown on December 3rd, proceeded a short distance, and was obliged due to weather to anchor within the limits of Char-lottetown harbour until December 4th. The Supreme Court of Canada found that the warranty in the policy on the vessel had not been breached as she had commenced her voyage on the 3rd of December. The warranty in the policy on freight had, however, been breached as the vessel was in Charlottetown harbour until December 4th and therefore the insurer was not liable.

A condition in a policy of insurance declared that the vessel was "prohibited from loading lime, from the river and gulf of St. Lawrence . . ., Northumberland Straits and Cape Breton, between October 31st and April 25th; permitted however to use gulf ports in Nova Scotia proper, up to November 15th, and the ports of Sydney, N.B., and Pictou, N.S., until November 25th and March 31st; from Newfoundland between November 25th and March 31st; from ports in Greenland or Iceland or being engaged in sealing; from the coast of Labrador, between September 15th and May 15th."[33] The vessel was lost in the Straits of Northumberland. The court found that the prohibition applied to the use of prohibited waters for any pur-poses during the periods mentioned and was not limited to the loading of lime at the ports mentioned.

In *Troop et al. v. Union Insurance Co.*,[34] a policy contained the words "prohibited . . . the Gulf of Campeachy". The court did not allow evidence of the usage in the port of Saint John of the word "prohibited" to contradict the meaning of the words in the contract.

A policy of insurance prohibited a vessel from using certain waters from January 1st to May 1st.[35] The vessel was unable to leave a port in these waters until January 3rd owing to the condition of the weather. The court found that there had been a breach of warranty and the assured was unable to recover for the loss.

In *Fallas v. Continental Insurance Co.*,[36] a policy prohibited a vessel from navigating outside certain "trading limits" as laid down in the policy. The assured approached his insurance agent and advised him he wished to use the boat outside the limits. The agent said that this would be all right. The insurer only became aware of this arrangement after the vessel was damaged in a storm outside the

32. *Robertson et al. v. Pugh* (1888), 15 S.C.R. 706.
33. *O'Leary v. Pelican Insurance Co.* (1889), 29 N.B.R. 510 (C.A.).
34. (1893), 32 N.B.R. 135 (C.A.).
35. *Richard SS. Co. Ltd., et al. v. China Mutual Insurance Co.* (1907), 42 N.S.R. 240 (C.A.).
36. [1973] 6 W.W.R. 379, [1973] I.L.R. 1-558 (B.C. S.C.).

trading limits. The court allowed the claim of the assured finding
that the insurer had held out the agent as having the authority to
bind it. Justice Berger stated:[37]

> There was a holding out by the defendant. Mr. Fallas was led to believe
> that Mr. McGaw had the power to waive the warranty. The policy itself said
> it was not valid "unless countersigned by the duly Authorized Representative
> of the Company". Facsimilies of the signatures of the president of the company
> and the secretary appear. Then it says, "Countersigned at Vancouver, B.C.
> this 28th day of April, 1970". Over the words "Authorized Representative",
> McGaw's stamp has been imprinted . . .
>
> In my view, the company cannot issue a policy to an applicant which on
> its face declares McGaw to be its authorized representative, which depends
> for its validity upon Mr. McGaw's signature, and then turn around and say,
> "McGaw wasn't our agent, he was yours."

A policy provided "warranted confined to the navigable water
of the Province of Manitoba."[38] The boat was destroyed by fire in
a parking lot in Calgary. Prior to the loss the boat had been used
in a lake in British Columbia. Judge Jewers of the Manitoba County
Court found that the clause in question was not a true warranty
but only a limitation of risk. Judge Jewers' reasoning on this point
is the exact reasoning used by the British Columbia Court of Appeal
in *Case Existological Laboratories Ltd. v. Foremost Insurance Co.
et al.*,[39] which was heard one year later. It appears from the reported
decision that the British Columbia Court of Appeal did not have
the benefit of the reasons of Judge Jewers, and *vice versa*. County
Court Judge Jewers said:[40]

> The clause does contain the term "warranted". It would perhaps, be not
> unreasonable to infer that, if the parties chose to employ that term in the contract,
> it was intended that the clause should be a "warranty". On the other hand,
> as mentioned in the above quotation from *MacGillivray and Parkington*, "there
> is no magic" in the use of the term, and, in my opinion, one must attempt
> to determine the true effect of the clause from a consideration of what is stated
> in it and its purpose and not by what the parties chose to call it . . .
>
> In this case, the fact that the word "warranted" appears in the clauses
> loses at least some of its force and significance because that very word also
> appears in other clauses in the policy in a context which makes it clear that
> the word is not used to imply a true warranty.

Judge Jewers continued:[41]

> It is suggested in *MacGillivray and Parkington* . . . that, in determining
> whether a clause should be construed as a continuing warranty, the courts

---

37. *Ibid.*, at 713, [1973] I.L.R.
38. *Britsky Building Movers Ltd. v. Dominion Insurance Corp.*, [1981] I.L.R. 1-1420 (Man. Co.
    Ct.).
39. 133 D.L.R. (3d) 727, [1982] I.L.R. 1-1567 (B.C.C.A.); affd [1983] 2 S.C.R. 47 (*sub nom. Century
    Insurance Co. of Canada v. Case Existological Laboratories Ltd.*), 48 B.C.L.R. 273, [1984]
    1 W.W.R. 97.
40. *Supra*, note 38, at 437.
41. *Supra*, at 437.

have emphasized, amongst others, the consideration as to whether a breach of the clause would permanently prejudice the insurers, even if it were subsequently remedied. They use the example that it would be unduly harsh on the owner of a commercial vehicle, who had stated the user as "goods carrying", that he should find his policy avoided utterly because he stopped to take the victim of a road accident to hospital.

Judge Jewers concluded that:[42]

> The defendant insurers would not be in any way continually prejudiced by the navigation of the boat outside of the limits in the policy: they would not be prejudiced when the boat was being navigated outside of the navigation limits because the coverage would not be in force; they would not subsequently be prejudiced when the boat was later being used within the risks covered because these risks would not have been materially affected and increased by the previous navigation outside the limits.

Judge Jewers felt that the parties might have put their intentions beyond all doubt simply by expressly stating that in the event the clause was breached by the navigation of the boat outside of the limits, that breach would entitle the insurers to avoid the policy, and the coverage would come to an end. Similarly, the parties could have stated that the clause was to be construed as a warranty within the terms of the *Marine Insurance Act.*[43]

(4) "Other" Warranties

A condition in a policy that particulars of the loss were to be given to the insurer under oath within a specified time after the loss occurred was held to be a warranty, a breach of which vitiated the policy.[44]

The submission of a proof of loss was held to be a condition precedent to the assured's right to recovery in a policy containing a proviso that the loss was to be paid within 60 days after proof of loss was given.[45]

A condition in a policy that a vessel was not to be below "Class B1" was held to mean "not to be below the class of vessels recognized by mariners as B1, if such a class existed."[46]

A policy contained the words "warranted no other insurance". The court held that these words meant that there should be no other insurance on the vessel during the continuance of the risk.[47]

---

42. *Supra,* at 439.
43. R.S.M. 1970, c. M40.
44. *McFaul v. Montreal Inland Insurance Co.* (1845), 2 U.C.Q.B. 59 (C.A.).
45. *Robertson v. N.B. Marine Assurance Co.* (1856), 8 N.B.R. 333 (C.A.).
46. *Cusack v. Mutual Insurance Co.* (1862), 6 L.C. Jur. 97, 10 R.J. R.Q. 194.
47. *Butler v. Merchants' Marine Insurance Co.* (1884), 17 N.S.R. 301 (C.A.); affd Cass. S.C. 390.

A policy which contains a condition that all claims under it are to be prosecuted within one year from the date of the loss is a valid policy with a valid condition.[48]

A marginal endorsement on a policy warranted that the yacht was to be used solely for private purposes.[49] Justice Kerwin, of the Supreme Court of Canada, stated:[50]

> [I] cannot read the statement in the margin of the policy as a condition that upon the yacht being used for other than private pleasure purposes the policy would be avoided even though at the time a loss was suffered the yacht was not being so used.

Justice Kerwin treated the promises of the assured as merely descriptive of the risk and not that "a certain state of things should continue, or a certain course of conduct be pursued during the whole period covered by the policy so that, if the particular promise be not kept, the policy was invalidated."[51]

Where an insurer insures a vessel both before and after it is transferred to a new owner, the new owner will not be charged with the implied warranties given by the prior owner.[52]

An assured's failure to have carried out the recommendations of a survey made after insurance coverage was issued in the form of a binder was not a breach of warranty entitling the insurer to repudiate liability.[53]

---

48. *Allen v. Merchants' Marine Insurance Co. of Canada* (1888), 15 S.C.R. 488.
49. *Staples v. Great American Insurance Co., New York*, [1941] S.C.R. 213, [1941] 2 D.L.R. 1, 8 I.L.R. 98.
50. *Ibid.*, at 222, [1941] S.C.R.
51. *Ibid.*, at 221.
52. *Berner & Bradley Finance Ltd. v. Sun Insurance Office Ltd.*, [1952] I.L.R. 1-069 (Ont. H.C.).
53. *Stevenson v. Continental Insurance Co. and Breen Agencies Ltd.*, [1973] I.L.R. 1-553, [1973] 6 W.W.R. 316 (B.C. S.C.).

16

Warranty of Neutrality

s. 37: (1) Where insurable property, whether ship or goods, is expressly warranted "neutral", there is an implied condition that the property shall have a neutral character at the commencement of the risk, and that, so far as the assured can control the matter, its neutral character shall be preserved during the risk.

(2) Where a ship is expressly warranted "neutral", there is also an implied condition that, so far as the assured can control the matter, she shall be properly documented, that is to say, that she shall carry the necessary papers to establish her neutrality, and that she shall not falsify or suppress her papers or use simulated papers and if any loss occurs through breach of this condition, the insurer may avoid the contract.

17

Warranty of Nationality

s. 38: There is no implied warranty as to the nationality of a ship, or that her nationality shall not be changed during the risk.

In *West v. Seaman*,[1] a ship's husband insured a vessel sailing under the Haitian flag without communicating this fact to the underwriters. The court found that there was no obligation to disclose the nationality of the vessel, there being no representation or warranty required respecting it by the policy, and no circumstances within the knowledge of the ship's husband attaching to the national character of the vessel exposing her to detention and capture.

---

1. (1885), Cass. S.C. 388.

18

Warranty of Good Safety

s. 39: Where the subject-matter insured is warranted "well" or "in good safety" on a particular day, it is sufficient if it is safe at any time during the day.

A policy contained the words "the said vessel being warranted by the insured to be then in safety".[1] The court found that in a voyage policy, the warranty of safety "refers only to the commencement of the voyage and not to the time of the insurance."[2]

---

1. *Anchor Marine Insurance Co. v. Keith* (1884), 9 S.C.R. 483.
2. *Ibid.*, at 487.

19

Warranty of Seaworthiness of Ship — Generally

s. 40: (1) In the voyage policy there is an implied warranty that at the commencement of the voyage the ship shall be seaworthy for the purpose of the particular adventure insured.

(2) Where the policy attaches while the ship is in port, there is also an implied warranty that she shall at the commencement of the risk be reasonably fit to encounter the ordinary perils of the port.

(3) Where the policy relates to a voyage that is performed in different stages during which the ship requires different kinds of or further preparation or equipment, there is an implied warranty that at the commencement of each stage the ship is seaworthy in respect of such preparation or equipment for the purposes of that stage.

(4) A ship is deemed to be seaworthy when she is reasonably fit in all respects to encounter the ordinary perils of the seas of the adventure insured.

(5) In a time policy there is no implied warranty that the ship shall be seaworthy at any stage of the adventure but where, with the privity of the assured, the ship is sent to sea in an unseaworthy state, the insurer is not liable for any loss attributable to unseaworthiness.

The unseaworthiness of a vessel may become an issue between an assured and an insurer in three types of situations. In a voyage policy, the insurer may allege that the vessel was unseaworthy at the commencement of the voyage. In a time policy, the insurer may allege that the ship was sent to sea in an unseaworthy condition with the privity of the assured and the loss was attributable to that unseaworthiness. An insurer may also seek to demonstrate that the loss was not due to a peril insured against but was due to the unseaworthy state of the vessel. Unseaworthiness, will therefore be tied in to the question of the proximate cause of the loss.[1]

In an action on a policy of insurance, the assured, to be successful must prove, on the balance of probabilities, that the loss occurred as a result of a peril of the sea. For an insurer to succeed with a defence based on the unseaworthiness of the vessel he must demonstrate, on a balance of probabilities, that the vessel was unseaworthy at the commencement of the voyage (in a voyage policy) or that the vessel was sent to sea in an unseaworthy condition with the privity

---

1. See s. 56 (Chapter 26) and the cases decided under that section of the Act.

of the assured (in a time policy). Thus, in *Federal Business Development Bank v. Commonwealth Insurance Co. et al.*[2] where a tugboat capsized and was lost, the onus was on the assured to prove that the loss was caused by a peril insured against. Justice Toy stated:[3]

> The plaintiff, to be successful, must prove on the balance of probabilities that the sinking of the *"Tightline"* occurred as a result of a peril of the sea. Even if the plaintiff establishes that the loss was caused by a peril of the sea, the defendant alleges and relies on the defence that the *"Tightline"* was unseaworthy when it commenced the voyage on the afternoon of 22nd March 1976. In this connection, the defendant *must also establish that the owner-master, Mr. Mr. Adams, had knowledge of or was privy to the unseaworthy condition of the "Tightline"*. In connection with the defence, the onus of proof to the same standard is on the defendant.

In *N.V. Bocimar S.A. v. Century Insurance Co. of Canada*,[4] the Federal Court of Appeal had occasion to determine if a shipowner could recover a general average contribution from the issuer of a general average guarantee covering the cargo owners' liability. The ship was damaged by fire while carrying cargo from North America to Europe. The defendant alleged that the ship was unseaworthy in that the crew was poorly trained in firefighting. Justice Hugessen, speaking for the Court of Appeal, said:[5]

> The claim for general average being contested solely on the grounds of the ship's being unseaworthy, the defendant bore and bears the burden of proving the fact as well as of demonstrating that the proven unseaworthiness caused or contributed to the damage ... [T]hese are simply the normal civil burdens of bringing evidence which makes the facts sought to be proved more probable than not.

The Court of Appeal reversed the trial judge's finding that the training of the crew in firefighting was so inadequate as to make the ship unseaworthy. The court added:[6]

> Some mistakes are bound to occur in an emergency situation such as a fire at sea. Even the most highly trained crew of firefighters are not going to do everything perfectly. The trial Judge recognized this and it is for this reason that he emphasizes the great number of errors which he thought had been committed. For my own part, I can only say that I am not persuaded that the relatively few well founded criticisms of the ship's firefighting efforts are of such number and gravity as to indicate that the crew was so poorly trained as to make the ship unseaworthy. The mistakes that were made seem

---

2. (1979), 13 B.C.L.R. 376 (S.C.).

3. *Ibid.*, at 378. (Emphasis added).

4. (1984), 7 C.C.L.I. 165, 53 N.R. 383 (C.A.). Leave to Appeal to S.C.C. granted 57 N.R. 80*n* (S.C.C.).

5. *Ibid.*, at 169, 7 C.C.L.I.

6. *Ibid.*, at 176.

to me to be at least as consistent with simple human error committed in a situation of great stress.

Although the burden of proof rests with the assured to demonstrate that the loss was caused by a peril insured against, this burden may be discharged by inference. The assured may be able, by positive and convincing proof of seaworthiness, to show that any other cause was improbable. In *H.B. Nickerson & Sons Ltd. v. Insurance Co. of North America et al.*,[7] a trawler sank while berthed alongside a dock at Riverport, Nova Scotia. She had been observed to have a small list to port on the previous day after unloading a catch of fish. The list gradually increased so as to permit the incursion of sea water into the ship through her scuppers. The evidence did not disclose why the vessel listed and sank. At issue was whether the evidentiary burden of proof on the assured had been discharged by inference. On this point, Justice Pratte said:[8]

> [T]he question to be answered is whether the evidence, as we read it, established the seaworthiness of the ship.... [T]he only indications of her seaworthiness were that she had not been found unseaworthy before the accident and that those who had the occasion to examine her after the accident failed to find anything wrong with her. This is insufficient, in my view, to conclude that she was seaworthy. The evidence does not disclose in any way the kind of examination that was made of the ship after the accident and none of those who had examined her testified that she was seaworthy.

If an underwriter appoints a surveyor and his report concludes that the vessel is seaworthy at a particular time, this will be binding upon the underwriter. Thus, in *Daneau v. Laurent Gendron Ltée et al.*,[9] where a scow was examined by a surveyor on behalf of underwriters and the report noted that "the scow was examined and found in good condition" the insurer was precluded from arguing that the assured had failed to supply a seaworthy vessel. Similarly, in *Riverside Landmark Corp. v. Northumberland General Insurance*,[10] the court held that as a matter of contract, the survey performed by the surveyor named in the policy was binding on the insurer "unless it is shown that the certificate [of seaworthiness] was not given in good faith."[11]

A policy of insurance contained an endorsement stating that "the

---

7. [1984] 1 F.C. 575, 49 N.R. 321, 3 C.C.L.I. 78 (C.A.); leave to appeal to the S.C.C. refused 54 N.R. 80*n* (S.C.C.).
8. *Ibid.*, at 323, 49 N.R.
9. [1964] 1 Lloyd's L.R. 220 (Ex. Ct.).
10. (1984), 8 C.C.L.I. 118 (Ont. H.C.).
11. *Ibid.*, at 142. See, however, *Lemelin v. Montreal Assurance Co.* (1873), 1 Q.L.R. 337 (Que. S.C.) where it was held that a survey of a vessel for underwriters did not constitute a waiver of the implied warranty of seaworthiness in a voyage policy.

seaworthiness of the vessel, as between the assured and the assurers is hereby admitted."[12] The assured was aware that the vessel was an uninsurable craft but not that it was unseaworthy. The court held that the uninsurability of a vessel has no connection with her seaworthiness.

In *Atwood v. The Queen*,[13] a vessel insured under the Fishing Vessel Insurance Plan was lost by a fire initiated from a spark when the assured tried to start the engine by bridging the points on the starter with a screwdriver. The plan was operated by the Federal Government of Canada under the Fishing Vessel Insurance Regulations.[14] The court found that there was no express warranty of seaworthiness in the policy. The court also held that the insurer could not rely upon the implied warranty provisions of the provincial marine insurance statute as the Fishing Vessel Insurance Regulations did not provide that policies issued pursuant to these regulations included the applicable provincial statutory sections. Justice Collier further added that if there was an obligation that the vessel be seaworthy when sent to sea, this obligation had been met. He stated:[15]

> [I] find no breach of the requirement. The unseaworthiness asserted was the faulty condition of the solenoid starter. The faulty solenoid was not, to my mind, a proximate cause of the loss. It did not cause the fire. The plaintiff used a different method of starting the engine. The cause of the fire was a spark into the bilge.

Where there is an express provision in a policy that a vessel shall be seaworthy at all times during the continuance of the policy, such a condition must be shown to have "been faithfully observed" to entitle the assured to recover under the policy.[16]

(1) Vessels Lost Within a Short Time After Leaving Port and Unexplained Sinkings

In the *H.B. Nickerson*[17] case, the vessel sank at her berth on a calm night. There was no explanation as to the cause of the sinking and the court decided the matter according to where the onus of proof lay. In *Marion Logging Co. Ltd. v. Utah Home Fire Insurance Co.*,[18] an earlier decision of the Supreme Court of British Columbia,

---

12. *Standard Marine Insurance Co. v. Whalen Pulp and Paper Co.*, 64 S.C.R. 90, [1922] 3 W.W.R. 211, 68 D.L.R. 269.
13. (1985), 10 C.C.L.I. 62 (F.C. T.D.).
14. C.R.C. 1978, c. 325.
15. *Supra*, note 13, at 68.
16. *Mittleberger v. British America Fire and Life Insurance Co.* (1846), 2 U.C.Q.B. 439 (C.A.).
17. *Supra*, note 7. See, however, *Young v. Dale & Co. Ltd. et al.*, [1968] I.L.R. 1-200 (B.C. S.C.).
18. (1956), 5 D.L.R. (2d) 700 (B.C. S.C.).

the court was required to determine the same issue. A ship moored to a dock partly sank and no explanation was given as to the cause of the sinking. Justice Macfarlane stated:[19]

> [I] am unable to find the means by which the water, which eventually caused the sinking of the boat, entered it. As I have already said, no explanation of the sinking of the ship was found in the evidence. It seems then to me to be a case which must be decided according to where the onus of proof lies. On the question of the onus of proof, the ordinary rule is where upon the evidence the Court is left in doubt whether the loss was due to a peril insured against or to a cause not covered by the policy, then the plaintiff having failed to discharge the burden which lies upon him of proving his case, there must be judgment for the defendant underwriter.

Earlier cases have also dealt with vessels sinking without explanation shortly after leaving port. In *Dawson v. Home Insurance Co.*,[20] a vessel left port and shortly after sailing was lost. The underwriters alleged that the assured had not given a sufficient reason for the sinking of the vessel and that in the absence of a reasonable cause, a presumption of unseaworthiness was raised. The court held that this presumption had been met by the evidence given by a shipwright that she was in a very good condition and seaworthy when she left port.

The principle enunciated above was also applied in *Ewart et al. v. Merchants' Marine Insurance Co.*[21] A vessel left port and after two days became leaky and floundered. The presumption of unseaworthiness was rebutted by direct evidence that "she was in good condition and seaworthy when she sailed."[22] Similarly, in *Irvine v. N. S. Marine Insurance Co.*,[23] in *Leduc v. Western Assurance Co.*,[24] and in *Morrison et al. v. N. S. Marine Insurance Co. Ltd.*,[25] the courts have weighed the evidence before them in determining whether the assured has met the presumption of unseaworthiness which has been raised by the unexplained loss shortly after the vessel leaving port.

(2) Improper Equipment, Crew, Documentation

In a voyage policy where there are distinct stages of navigation, the vessel must be seaworthy at the commencement of each stage. Where the distinct stages involve the necessity of different equipment

---

19. *Ibid.*, at 703.
20. (1870), 21 U.C.C.P. 20 (C.A.).
21. (1879), 13 N.S.R. 168 (C.A.).
22. *Ibid.*, at 172.
23. (1872), 8 N.S.R. 510 (C.A.).
24. (1880), 25 L.C. Jur. 55, 3 L.N. 124 (C.A.).
25. (1896), 28 N.S.R. 346 (C.A.).

the vessel must be so equipped for that stage, otherwise the warranty of seaworthiness is not complied with. Thus, where a vessel commenced a voyage in a river, and proceeded into salt water with boilers that were unfit for seawater, the implied warranty of seaworthiness had not been complied with.[26]

In *Woodhouse v. Provincial Insurance Co.*,[27] a vessel went to sea with a partial mainsail in a fresh wind. The insurer denied liability on the ground that the vessel was unseaworthy as it did not have a proper mainsail. The master gave evidence that he did not think the vessel was seaworthy but stated that he did not think he could have saved the vessel with any sail having regard to the wind conditions. The court found that the proximate and immediate cause of the loss of the vessel was not the alleged unseaworthiness but the weather.

In *Phoenix Insurance Co. v. Anchor Insurance Co.*,[28] a vessel lost one anchor during a voyage and failed to replace it at its next port of call. The vessel was insured under a time policy with no express warranty of seaworthiness. The insurers were unable to succeed on the defence of unseaworthiness. The court found that it could not conclude that the stranding of the vessel was caused by the absence of the second anchor.

In *Pacific Coast Freighters Ltd. v. Westchester Fire Insurance Co.*,[29] an insurer defended an action on a time policy of insurance on the ground that the vessel was unseaworthy through being overloaded. The assured was entitled to recover for the loss as the vessel was on charter and the overloading had been done by the charterers without the knowledge or privity of the assured.

In *Parrish & Heimbecker Ltd. et al. v. Burke Towing & Salvage Co. Ltd.*,[30] the court found that the ship was not unseaworthy because she was not provided with either longitudinal bulkheads in the cargo holds or with shifting boards. In reaching this conclusion, the court relied upon the "absence of any enactment or regulation in Canada requiring shifting boards, or some equivalent, in grain carrying ships on the Great Lakes".[31]

In *Berner & Bradley Finance Ltd. v. Sun Insurance Office Ltd.*,[32] the insurer resisted payment on the ground the vessel was unsea-

---

26. *Quebec Marine Insurance Co. v. Commercial Bank of Canada* (1870), 3 L.R.P.C. 234, 19 R.J.R.Q. 372 (J.C.P.C.).
27. (1871), 31 U.C.Q.B. 176 (C.A.).
28. (1884), 4 O.R. 524.
29. 38 B.C.R. 315, [1927] 1 W.W.R. 878, [1927] 2 D.L.R. 590 (C.A.).
30. [1942] Ex. C.R. 159; affd [1943] S.C.R. 179, 55 C.R.T.C. 388, [1943] 2 D.L.R. 193.
31. *Ibid.*, at 174, Ex. C.R.
32. [1952] I.L.R. 1-069 (Ont. H.C.).

worthy by virtue of an auxiliary air-cooled motor being maintained and operated below deck, and also by virtue of insufficient crew on board to properly man the vessel. The vessel was destroyed by fire. In finding for the assured, the court found that there was no evidence that the loss of the vessel by fire was caused by an inadequate crew. As well, the court held that the auxiliary motor:[33]

> "[W]as installed by competent boat builders. I cannot believe that they would install it if there was any prohibition against its installation, or that its installation would render the vessel unseaworthy.

A ship that is sent on a voyage with leaks and admitting seawater is unseaworthy.[34]

A ship that is sent into an area where ice is expected at that time of year, without being fit to encounter ice, is unseaworthy.[35]

Where an assured was aware that gasoline fumes accumulated in his boat and operated the boat, he was not allowed to recover for the loss of the boat by fire as he was privy to its unseaworthiness.[36]

Seepage of 8 to 10 gallons of water entering a vessel per hour is not necessarily indicative that a vessel is unseaworthy, especially where expert evidence is given that such seepage is not uncommon for a particular type of vessel.[37]

The fact that a vessel is not equipped with the best or latest apparatus will not necessarily mean that she is unseaworthy. In *Case Existological Laboratories Ltd. v. Foremost Insurance Co.*,[38] the insurer alleged the vessel to be unseaworthy in that she was not equipped with proper alarms and flotation devices that would prevent her from sinking even if deck valves controlling water levels remained fully open indefinitely. The alarm signals and flotation devices were all provided after the vessel was refloated and put back into service. The court found that the allegations made by the insurers did not relate to the seaworthiness of the vessel:[39]

> It is true that the vessel would sink if the deck valves were left open, but a conventional ship would also sink if the sea cocks were opened. In that sense both are inherently unseaworthy since they are heavier than water.

---

33. *Ibid.*, at 292.
34. *Canadian Industries Ltd. et al. v. Continental Explosives Ltd.* (1962), 35 D.L.R. (2d) 363, 83 C.R.T.C. 332 (B.C. S.C.).
35. *C.N.R. v. E. & S. Barbour Ltd.*, [1963] S.C.R. 323, 48 M.P.R. 319, 40 D.L.R. (2d) 668.
36. *Lamoureux v. Coast Underwriters Ltd. et al.*, [1977] I.L.R. 1-840 (B.C. S.C.).
37. *Central Native Fishermen's Co-Operative v. Commonwealth Insurance Co. et al.*, [1979] I.L.R. 1-1091 (B.C. S.C.).
38. 133 D.L.R. (3d) 727, [1982] I.L.R. 1-1567 (B.C. C.A.); affd [1983] 2 S.C.R. 47. (*sub nom. Century Insurance Co. of Canada v. Case Existological Laboratories Ltd.*), 48 B.C.L.R. 273, [1984] 1 W.W.R. 97, 150 D.L.R. (3d) 9, 49 N.R. 19, [1983] I.L.R. 1-1698.
39. *Ibid.*, at 737, 133 D.L.R.

The fact that a Canada Steamship Inspection Certificate has expired is not evidence of unseaworthiness.[40]

---

40. *Gould r. Cornhill Insurance Co. Ltd.*, 43 Nfld. & P.E.I.R. 355, 127 A.P.R. 355, 1 D.L.R. (4th) 183, 2 C.C.L.I. 148, [1983] I.L.R. 1-1715 (C.A.). Leave to appeal to S.C.C. refused 44 Nfld. & P.E.I.R. 270, 130 A.P.R. 270 (S.C.C.).

20

Warranty of Seaworthiness of Goods

s. 41: (1) In a policy on goods or other movables there is no implied warranty that the goods or movables are seaworthy.

(2) In a voyage policy on goods or other movables there is an implied warranty that at the commencement of the voyage the ship is not only seaworthy as a ship but also that she is reasonably fit to carry the goods or other movables to the destination contemplated by the policy.

21
Warranty of Legality

s. 42: There is an implied warranty that the adventure insured is a lawful one, and that, so far as the assured can control the matter, the adventure shall be carried out in a lawful manner.

The fact that a vessel has no current certificate as required by the *Canada Shipping Act* or that there has not been an inspection as required by the *Canada Shipping Act* for more than a year prior to the loss will not make the voyage an illegal voyage allowing the insurer to avoid the policy.[1]

However, where an assured was engaged in the unlawful business of boat building in a building in which it was forbidden by municipal by-law because it did not meet the standards for that use, the assured was denied recovery for a loss caused by fire. Thus, in *James Yachts Ltd. v. Thames and Mersey Marine Insurance Co. Ltd. et al.,*[2] the court found that the assured's behaviour in carrying on business where it did was in breach of the implied warranty of legality. The insurer was entitled to avoid the contract of insurance.

In *Federal Business Development Bank v. Commonwealth Insurance Co. et al.,*[3] a tugboat towing a jet boat loaded with a cargo of shingle bolts cut from cedar stumps was swamped by a large wave and sank. One of the defences raised by the insurers was that the voyage was an illegal voyage. The insurer submitted that the assured had sawed up cedar logs as opposed to cedar stumps, and, therefore were guilty of theft pursuant to s. 299 of the *Criminal Code*[4] of Canada as well as offences against the *Ministry of Forests Act*[5]. The court found that there had not been a breach of the *Criminal Code*[6] of Canada. The court was prepared to assume that there was a technical breach of ss. 65 and 66 of the *Ministry of Forests Act*[7] in that the stumps were not scaled before being cut or the shingle bolts were not scaled forthwith. However, the court was not prepared

---

1. *Atlantic Freighting Co. Ltd. v. Provincial Insurance Co. Ltd.* (1956), 5 D.L.R. (2d) 164, [1956] I.L.R. 1-245 (N.S. S.C.).
2. [1976] I.L.R. 1-751 (B.C. S.C.).
3. (1979), 13 B.C.L.R. 376 (S.C.).
4. R.S.C. 1970, c. C-34.
5. R.S.B.C. 1960, c. 153.
6. *Supra*, note 4.
7. *Supra*, note 5.

to find that there was a breach of the implied warranty of legality. Justice Toy stated:[8]

> [J]ames Yachts Ltd. v. Thames & Mersey Marine Ins. Co., ... in my view, is distinguishable in that the unlawful adventure was being deliberately carried on by the plaintiff after he had been advised that such a business was unlawfully being conducted on the premises that the plaintiff sought to insure with the defendant. In this case, there is no evidence of any such state of mind on the part of Mr. Adams ... The case is further distinguishable on the basis that, unlike the case at bar, there was a direct relationship between the unlawful use of the building because it did not meet acceptable safety standards and the fire risk which was assumed as the adventure insured. In the case at bar, the failure to scale stumps or shingle bolts is quite remote from the adventure insured, i.e., the risk of perils of the sea.

---

8. *Supra*, note 3, at 389-90.

22

The Voyage[1]

s. 43: (1) Where the subject-matter is insured by a voyage policy "at and from" or "from" a particular place, it is not necessary that the ship should be at that place when the contract is concluded, but there is an implied condition that the adventure shall be commenced within a reasonable time and that if the adventure is not so commenced the insurer may avoid the contract.
(2) The implied condition may be negatived by showing that the delay was caused by circumstances known to the insurer before the contract was concluded or by showing that he waived the condition.

s. 44: Where the place of departure is specified in the policy and the ship, instead of sailing from that place, sails from any other place, the risk does not attach.

s. 45: Where the destination is specified in the policy and the ship, instead of sailing for that destination, sails for any other destination, the risk does not attach.

s. 46: (1) Where, after the commencement of the risk, the destination of the ship is voluntarily changed from the destination contemplated by the policy, there is said to be a change of voyage.
(2) Unless the policy otherwise provides, where there is a change of voyage, the insurer is discharged from liability as from the time of change, that is to say, as from the time when the determination to change it is manifested; and it is immaterial that the ship may not in fact have left the course of the voyage contemplated by the policy when the loss occurs.

A policy of insurance upon a vessel was for a voyage "at and from St. John, N.B., to a port of call and discharge and loading in the West Indies, and from thence to a port of call and discharge in the United Kingdom."[2] The issue was whether this meant one port for discharge and loading, or one port for discharge and another for loading. The court found that there was not ambiguity in the words and held that it meant one port for discharge and loading. It added:[3]

---

1. See also s. 36 and chapter 15(3) "Navigation" Warranties.
2. *M'Givern v. Provincial Insurance Co. of Toronto* (1858), 9 N.B.R. 64 (C.A.).
3. *Ibid.*, at 69.

We are not prepared to say that if a peculiar meaning were, by the usage
in reference to contracts of this description, attached to the terms "a port of
call" and "discharge and loading," it might not have been open to the plaintiff
to have given evidence of such usage, according thereto ...

The only usage which would have aided him, would have been one by which
it would have appeared that this mode of expression when used in policies
of insurance, meant by the understanding of the assurers and assured, not
one port both for discharge and loading, but one port for discharge and another
for loading. But he proved nothing of this kind.

A cargo was insured "at and from Arichat to Halifax."[4] It was
shipped from a port nine miles distant from Arichat. The usage
of the trade in the county where both ports were situated appeared
to be that they were treated by merchants in the area, by masters
of coasting vessels and by merchants in Halifax to be the one and
the same port. The court found that this usage did not bind the
underwriters unless it was known to or recognized by them.

Where a policy of insurance covers a voyage "at and from Buenos
Ayres to Matanzas Cuba" and there is an endorsement on the policy
granting permission for the vessel to proceed "from Monte Video
to Cardenas, calling at Barbados for orders instead of Buenos Ayres
to Matanzas" the policy and endorsement must be read together.[5]
The policy was construed as covering a voyage from Buenos Ayres
to Cardenas with liberty to go to Monte Video as an intermediate
port.

In *Wylde v. Union Marine Insurance Co.*[6] freight was insured
"at and from Block House Mines to Montreal". In issuing the policy
the insurers inserted the words "beginning the adventure upon the
said freight from and immediately following the loading thereof on
board." The vessel was lost at Block House Mines before she commenced loading cargo on board. The court found that where freight
is insured at and from a given port, it is insured so long as the
ship is at the port and allowed the assured to recover.

Similarly, in *Lord v. Grant*[7] the risk in a policy of insurance
on freight "at and from Pictou, to and at Aspinwall" was found to
attach when the ship was ready to take in the cargo. Justice Mc-
Donald, delivering the judgment of the court said:[8]

[I]n cases of insurance upon fixed sums stipulated to be paid to the ship-owner
as freight for the whole voyage by the terms of a charter-party, the amount

4. *Hennessy v. New York Mutual Insurance Co.* (1863), 5 N.S.R. 259 (C.A.).
5. *Wilson v. Merchants' Marine Insurance Co.* (1872), 9 N.S.R. 81.
6. (1875), R.E.D. 203; affd 10 N.S.R. 205 (C.A.).
7. (1875), 10 N.S.R. 120 (C.A.).
8. *Ibid.*, at 125.

insured on such freight at and from a certain place may be recovered, if ...
the voyage commenced and that the ship was ready to take in the cargo ...

A policy of insurance specified that the loading of the vessel
was to be at a "loading port on the western coast of South America."[9]
The vessel loaded at Lobos, in the Guano Islands, some 25 to 40
miles off the coast. Evidence was given by shipowners and mariners
that according to commercial usage, the description in the policy
would include the Guano Islands. In allowing the assured to recover
for the loss, the court stated that the words in the policy must be
taken to have been used in a commercial sense and as understood
by shippers, shipowners and underwriters.

A policy of insurance insured a ship on a voyage "at and from
Sydney to St. John, N.B."[10] The vessel went to Sydney for orders
but did not enter the port as she was able to receive her orders
by signal. Evidence was given that vessels going to Sydney never
entered the harbour, whose entrance was five or six miles further
inland. In finding that the vessel arrived at Sydney, the court stated:[11]

> Walter McLean, also called for defendants, a master mariner for 12 years,
> says that he had been in Sydney harbour about six times and only once went
> inside the bars, being then chartered to load there; that Sydney is a port to
> which many vessels go for orders; that in anchoring outside he always considered
> he was in Sydney harbour.
>
> Now this is indeed the testimony of navigators rather than of shipowners
> and underwriters, but practices so uniform and reasonable and founded on
> consideration for the shipowner's benefit may fairly be presumed to be known
> to and approved of by them.... [T]his uniform practice of navigators might
> reasonably be known to persons engaged in the business of underwriting.

A policy of insurance did not cover any loss of a vessel while
on any voyage "to or from any foreign port."[12] The vessel was lost
on a voyage from North Sydney, Cape Breton to Newfoundland. The
insurer was a local company in Newfoundland insuring local vessels.
The vessel was lost on December 21, 1950. Newfoundland joined
Canada on the 30th of March 1949. The question arose as to whether
North Sydney was a foreign port at the time of the loss. The court
held that for the purposes of the policy, North Sydney was a foreign
port. It reasoned that:[13]

---

9. *Providence Washington Insurance Co. v. Gerow* (1890), 17 S.C.R. 387.
10. *Saint Paul Fire and Marine Insurance Co. v. Troop and Irvine* (1896), 26 S.C.R. 5.
11. *Ibid.,* at 10-11.
12. *Re an Arbitration between Terra Nova Mutual Marine Insurance Co. Ltd. and Blackwood,*
    [1952] I.L.R. 1-074 (Nfld. S.C.).
13. *Ibid.,* at 305.

On the whole, and taking into consideration both the normal connotation of the word "foreign" and the general character of the company and its operations, we do not feel bound to interpret the word "foreign" in its political sense; we think that in this connection and in the contemplation of the parties it meant "external to this Island."

In *Central Native Fishermen's Co-operative v. Commonwealth Insurance Co. et al.*,[14] the insurer denied liability on the basis that the risk did not attach because the vessel, when lost, was not on a voyage covered in the insurance policy, namely "between Bella Bella, B.C. and Vancouver, B.C." but rather had departed from Shearwater, B.C. The assured's position was that in the common parlance of the fishing industry, Shearwater and Bella Bella were the same and were used interchangeably. The court accepted the assured's evidence and extended the term "Bella Bella" in the policy to include "Shearwater".

---

14. [1979] I.L.R. 1-1091 (B.C. S.C.).

23

Deviation and Delay

s. 47: (1) Where a ship, without lawful excuse, deviates from the voyage contemplated by the policy, the insurer is discharged from liability as from the time of deviation and it is immaterial that the ship may have regained her route before any loss occurs.

(2) There is a deviation from the voyage contemplated by the policy,

(*a*) where the course of the voyage is specially designated by the policy and that course is departed from; or

(*b*) where the course of the voyage is not specifically designated by the policy but the usual and customary course is departed from.

(3) The intention to deviate is immaterial and there must be a deviation in fact to discharge the insurer from his liability under the contract.

s. 48: (1) Where several ports of discharge are specified by the policy, the ship may proceed to all or any of them, but, in the absence of any usage or sufficient cause to the contrary, she must proceed to them, or such of them as she goes to, in the order designated in the policy, and if she does not there is a deviation.

(2) Where the policy is to "ports of discharge", within a given area, which are not named, the ship must, in the absence of any usage or sufficient cause to the contrary, proceed to them, or such of them as she goes to, in their geographical order, and if she does not there is a deviation.

s. 49: In the case of a voyage policy, the adventure insured must be prosecuted throughout its course with reasonable dispatch, and, if without lawful excuse it is not so prosecuted, the insurer is discharged from liability as from the time when the delay became unreasonable.

s. 50: (1) Deviation or delay in prosecuting the voyage contemplated by the policy is excused,

(*a*) where authorized by any special term in the policy; or

(*b*) where caused by circumstances beyond the control of the master and his employer; or

(*c*) where reasonably necessary in order to comply with an express or implied warranty; or

(*d*) where reasonably necessary for the safety of the ship or subject-matter insured; or

(*e*) for the purpose of saving human life or aiding a ship in distress where human life may be in danger; or

(*f*) where reasonably necessary for the purpose of obtaining medical or surgical aid for any person on board the ship; or (*g*) where caused by the barratrous conduct of the master or crew, if barratry is one of the perils insured against.

(2) When the cause excusing the deviation or delay ceases to operate, the ship must resume her course and prosecute her voyage with reasonable dispatch.

In s. 46 of the Act if after the commencement of the risk the destination of the ship is voluntarily changed the insurer is discharged from liability as from the time when the determination to change is manifested whether or not the ship has in fact left the course of the voyage contemplated in the policy when the loss occurs. In s. 47, the insurer is discharged from liability for a loss after a deviation only when a deviation in fact has occurred. The intention to deviate is immaterial. Sections 44-47 of the Act have been distinguished as follows:[1]

> First, the ship may sail on a voyage not contemplated by the policy. In that case the risk does not attach. See ss. [44] and [45]. Secondly, a ship may commence the adventure insured, but afterwards change her destination. There is then a change of voyage, [s. 46]. In that case the risk attaches, but is afterwards avoided. Thirdly, a ship may proceed from the terminus *a quo* to the terminus *ad quem*, but sail thither by an unauthorized route. In that case there is a deviation, [s. 47].

In *Crowell v. Geddes*[2] a policy of insurance provided coverage for a vessel on a voyage from Halifax to Nassau, in the Island of New Providence, and back to Halifax. The vessel sailed to Nassau, where she took on board cargo for New York and none for Halifax. Before leaving Nassau the captain had expressed his determination to return to Nassau or some other West Indies Island from New York if he could obtain freight. He also expressed his disinclination to return to Halifax. The vessel was lost on its route to New York, a route which was common both to New York and Halifax. The court held that there had been a change in the voyage and not merely a deviation and the underwriters were not liable. In so holding, the court stated:[3]

> If this were a case merely of an intention to deviate, then as the loss took place before the dividing point of the voyage had been reached, it is clear, under the decisions which have been given, that the underwriters would be liable.... [I]n deviation, the *terminus a quo* and that *ad quem* are the same; or, as it was put by counsel in argument ... in case of a deviation, the *termini*

1. E.R.H. Ivamy, *Chalmers' Marine Insurance Act 1906*, 8th ed. Butterworths & Co. (Publishers) Ltd., London, 1976, at 64.
2. (1862), 5 N.S.R. 184 (C.A.).
3. *Ibid.*, at 185.

of the voyage remain, though the course, by which the *terminus ad quem* is sought, be changed. But when the *terminus ad quem* is changed, it is not a deviation but an abandonment of the voyage; and such an abandonment, at whatever time it takes place, whether before or after the arrival of the ship at the dividing point, discharges the underwriters.

Where a partial loss occurs prior to a deviation the insurers will be liable for that partial loss.[4]

In *Fisher v. Western Assurance Co.*[5] a cargo of wheat was insured from Port Darlington to Kingston and from there to Montreal. The wheat was discharged three miles below Kingston onto a barge. The barge was returning to Kingston to complete her cargo to then proceed to Montreal when she was lost. The court found that there was a deviation and that the assured failed to demonstrate that there was a custom or usage to do what was done.

To succeed on a defence of unnecessary or unreasonable delay it is not necessary that insurers demonstrate that the delay amounted to a deviation. There may be unreasonable delay without deviation.[6]

Where a vessel starts her voyage and at the intermediate port is put on blocks, detained for 17 days, repaired and reclassed, this will constitute unreasonable delay and the insurer is entitled to avoid the policy.[7]

A vessel was insured for a voyage from Cardiff to Aden and then to India. She set sail for Aden with the intention of proceeding to Chincha instead of India. She was lost before reaching Aden. The court found that there had been no deviation and that the underwriters were liable for the loss.[8]

In *Rodgers v. Jones*,[9] a cargo of fish was insured at and from Eel Brook to Halifax. The vessel loaded at Eel Brook and proceeded to two other ports to load supplies. The court held that there was a deviation, unexplained by any evidence, and this rendered the policy void.

In *Spinney and Oliver v. Ocean Mutual Marine Insurance Co.*,[10] a vessel sailed on December 15th from Pubnico, Nova Scotia towards Halifax. The vessel put into Shelbourne harbour and remained there until January 4th. She sailed out on the 4th and was lost. It was shown that during this time period other vessels bound on the same

---

4. *Fairbanks et al. v. Union Marine Insurance Co.* (1854), 2 N.S.R. 271 (C.A.).
5. (1854), 11 U.C.Q.B. 255 (C.A.).
6. *Orchard v. Aetna Insurance Co.* (1856), 5 U.C.C.P. 445, at 449 (C.A.).
7. *Reed v. Weldon* (1869), 12 N.B.R. 460 (C.A.); *Reed v. Philps* (1870), 13 N.B.R. 171 (C.A.).
8. *Ibid.*, 12 N.B.R. 460. The court found as a fact that the intention to deviate had only been formed after the risk attached. Hence, it was not a change of voyage.
9. (1883), 16 N.S.R. 96 (C.A.).
10. (1890), 17 S.C.R. 326.

course did proceed after seeking shelter in Shelbourne. In deciding that the insurer was entitled to avoid the policy, Chief Justice Ritchie of the Supreme Court of Canada, said:[11]

> There can be no doubt that the understanding implied in the contract is not only that the voyage shall be accomplished in the track or course of navigation in which it ought to be pursued, but also that the voyage shall be commenced and completed with all reasonable expedition, that is, with all reasonable and ordinary diligence, and that any unreasonable or unexcused delay, either in commencing or prosecuting the voyage insured, alters the risk and absolves the underwriter from his liability for any subsequent loss. No doubt, it must be an unreasonable or inexcusable delay, that is, a wilful and unnecessary waste of time. In like manner as in the case of a departure from the usual course of navigation it is not necessary to prove that the peril has been enhanced, so it is equally clear that the same principle applies in case of deviation by delay.

In *Eisenhauer et al. v. Nova Scotia Marine Insurance Co.*,[12] the Court of Appeal for Nova Scotia distinguished the *Spinney*[13] decision and held that where a master put his vessel into an intermediate port overnight to escape threatened bad weather there was no deviation. The delay was neither "wilful or unnecessary."[14]

In *Mannheim Insurance Co. et al. v. Atlantic and Lake Superior Railway Co.*,[15] Justice Hall aptly summarized the reason for strictness of the law with respect to deviations and delays:[16]

> [The] authorities almost shock one's sense of justice, upon the first consideration of them, by the strictness and exactitude with which these rules are enforced. Upon second thought, however, one realizes the reason and justice of them. Marine insurance is undertaken by the underwriters upon the chances of a vessel making a safe voyage between two stipulated ports over the usual and well established route. For the safety of the ship or cargo under these conditions, they will undertake insurance at a stipulated rate. They are equally ready to insure under an almost infinite variety of other conditions; *e.g.*, for an alternative or additional port *ad quem*; for right to touch at one or all intermediate ports for supplies, or to discharge or add to cargo; for a time limit, or for the purpose of the venture whatever time may be required, but each variation in the conditions carries with it the right to vary the rate of premium and the nature and extent of insurance. Each additional landing which the vessel may make is considered to add slightly or otherwise to the risk, and an additional rate, 1/8 or 1/4 of 1 per cent for each is usually added to the ordinary premium for a straight voyage between two ports. When, therefore, the owner of the ship or cargo secures insurance upon the basis of a direct voyage between

---

11. *Ibid.*, at 328-29.
12. (1892), 24 N.S.R. 205; affd Cout. S.C. 811.
13. *Supra*, note 10.
14. *Supra*, note 12, at 212, 24 N.S.R.
15. (1900), 11 Que. K.B. 200 (C.A.).
16. *Ibid.*, at 206-207.

two named ports, one of the essential conditions of that contract is violated if the vessel adopts a different route from the usual one, or if she puts in to an intermediate harbour and thereby adds to the risk not only by the increased danger of approaching the land, but by prolonging the time within which the voyage should have been made. Even if the risk be not increased, the contract has been varied, and is held to be at an end the moment such variation or deviation occurred. It strikes one at first thought that if the subsequent loss be proved not to have resulted from the deviation, the insurer should be held to make it good, but the authorities make it clear that the time or manner of such subsequent loss has no influence on the question of liability. The insurance absolutely ceased at the time of the deviation, and whether or not a loss subsequently occurred, or when, or how, is as completely indifferent to the underwriter as though he had never assumed the risk.

A policy of insurance may permit, by way of a "deviation clause", a vessel to deviate from the course contemplated in the policy upon payment of additional premium.[17]

---

17. See *Chartered Bank of India v. Pacific Marine Insurance Co.*, 33 B.C.R. 91, [1924] 1 W.W.R. 114, [1923] 4 D.L.R. 942 (C.A.), where Justice Macdonald stated at 943, D.L.R., "The law permits deviation of necessity. The clause in question here permits deviation not of necessity and it provides for compensation to the insurer for such deviations when they occur."

24

Assignment of the Policy

s. 51: (1) A marine policy is assignable unless it contains terms expressly prohibiting assignment and it may be assigned either before or after loss.

(2) Where a marine policy has been assigned so as to pass the beneficial interest in such policy, the assignee of the policy is entitled to sue thereon in his own name, and the defendant is entitled to make any defence arising out of the contract that he would have been entitled to make if the action had been brought in the name of the person by or on behalf or whom the policy was effected.

(3) A marine policy may be assigned by endorsement thereon or in other customary manner.

s. 52: Where the assured has parted with or lost his interest in the subject-matter insured, and has not, before or at the time of so doing, expressly or impliedly agreed to assign the policy, any subsequent assignment of the policy is inoperative; provided that nothing in this section affects the assignment of a policy after loss.

In *Re SS "Dorin"*,[1] a marine policy was assigned to a bank, which was a creditor of the owner of the vessel. The vessel had been mortgaged and the mortgagee had assigned his interest to a third party. In an action to determine who was entitled to the proceeds of insurance after a loss of the vessel, the court found that the bank had the same rights as the owner, and the third party had the same rights as the mortgagee. The third party (mortgagee) was entitled to be paid first, and the bank was entitled to any surplus. The parties had no greater and no lesser rights than what had been assigned to them.

---

1. [1935] 4 D.L.R. 526 (N.S. S.C.); affd 10 M.P.R. 325 (*sub nom. Canada S.K.F. Co. v. Royal Bank*), [1936] 2 D.L.R. 40, 3 I.L.R. 309 (N.S. C.A.).

25

The Premium[1]

s. 53: Unless otherwise agreed, the duty of the assured or his agent to pay the premium and the duty of the insurer to issue the policy to the assured or his agent are concurrent conditions, and the insurer is not bound to issue the policy until payment or tender of the premium.

s. 54: (1) Unless otherwise agreed, where a marine policy is effected on behalf of the assured by a broker, the broker is directly responsible to the insurer for the premium and the insurer is directly responsible to the assured for the amount that may be payable in respect of losses or in respect of returnable premium.
(2) Unless otherwise agreed, the broker has, as against the assured, a lien upon the policy for the amount of the premium and his charges in respect of effecting the policy, and, where he has dealt with the person who employs him as a principal, he has also a lien on the policy in respect of any balance on any insurance account that may be due to him from such person, unless when the debt was incurred he had reason to believe that such person was only an agent.

s. 55: Where a marine policy effected on behalf of the assured by a broker acknowledges the receipt of the premium, such acknowledgment is, in the absence of fraud, conclusive as between the insurer and the assured, but not as between the insurer and broker.

Sections 53, 54 and 55 are a codification of the custom in England which was in existence at least 100 years prior to codification. Justice Rose in *O'Keefe and Lynch of Canada Ltd. v. Toronto Insurance and Vessel Agency Ltd.*[2] stated:[3]

> In England, by custom which was proved so often that the courts took judicial notice of it, when marine insurance was effected through a broker, the broker and not the assured was liable to the underwriter for the premium, while the underwriter was directly responsible to the assured for the loss; and this was the case even when the policy recited an undertaking on the part of the assured to pay the premium. As between the underwriter and the assured (who often was unknown to the underwriter) the broker was deemed to have paid the premium (with money which he had borrowed from the underwriter). As between the broker and the assured, the broker was deemed to have paid

---

1. See also s. 32 and ss. 83-85.
2. 59 O.L.R. 235, [1926] 4 D.L.R. 477.
3. *Ibid.*, at 240, O.L.R.

the premium for and at the request of the assured ... Since 1906, "unless otherwise agreed," the rights of the underwriter, the assured, and the broker have been by statute what they were by custom: The Marine Insurance Act[4].

Where a vessel was lost at sea and at the time the assured was not in default of payment of the premium but when the action was commenced the premium payment was in default, this did not constitute a defence under the policy.[5]

A guarantee to secure the payment of premium has been held to be equivalent to actual payment of the premium and the insurers could not avoid the policy.[6]

Similarly, a promise to pay the premium has been held to be good and sufficient consideration in a contract of marine insurance.[7]

4. 1906, 6 Edw. VII, c. 41, ss. 52-54.
5. *Meagher v. Home Insurance Co.* (1860), 10 U.C.C.P. 313 (C.A.).
6. *Anchor Marine Insurance Co. v. Corbett* (1882), 9 S.C.R. 73.
7. *Osborne v. The Queen in right of Canada*, [1984] I.L.R. 1-1724 (F.C. T.D.).

26

Perils Insured Against

s. 56: (1) Subject to the provisions of this Act and unless the policy otherwise provides, the insurer is liable for any loss proximately caused by a peril insured against, but, subject as aforesaid, he is not liable for any loss that is not proximately caused by a peril insured against.
(2) In particular,
(*a*) the insurer is not liable for any loss attributable to the wilful misconduct of the assured, but, unless the policy otherwise provides, he is liable for any loss proximately caused by a peril insured against, even though the loss would not have happened but for the misconduct or negligence of the master or crew;
(*b*) unless the policy otherwise provides, the insurer on ship or goods is not liable for any loss proximately caused by delay, although the delay is caused by a peril insured against;
(*c*) unless the policy otherwise provides, the insurer is not liable for ordinary wear and tear, ordinary leakage and breakage, inherent vice or nature of the subject-matter insured, or for any loss proximately caused by rats or vermin, or for any injury to machinery not proximately caused by maritime perils.

The average policy of insurance will be similar in form to that found in the Schedule to the Act. The form of policy in the Schedule is the Lloyd's S.G. policy which has been in use for over 200 years. The assurers will pay for any losses proximately caused by perils "of the seas, men-of-war, fire, enemies, pirates, rovers, thieves, jettisons, letters of mart and countermart, surprisals, takings at sea, arrests, restraints, and detainments of all kings, princes, and people, of what nation, condition, or quality soever, barratry of the master and mariners, and of all other perils, losses and misfortunes, that have or shall come to the hurt, detriment, or damage of the said goods and merchandises, and ship, *etc.*, or any part thereof." The Rules for Construction of the Policy found in the Schedule define some of these terms such as "perils of the seas", "fire", "barratry", *etc.*

(1) Onus of Proof

The burden of proof that the loss arose from a peril covered by the policy is on the assured.[1] The burden has been described as

---

1. See *Myles v. Montreal Insurance Co.* (1870), 20 U.C.C.P. 283, at 287 (C.A.); *Stad v. Firemans Fund Insurance Co. et al.*, [1979] I.L.R. 1-1070, at 66 (B.C. S.C.); *Marion Logging Co. Ltd.*

follows:[2]

> The onus is of establishing that a peril of the sea was at the origin of the loss, not of identifying the exact cause, and the standard of proof applicable is only that of a balance of probabilities.

The burden can be met by inference. Thus:[3]

> If the owner, although unable to put his finger on the precise cause of the loss, can nevertheless demonstrate on a balance of probabilities that, because of the circumstances of the case and the clear seaworthiness of the vessel, most of the events that could not be included into the concept of peril of the sea have to be disregarded as possible causes, he may very well satisfy the onus that rested upon him. This is so, obviously, because proof by inference or presumption is a perfectly valid means of evidence and the inference relied upon here may be quite reasonable.

(2) Proximate Cause

In *Canada Rice Mills Ltd. v. Union Marine & General Insurance Co.*[4] the Judicial Committee of the Privy Council had occasion to comment on the concept of proximate cause. The action was on a marine insurance policy for damages to a shipment of rice. The rice was stored in the vessel's holds and required ventilation. During a storm, the ventilator covers were closed to prevent the incursion of seawater into the holds. The interruption of ventilation caused the heating and fermentation of the rice thereby damaging it. The court found that the loss had been proximately caused by a peril of the sea. The damage was caused by an action taken to prevent the incursion of sea water. This action was not to be "regarded as a separate or independent cause, interposed between the peril of the sea and the damage, but as being such a mere matter of routine seamanship necessitated by the peril that the damage can be regarded as the direct result of the peril."[5] Lord Wright, speaking for the court, stated:[6]

> [I]t is now established by such authorities as *Leyland v. Norwich Union F. Ins. Soc.*, [1918] A.C. 350 and many others that *causa proxima* in insurance

---

   v. Utah Home Fire Insurance Co. (1956), 5 D.L.R. (2d) 700, at 703-704 (B.C. S.C.); *H.B. Nickerson & Sons Ltd. v. Insurance Co. of North America et al.*, [1984] 1 F.C. 575, 49 N.R. 321, at 330 (C.A.); *Coons v. Aetna Insurance Co.* (1868), 18 U.C.C.P. 305, at 311; *Creeden & Avery Ltd. v. North China Insurance Co.*, 24 B.C.R. 335, [1917] 3 W.W.R. 33, 36 D.L.R. 359, at 363 (C.A.).

2. *H.B. Nickerson & Sons Ltd. v. Insurance Co. of North America et al.*, [1984] 1 F.C. 575, 49 N.R. 321, at 330, 3 C.C.L.I. 78 (C.A.); leave to appeal to the S.C.C. refused 54 N.R. 80 (S.C.C.).

3. *Ibid.*, p. 330, 49 N.R.

4. [1941] 3 W.W.R. 401, [1941] 1 D.L.R. 1, 8 I.L.R. 1 (J.C. P.C.).

5. *Ibid.*, at 11, 1 D.L.R.

6. *Ibid.*, at 11.

law does not necessarily mean the cause last in time but what is "in substance" the cause, per Lord Finlay at p. 355, or the cause "to be determined by commonsense principles," per Lord Dunedin at p. 362. ...Their Lordships agree with this expression of opinion.

In *H.B. Nickerson & Sons Ltd. v. Insurance Co. of North America et al.*,[7] Justice Marceau commented on what is meant by "proximate cause":[8]

> It is likewise beyond question that in order to establish that the loss occurred from a peril insured against, the insured has to prove ... that the "proximate cause" of the loss was a peril of the sea, the words "proximate cause" referring not necessarily to the ultimate or immediate cause of the loss in a possible succession of causes, the ultimate effect of which was the loss, but referring rather to the dominant and effective cause, the one that has really triggered the natural sequence of causes that led to the loss.

In *Case Existological Laboratories v. Foremost Insurance Co. et al.*,[9] Justice Lambert of the British Columbia Court of Appeal referred to proximate cause as the "efficient" cause. Thus, the negligent failure of a crew member to close the deck valves of the *Bamcell II* and so prevent the continued entry of sea water into the vessel was held to be the efficient cause for the sinking of the vessel.

In *Williams v. The Queen*[10], a matter involving the sinking of a fishing vessel, Justice McNair of the Federal Court, Trial Division found that the proximate cause of the sinking was the incursion of seawater into the vessel. He then went on to consider the "primary cause" of the loss. Justice McNair stated:[11]

> In my judgment, the loss in this case was proximately caused by a 'peril of the seas'. The fortuitous accident or event was the fracturing of the sea intake pipe which led to the incursion of seawater into the vessel in circumstances where that happening could not have been inevitably foreseen. The incursion of seawater resulting from the fractured pipe is the fortuitous occurrence which was the proximate cause of the loss. It becomes necessary to determine 'the cause of that cause' only insofar as it relates to the ordinary wear-and-tear exclusion. I have no difficulty in finding on the reasonable balance of probability that the primary cause of the fracture of the sea intake pipe was the striking of the submerged object.

---

7. *Supra*, note 2.
8. *Supra*, p. 326, 49 N.R.
9. 133 D.L.R. (3d) 727, [1982] I.L.R. 1-1567 (B.C. C.A.); affd [1983] 2 S.C.R. 47 (*sub nom. Century Insurance Co. of Canada v. Case Existological Laboratories Ltd.*), 48 B.C.L.R. 273, [1984] 1 W.W.R. 97, 150 D.L.R. (3d) 9, 49 N.R. 19, [1983] I.L.R. 1-1698.
10. (1984), 7 C.C.L.I. 198 (F.C. T.D.).
11. *Ibid.*, at 210.

Applying the reasoning in earlier cases, one would have thought that Justice McNair would have found the proximate cause to have been the intake pipe striking the submerged object.[12]

(3) Perils of the Sea

Rule 7 of the *Rules for the Construction of the Policy* found in the Schedule to the Act[13] provides that:

> The term 'perils of the sea' refers only to fortuitous accidents or casualties of the seas. It does not include the ordinary action of the winds and waves.

British and Canadian courts have distinguished between that which is accidental or fortuitous and that which is natural, ordinary or expected in its nature having regard to the particular circumstances of the case.

(3.1) U.K. Decisions Considered by Canadian Courts

There are a number of British decisions which have been the basis for nearly all of the Canadian cases dealing with perils of the sea. The words used by the English judges in these important decisions have been often repeated by Canadian courts.

In *Thames & Mersey Marine Insurance Co. Ltd. v. Hamilton, Fraser & Co. (The Inchmaree)*,[14] an engine was damaged when a valve was mistakenly left closed. The court found that the insurer was not liable as the accident was not incidental to a sea voyage. The loss did not fall under the words "perils of the sea" nor under the words "all other perils." Lord Herschell said:[15]

> To which of the specially enumerated perils is it similar? The only one that could be suggested is "perils of the seas". The damage here arose from the air-chamber of the donkey-pump giving way under an excessive pressure of water, owing to the proper outlet being closed. It is, I think, impossible to say that this is damage occasioned by a cause similar to "perils of the sea,"

---

12. See also *Coast Ferries Ltd. v. Century Insurance Co. of Canada et al.* (1974), 48 D.L.R. (3d) 310, [1974] I.L.R. 1-612 (S.C.C.) where the proximate cause of a vessel's casualty was found to be the unseaworthiness of the vessel caused by improper loading for which the master was to blame.

13. *Marine Insurance Act*, R.S.O. 1980, c. 255.

14. (1887), 12 App. Cas. 484, 36 W.R. 337 (H.L.). This case gave rise to the use of the "Inchmaree Clause". This clause now covers, for example, the negligence of a master or crew provided the owners did not cause the loss or damage by failing to exercise due diligence. See chapter 48 and Appendix D.

15. *Ibid.*, at 498.

on any interpretation which has ever been applied to that term. It will be observed that Lord Ellenborough limits the operation of the clause to "marine damage". By this I do not understand him to mean only damage which has been caused by the sea, but damage of a character to which a marine adventure is subject. Such an adventure has its own perils, to which either it is exclusively subject or which possess in relation to it a special or peculiar character. To secure an indemnity against these is the purpose and object of a policy of marine insurance.

In *Wilson, Sons & Co. v. The Xantho*,[16] two ships collided and the "*Xantho*" foundered. The court found that the loss was proximately caused by a peril of the sea, *i.e.* foundering.[17] Lord Herschell stated:[18]

> I think it clear that the term "perils of the sea" does not cover every accident or casualty which may happen to the subject-matter of the insurance on the sea. It must be a peril "of" the sea. Again, it is well settled that it is not every loss or damage of which the sea is the immediate cause that is covered by these words. They do not protect, for example, against that natural and inevitable action of the winds and waves which result in what may be described as wear and tear. There must be some casualty, something which could not be foreseen as one of the necessary incidents of the adventure. The purpose of the policy is to secure an indemnity against accidents which may happen, not against events which must happen. It was contended that those losses only were losses by perils of the sea, which were occasioned by extraordinary violence of the winds or waves. I think this is too narrow a construction of the words and it is certainly not supported by the authorities or by common understanding. It is beyond question, that if a vessel strikes upon a sunken rock in fair weather and sinks, this is a loss by perils of the sea.

In *Hamilton, Fraser & Co. v. Pandorf & Co.*,[19] rats gnawed a hole in a pipe on board a ship, whereby seawater escaped and damaged a cargo of rice. The court found that the loss had been caused by a peril of the sea. Lord Watson said:[20]

> If the respondents were preferring a claim under a contract of marine insurance, expressed in ordinary terms I should be clearly of the opinion that they were entitled to recover on the ground that their loss was occasioned by a peril of the sea within the meaning of the contract. When a cargo of rice is directly injured by rats, or by the crew of the vessel, the sea has no share

---

16. (1887), 12 App. Cas. 503 (H.L.).
17. The court found that the meaning of "perils of the seas" in bills of lading and in policies of insurance is the same. In a marine policy the court will regard only the *causa proxima*, whereas in a bill of lading the court will consider also the *causa sine qua non*. (*Ibid.*, at 510 and 514.) Therefore "the effect of such matters as negligence of the master or crew and conduct of the owner may produce a different result in the application of the words to one kind of case than to the other." (*per* Lambert J.A., *supra*, note 9, at 733, 133 D.L.R. (3d)).
18. *Supra*, note 16, at 509.
19. (1887), 12 App. Cas. 518 (H.L.).
20. *Ibid.*, at 525.

in producing the damage which in that case is wholly due to a risk not peculiar to the sea, but incidental to the keeping of that class of goods, whether on shore or on board of a voyaging ship. But in the case where rats make a hole or where one of the crew leaves a port-hole open, through which the sea enters and injures the cargo, the sea is the immediate cause of mischief and it would afford no answer to the claim of the insured to say that, had ordinary precaution been taken to keep down vermin, or had careful hands been employed, the sea would not have been admitted and there would have been no consequent damage.

In *Samuel (P.) & Co. Ltd. v. Dumas,*[21] the House of Lords held that a loss of a vessel by scuttling was not a peril of the sea. Viscount Cave stated:[22]

> Then, was the loss by perils of the sea? Surely not. The term "perils of the seas" is defined in Sched. 1 to the Act as referring only to "fortuitous accidents or casualties of the seas." The word "accident" may be ambiguous, and has even been held in another connection to include wilful murder: *Trim Joint District School Board of Management v. Kelly,* [1914] A.C. 667 (H.L.), but the word "fortuitous", which is at least as old as *Thompson v. Hopper* (1856), 6 E. & B. 172, involves an element of chance or ill luck which is absent where those in charge of a vessel deliberately throw her away. In *Wilson, Sons & Co. v. Xantho (Cargo Owners)* (1887), 12 A.C. 503, Lord Herschell said that in order that there might be a peril of the seas "there must be some casualty, something which could not be foreseen as one of the necessary incidents of the adventure. The purpose of the policy is to secure an indemnity against accidents which may happen, not against events which must happen." In *Hamilton, Fraser & Co. v. Pandorf & Co.,* (1887), 12 A.C. 518, Lord Bramwell approved the definition of Lopes, L.J., "it is a sea damage occurring at sea and nobody's fault". In *E.D. Sassoon & Co. v. Western Assurance Co.,* [1912] A.C. 561, Lord Mersey, in delivering the judgment of the Judicial Committee of the Privy Council, adopted a similar view, which is also to be found in the judgment of the Judicial Committee in *Grant Smith & Co. and McDonnell, Ltd. v. Seattle Construction and Dry Dock Co.,* [1920] A.C. 162. On this view the expression "perils of the sea", while it may well include a loss by accidental collision or negligent navigation, cannot extend to a wilful and deliberate throwing away of a ship by those in charge of her.

In *Cohen, Sons & Co. v. National Benefit Assurance Co. Ltd.,*[23] the assured claimed for a loss involving a German submarine that sank in a dock while being in the process of broken up. In holding that the loss was caused by a peril of the sea, Justice Bailhache observed:[24]

> In my view, the unintentional admission of sea water into a ship, whereby the ship sinks, is a peril of the sea. There is no warranty in this policy against

---

21. [1924] All E.R. Rep. 66, [1924] A.C. 431 (H.L.).
22. *Ibid.,* at 76.
23. (1924), 40 T.L.R. 347, 18 Lloyd's L.R. 199 (K.B.).
24. *Ibid.,* at 202.

negligence; there is no exception of negligence; and the fact that the unintentional admission of water into the ship is due to negligence is, in my opinion, totally and absolutely immaterial. There is a peril of the sea whenever a ship is afloat in the sea, and water from the sea is unintentionally admitted into her which causes a loss, either to the cargo or to the ship.

In the *Canada Rice Mills*[25] decision, the court held that damage caused by an action to prevent the incursion of sea water was recoverable as a loss by perils of the sea. Lord Wright, commenting on the meaning of the words "perils of the sea", observed:[26]

> In *Thames & Mersey Marine Ins. Co. v. Hamilton, Fraser & Co.* (1887), 12 App. Cas. 484 at p. 502 Lord Macnaghten said that it was impossible to frame a definition of the words. In *Hamilton, Fraser & Co. v. Pandorf* (1887), 12 App. Cas. 518, where a rat had gnawed a hole in a pipe, whereby seawater entered and damaged the cargo, there was no suggestion that the ship was endangered, but the damage to the cargo of rice was held to be due to a peril of the sea. There are many contingencies which might let the water into the ship besides a storm and in the opinion of Lord Halsbury in the case last cited any accident that should do damage by letting in sea into the vessel should be one of the risks contemplated.
>
> Where there is an accidental incursion of seawater into a vessel at a part of the vessel and in a manner where seawater is not expected to enter in the ordinary course of things and there is consequent damage to the thing insured, there is *prima facie* a loss by perils of the seas. The accident may consist in some negligent act, such as improper opening of a valve, or a hole made in a pipe by mischance, or it may be that sea water is admitted by stress of weather or some like cause bringing the sea over openings ordinarily not exposed to the sea or, even without stress of weather, by the vessel heeling over owing to some accident or by the breaking of hatches or other coverings. These are merely a few amongst many possible instances in which there may be a fortuitous incursion of seawater. It is the fortuitous entry of the seawater which is the peril of the sea in such cases.

(3.2) The "Bamcell II"

In *Case Existological Laboratories v. Foremost Insurance Co. et al.*,[27] the British Columbia Court of Appeal had occasion to express its views on the meaning of the words "perils of the sea". This decision went to the Supreme Court of Canada wherein Justice Ritchie, speaking for the court, approved the reasoning of Justice Lambert in the Court of Appeal.[28] The case involved a hull policy on the vessel *Bamcell II*. The facts were summarized by Justice Lambert as follows:[29]

---

25. [1941] 3 W.W.R. 401, 1 D.L.R. 1, 8 I.L.R. 1 (J.C. P.C).
26. *Ibid.*, at 9, 1 D.L.R.
27. *Supra*, note 9.
28. *Supra*, note 9.
29. *Supra*, note 9, at 730, 133 D.L.R. (3d).

[T]he *"Bamcell II"*, was a converted barge of unique design, partially open to the sea on her bottom, and kept afloat by an airtight deck. The vessel sank when a member of her crew intentionally opened the deck valves to let out the air trapped in the hull so that the stern would settle, and then negligently failed to close the valves again. The only other person on board the vessel at the time was a second crew member who was a novice. The *"Bamcell II"* was permanently moored in Patricia Bay where a scientific experiment was being conducted. The opening of the valves was done in the course of the scientific work to permit a floating concrete ring weighing seven tons to be brought aboard the *"Bamcell II"* by floating it over the submerged stern and then raising the stern again.

The insurance policy was in the form set out in the Schedule to the Act.[30] In addition, the policy contained an Inchmaree clause. This clause provided that the insurance "includes loss of or damage to the subject-matter insured directly caused by negligence of the master, charterers other than the assured, officers, crews or pilots ... provided such loss or damage has not resulted from want of due diligence by the assured, owners or managers." No argument was made by the assured based on the Inchmaree clause. Presumably the assured could not demonstrate due diligence to prevent the loss. The assured sought recovery of the loss under the wording of "perils of the sea" in the policy.

Justice Lambert reviewed a number of English decisions on the meaning of "perils of the seas" and concluded that:[31]

> The accident must be "fortuitous", first in the sense that it is not caused intentionally by the assured and, second, in the sense that it is not the inevitable result of deterioration caused by normal action of wind, waves and time. . .
>
> In addition, the accident must be "of the seas" in the sense at least, that the damage is damage that would not have occurred in an accident on land, such as damage by sinking, or by foundering following a collision at sea or striking a rock.

The insurer agreed that the fact that there was negligence on the part of a member of the crew did not exclude liability on the policy. The insurer argued, however, that in addition to this negligence there has to be an operating peril of the seas of some category peculiar to marine operations. The insurer argued that where the negligence of the master or crew stands alone as the proximate cause of the loss, there is no liability under the policy because negligence, in itself, in not a peril of the seas. To succeed, the insurer argued, where negligence of the master or crew stands alone as the cause, the assured must come within the wording of the Inchmaree clause.[32]

---

30. *Marine Insurance Act*, R.S.O. 1980, c. 255.
31. *Supra*, note 9, at 733, 133 D.L.R. (3d).
32. *Supra*, note 9.

The assured argued that a sinking caused by a negligent act is a sufficient fortuitous accident of the sea. Justice Lambert resolved the issue by an analysis of the negligent act:[33]

> An act is not negligent in itself but only in relation to a foreseeable risk of harm. If that foreseeable risk of harm is a peculiarly marine risk, then the act, coupled with its foreseeable consequence, is a fortuitous accident of the seas and a peril of the seas and the proximate cause of the loss.
>
> That conclusion is sufficient to decide the first issue in this appeal. In this case there is no doubt that it was the risk of the *"Bamcell II"* sinking, and causing loss by that sinking, that made the failure to close the deck valves a negligent omission when there was duty to act. When that negligent omission is coupled with its foreseeable consequence, the proximate cause of the loss in this case was a peril of the seas, and as such, covered by the policy.

The *Bamcell II* decision is significant in that an assured will not have to rely solely on the Inchmaree clause where the loss is attributable to negligence. An assured will only be required to show that the loss was fortuitous, *i.e.* that the sinking resulted from negligence. There will be no need to show that the loss did not result from his want of due diligence. Future cases will have to determine if the *Bamcell II* decision is restricted to the negligence of the master or crew or whether the negligence of the assured is also covered.

(3.3) Other Canadian Decisions on Perils of the Sea

In 1868, in *Coons v. Aetna Insurance Co.*,[34] the Court of Common Pleas of Upper Canada was asked to determine if a vessel which began to leak 15 minutes after leaving port in calm weather and waters was lost due to a peril of the sea. The assured presented no evidence to rebut the presumption that the vessel was unseaworthy. The court held that the assured was thereby disentitled to recover for the loss. Judge Wilson, in delivering the judgment of the court observed:[35]

> The observations of Cockburn, C.J., in *Paterson v. Harris* (7 Jur. N.S. 1279), are very applicable here: "The purpose of insurance is to afford protection against contingencies and damages which may or may not occur: it cannot properly apply to a case where the loss or injury must take place in the ordinary course of things. The wear and tear of a ship, the decay of her sheathing, the action of worms on her bottom, have been properly held not to be included

---

33. *Supra*, note 9, at 735.
34. (1868), 18 U.C.C.P. 305 (C.A.). An insurer may seek to demonstrate that the loss was not due to a peril of the sea but to the unseaworthy state of the vessel. The unseaworthiness of the vessel will therefore be tied in to the question of the proximate cause of the loss. In this regard see also Chapter 9 and the cases therein referred to.
35. *Ibid.*, at 309.

in the insurance against perils of the sea, as being the unavoidable consequences of the service to which the vessel is exposed: the insurer cannot be understood as undertaking to indemnify against losses which in the nature of things must necessarily happen."

In *Myles v. Montreal Insurance Co.*,[36] a vessel which had been sailing all day in a calm sea in a light breeze sank in the evening without explanation. The court referred to the *Coons v. Aetna*[37] decision and dismissed the assured's claim.

In 1875, in *Murray v. Nova Scotia Marine Insurance Co.*,[38] the assured claimed for damage to a cargo of supplies damaged by sea-water. The vessel had encountered heavy weather and put into port where she was found to be leaking. The court did not disturb the finding of the jury that the damage was occasioned by the leakage in the vessel resulting from boisterous weather encountered on the voyage. Sir William Young C.J. observed:[39]

> Now it is clear that [the words perils of the seas] only extend to cover losses really caused by sea damage, or the violence of the elements, "*ex marinae tempestatis discrimine;*" they do not embrace all losses happening upon the seas, comprehended under the general sweeping words in this as in most other policies, "of all other perils, losses or misfortunes, that have or shall come to the hurt detriment, or damage of the property assured." ...On the contrary the insured must prove an extraordinary peril of the kind assured against and a loss by that peril. It is a frequent subject of inquiry, whether the damage, which, as in this case is unquestionable as a fact, was caused by a peril insured against or by some other cause, and the burden of proof is of course on the insured.

A loss occasioned by the detention of a ship by ice is not a loss by "perils of the seas" covered by an ordinary marine policy.[40]

In 1886, in *Western Assurance Co. v. Scanlan*,[41] the assured claimed for the loss of a barge that sank as a result of water entering through an auger hole in the bilge which had been plugged up with a little wooden plug that had come out. The court found that the vessel had not been lost by a peril of the sea.

In 1917, the British Columbia Court of Appeal held that where cargo is damaged by sea water which has apparently been forced through the hatches of a ship during a storm, such injury is caused by a "peril of the sea".[42]

---

36. (1870), 20 U.C.C.P. 283 (C.A.).
37. *Supra*, note 34.
38. (1875), 10 N.S.R. 24 (C.A.).
39. *Ibid.*, at 27.
40. *Great Western Insurance Co. v. Jordon* (1886), 14 S.C.R. 734.
41. (1886), 13 S.C.R. 207, 33 L.C. Jur. 301.
42. *Creeden & Avery Ltd. v. North China Insurance Co.* (1917), 24 B.C.R. 335, 36 D.L.R. 359 [1917] 3 W.W.R. 33 (C.A.).

Where a sail is split, not as a result of its deterioration from use, but as a result of an accident, *i.e.* an unusual gale, there is a loss by a peril of the sea.[43] "If torn by an ordinary wind, it is not: this ordinary wind has revealed the deterioration of the sail by age and use, a thing not insured against."[44]

In *Keystone Transports Ltd. v. Dominion Steel & Coal Corp. Ltd.*,[45] an assured claimed for damage to a cargo of nails, staples and wires by contact with sea water which had infiltrated the hold during a storm. The storm had loosened the tarpaulins covering the hatch to the hold. The court held that the goods had been damaged by a peril of the sea. Justice Taschereau observed:[46]

> [T]o constitute a peril of the sea the accident need not be of an extraordinary nature or arise from irresistible force. It is sufficient that it be the cause of damage to goods at sea by the violent action of the wind and waves, when such damage cannot be attributed to someone's negligence.

The case of *Parrish & Heimbecker Ltd. et al. v. Burke Towing & Salvage Co. Ltd.*[47] involved a claim by a cargo owner against a shipowner for a loss of a cargo of wheat when the vessel *Arlington* foundered in a storm shortly after sailing. The court held that the loss was due to a peril of the sea. Justice Kerwin stated:[48]

> With respect to the interpretation of the words "perils of the sea", these remarks are just as applicable to and in fact appear in a bill of lading case. The results, of course, are not necessarily the same since negligence is immaterial in an insurance case.
>
> In the case at bar, there was more than a *prima facie* case of loss by perils of the sea, and negligence causing the loss was negatived. The evidence discloses that the storm was a severe one and the mere fact that none of the other ships in the vicinity suffered in the same way as did the *Arlington* does not detract from this evidence. The respondent has acquitted itself "of the onus of showing that the weather encountered was the cause of the damage and that it was of such a nature that the danger of damage to the cargo arising from it could not have been foreseen or guarded against as one of the probable incidents of the voyage."

In *Miskofski v. Economic Insurance Co. Ltd. et al.*,[49] the Court of Appeal for British Columbia took a very strict approach in denying the assured the right to recovery under a policy of marine insurance.

---

43. *Hill et al. v. Union Insurance Society of Canton Ltd.*, 61 O.L.R. 201, [1927] 4 D.L.R. 718 (C.A.).
44. *Ibid.*, at 724, [1927] 4 D.L.R.
45. [1942] S.C.R. 495, [1942] 4 D.L.R. 513.
46. *Ibid.*, at 505, [1942] S.C.R.
47. [1943] S.C.R. 179, [1943] 2 D.L.R. 193.
48. *Ibid.*, at 184, [1943] S.C.R.
49. 43 D.L.R. (2d) 281, [1964] I.L.R. 1-115 (B.C. C.A.).

The assured's tug had been "clandestinely" stolen from its wharf and abandoned at sea. The vessel was salvaged as it was sinking. Its toilet seacock had been deliberately left open. The court found that the loss was not by a peril of the sea in that it was not fortuitous but deliberate. Similarly, the loss did not come within the words "assailing thieves" in the policy as there was no evidence of violence and as the term does not cover clandestine theft.

In 1973, in *Stevenson v. Continental Insurance Co. et al.*,[50] an assured claimed for a loss to a 26-foot work boat which had been destroyed by fire. The assured had indicated that he noticed a fire start around the carburettor on top of the engine, that he shut off the motor and aimed a carbon dioxide fire extinguisher at the site of the fire apparently putting it out, that "the fire travelled down to the back of the motor and caught on gas in the bilge."[51] The insurer argued that, in the circumstances, the fire was to be expected and therefore was not fortuitous. The court was not prepared to find that the fire was not fortuitous and held that the loss fell within the peril of fire as insured against in the policy.

In *Central Native Fishermen's Co-Operative v. Commonwealth Insurance Co. et al.*,[52] the court found that the cause of a vessel's sinking was that:[53]

> [T]he sea and wind conditions, together with the speed at which the *Millbanke V* was being towed — in excess of 8 knots — caused the port forward towpost to be pulled forward with such force and to such extent that a substantial hole resulted in the deck. This hole allowed water to enter the hull in a quantity sufficient to cause a list to port to such a degree that the cargo was spilled out through the walls of the cargo shed ... [T]he loss was a result of a fortuitous accident or casualty of the sea...

The Supreme Court of British Columbia, in *Stad v. Fireman's Fund Insurance Co. et al.*,[54] reiterated the principle that the burden of proof is on the assured to show that the loss was due to a peril insured against. Thus, where a vessel was abandoned at sea in a partially submerged condition in the evening and the next morning was not located and the assured could not explain how the sea water got into the vessel in such quantity as to partially submerge it, the assured was denied recovery.

In *Federal Business Development Bank v. Commonwealth Insurance Co. et al.*,[55] Justice Toy of the British Columbia Supreme Court

---

50. [1973] 6 W.W.R. 316, [1973] I.L.R. 1-553 (B.C. S.C.).
51. *Ibid.*, at 321, [1973] 6 W.W.R.
52. [1979] I.L.R. 1-1091 (B.C. S.C.).
53. *Ibid.*, at 156.
54. [1979] I.L.R. 1-1070 (B.C. S.C.).
55. (1979), 13 B.C.L.R. 376 (S.C.).

applied the reasoning found in *The Xantho*[56] decision and allowed the owner of a tugboat which had capsized when hit by a large wave to recover for his loss.

In 1983, in *Williams v. The Queen*,[57] an assured claimed for a loss by sinking to his fishing boat caused by the fracturing of a sea intake pipe. The assured contended that the fracture had resulted from striking a submerged unknown object. The fracture of the pipe caused a small leakage in the early stages which accelerated at a more rapid rate later. The court accepted this evidence and the evidence of the assured's expert that corrosion was not a probable cause of the fracture. The court considered the *Bamcell II*[58] decision and the reasoning of Lord Wright in the *Canada Rice Mills*[59] case and found that the loss was fortuitous and due to a peril of the sea. Justice McNair, *in obiter*, observed:[60]

> [T]he primary thrust of the plaintiff's case, as I see it, is directed to the issue of whether the loss arose from a peril of the sea so as to come within the general risk insured against. The affirmative burden of proof of this rests with the plaintiff. In short, the plaintiff must make out a *prima facie* case that the loss was occasioned by a peril of the sea. The defendant has the burden of establishing the defences alleged to exclude the risk. One of these is ordinary wear and tear. The cause of the loss becomes a significant factor in determining whether or not the loss was proximately caused by a peril of the sea within the ambit of the coverage.
>
> The meaning of "perils of the seas" has been the subject of judicial interpretation for many years. The *Marine Insurance Acts* codified the earlier common law decisions on the subject but, as with most codifications, this did not put a complete end to the controversy.

In the *H.B. Nickerson & Sons Ltd.*[61] decision, the court summarized the relationship between s. 56 of the Act[62] and Rule 7 of the *Rules for Construction of Policy* in the Schedule to the Act.[63] Justice Marceau stated:[64]

> Rule 7 of the *Rules for Construction of Policy* set out in the First Schedule to the *Marine Insurance Act, 1906 (U.K.)* states that: "The term 'perils of the

---

56. (1887), 12 App. Cas. 503 (H.L.).
57. (1984), 7 C.C.L.I. 198 (F.C. T.D.).
58. (1982), 133 D.L.R. (3d) 727, [1982] I.L.R. 1-1567 (B.C. C.A); affd [1983] 2 S.C.R. 47 (*sub nom. Century Insurance Co. of Canada v. Case Existological Laboratories Ltd.*), 48 B.C.L.R. 273, [1984] 1 W.W.R. 97, 150 D.L.R. (3d) 9, 49 N.R. 19, [1983] I.L.R. 1-1698.
59. [1941] 3 W.W.R. 401, [1941] 1 D.L.R. 1, 8 I.L.R. 1 (J.C. P.C.).
60. *Supra*, note 57, at 205.
61. [1984] 1 F.C. 575, 49 N.R. 321, 3 C.C.L.I. 78 (C.A.); leave to appeal to S.C.C. refused (1984), 54 N.R. 80 (S.C.C.).
62. *Marine Insurance Act*, R.S.O. 1980, c. 255.
63. *Ibid.*
64. *Supra*, note 61, at 326, 49 N.R.

seas' refers only to fortuitous accidents or casualties of the seas. It does not include the ordinary action of the winds and waves." Consequently, not every loss caused by the entry of seawater into a vessel is a loss caused by the direct operation of a peril of the sea; it may be due to some other cause neither accidental nor fortuitous such as the ordinary action of the wind and waves or wear and tear. If the assured fails to prove satisfactorily that the loss was due to a fortuitous accident or casualty of the sea, a doubt will remain as to whether it was one that the insurers had agreed to bear and the right to indemnity will not have been established.

Counsel and even the courts often equate "peril insured against" with "peril of the sea". Thus, in *Atwood v. The Queen*,[65] a loss by fire, a named peril in the policy, was characterized as a "peril of the sea".[66] However, in *O'Connor v. Merchants Marine Insurance Co.*,[67] the Supreme Court of Canada made it quite clear that "perils of the seas" does not encompass the other expressed perils such as barratry or fire. Thus, where a vessel was lost due to the barratrous conduct of the master and the policy covered perils of the sea but did not expressly insure against barratry, the assured was unable to recover for the loss.

(4) All Risks Policies[68]

In *Boyda v. Saxbee Insurance Agencies (1975) Ltd. et al.*,[69] an assured claimed for a loss of a sailboat which had sunk. The court found on the evidence that the sailboat had been intentionally sunk, on the third attempt, by the assured. The vessel was insured under an "all risks" coverage. Justice McKenzie, in describing the case as a "black farce about the efforts of three oddly-assorted characters to rid themselves of an unwanted sailboat at the expense of the insurance company," concluded:[70]

> There are many reasons why this action must fail, but it is sufficient to find that the vessel did not sink from any external cause. The all-risk coverage extends only to "direct physical loss from any external cause." It was deliberately sunk.

In *Richardson (James) & Sons Ltd. v. Standard Marine Insurance Co.*,[71] a marine policy insured a cargo of wheat against "loss or damage from any external cause." The court held that this clause enabled

---

65. (1985), 10 C.C.L.I. 62 (F.C. T.D.).
66. *Ibid.*, at 64.
67. (1889), 16 S.C.R. 331. See also *Wolff v. Merchants Insurance Co.* (1892), 31 N.B.R. 577 (C.A.).
68. See also chapter 48.
69. [1984] I.L.R. 1-1775, 4 C.C.L.I 26 (B.C. S.C.).
70. *Ibid.*, at 6843-44.
71. [1936] S.C.R. 573, [1936] 3 D.L.R. 513, 3 I.L.R. 494.

the assured to recover for depreciation of the wheat from excessive moisture caused by rain.

Even in an "all risks" policy the burden of proof is on the assured to prove that the loss suffered was proximately caused by a risk covered by the policy. Thus, even in such a policy, the risk must relate to a marine risk.[72]

(5) The Exceptions

The insurer is not liable for any loss attributable to the wilful misconduct of the assured, for any loss caused by delay, or resulting from ordinary wear and tear, ordinary leakage and breakage, inherent vice, *etc.*

The burden of proof is on the insurer to prove that the loss falls within an express exception to the policy or within s. 56(2) of the Act.[73]

In *Williams v. The Queen*,[74] the insurer alleged that a fracture, in a sea intake pipe, had been caused by ordinary wear and tear. The court found that the defendant insurer had failed to demonstrate that the loss was caused by ordinary wear and tear. Justice McNair observed:[75]

> In my view, the following passage from Arnould, *The Law of Marine Insurance and Average* (16th ed.), para. 798, at p. 659 accurately states the law on this whole aspect: "Where the loss is not proximately caused by the agency of the winds and waves, but is merely the natural result of the action of seawater on the subject of insurance, or of the ordinary wear and tear of the voyage, it is not recoverable as a peril of the seas, nor indeed under the policy at all. It should be observed, however, that there have been relatively few decisions of the English courts where the issue of wear and tear or inherent vice has been determinative of a claim under a hull policy in modern times. Analogies from cases on sailing vessels or on wooden ships may be dangerous. Thus it is submitted, for example, that no analogy can necessarily be drawn between the case of a loss occasioned by the rotten condition of a wooden hull, and a case of metal fatigue in a modern vessel. The structure of metal ships may fail suddenly for a variety of causes, and it may not be possible to point to any unusual weather or sea conditions at or near the time of the occurrence. There is no recent decision of the English courts in which this point has been considered, although in several of the cases where scuttling was alleged it seems to have been assumed that a loss by the sudden incursion of water through the ship's side in calm seas, without contact with any external substance, was recoverable. It is submitted that the better view is probably that a defence of wear and tear or inherent vice is applicable to cases where the loss is attrib-

---

72. See *Star-Rite International Food Inc. v. Maritime Insurance Co. Ltd.*, unreported, December 12, 1984 (Ont. Co. Ct.); affd, not yet reported, June 10, 1986 (Ont. C.A.).

73. *Marine Insurance Act*, R.S.O. 1980, c. 255.

74. *Supra*, note 57.

75. *Supra*, at 208-209.

utable to a general debility of the vessel such as to make it plain that the loss was a certainty, whatever the state of the weather or the sea, but that the defence is unlikely to prevail in cases where there is a sudden failure of a part of the structure, even though this may have long-standing causes, or be due merely to metal fatigue, and though the weather and sea conditions at the time may be in no way unusual or extreme..."

In *Federation Insurance Co. of Canada v. Coret Accessories Inc. et al.*,[76] an insurer brought an action against an assured for the return of money paid under a policy of insurance. In May of 1966, the assured had imported a case of handbag parts from Barcelona to Montreal. The case was not delivered and a claim for the loss under the policy was paid by the insurer. Subsequently, in December of 1966, the case was found and delivered to the assured. The assured refused to accept the shipment on the grounds that the goods were seasonal, and could not be used. In holding that the loss was caused by delay and that the insurer was entitled to be reimbursed, Justice Collins of the Quebec Superior Court stated:[77]

> The plaintiff [insurer] only insured the goods which were permanently lost. It did not insure any goods which were delayed in transit or which were lost temporarily but which were subsequently delivered to the owner thereof. There was no complaint by the defendant [assured] that the handbag parts were damaged. The fact that the defendant was unable to use them when they were delivered because of their seasonal nature does not affect the legal situation. While the failure to deliver on time resulted in a monetary loss to the defendant such a loss was not insured against ... Loss or damage arising from loss of market as well as loss, damage or deterioration arising from delay are specifically excluded. It was delay which caused the loss or damage.

Inherent vice is a defence relied upon frequently by insurers on policies involving shipments of goods. The case of *Star-Rite International Food Inc. v. Maritime Insurance Co. Ltd.*,[78] involved a shipment of fresh produce from Costa Rica to Canada. The assured imported a container of coconuts and fresh ginger in a non-refrigerated container. The produce was damaged by the temperature changes experienced while on board the vessel. The produce arrived in a rotted condition. The insurer argued that the loss did not arise out of fortuitous circumstances. It argued that when this type of cargo, which requires proper ventilation, is shipped in a non-ventilated container, by the very nature of the subject-matter, the loss is not fortuitous but certain. The court relied on the evidence of the assured that it had successfully shipped the same type of produce in the same manner before. Judge Haley added:[79]

---

76. [1968] 2 Lloyd's L.R. 109 (Que. S.C.).
77. *Ibid.*, at 111.
78. *Supra*, note 72.
79. *Supra*.

Once the plaintiff has brought itself within a risk covered by the policy, the onus is on the defendant to prove that the loss falls within an exception to the policy or within s. 56(2) of the *Marine Insurance Act*. The defendant says that the loss of the cargo was not caused by an external force but by the very nature of the coconuts and the fresh ginger, *i.e.* their inherent vice. In *Soya G.m.b.H. Mainz Kommanditgesellschaft v. White* [1983] 2 Lloyd's Rep. 122, Lord Diplock discussed the meaning of inherent vice. He says at p. 126: "This phrase (generally shortened to "inherent vice") where it is used in s. 55(2)(c) refers to a peril by which a loss is proximately caused; it is not descriptive of the loss itself. It means the risk of deterioration of the goods shipped as a result of their natural behaviour in the ordinary course of the contemplated voyage without the intervention of any fortuitous external accident or casualty." On this definition I cannot find that the loss of the cargo was caused by inherent vice. I have found that the cargo was in good condition when it was placed in the carrier's hands and in damaged condition when it reached Halifax ... There was nothing in the nature of the cargo itself which created the heating and hence the deterioration. It would have been different if the defendant had convinced me that the method of shipping was unsuitable for the nature of the cargo as was the case in *Gee & Garnham Ltd. v. Whittall* [(1955) 2 Lloyd's Rep. 562] where damaged kettles were found to have been inadequately packed by the shipper and in *F.W. Berk & Co. Ltd. v. Style* [1956] 1 Q.B.D. 180 where bags containing kieselguhr were found to be unsuitable.

In *Balix Furniture & Appliances Ltd. v. Maritime Insurance Co.*,[80] an assured claimed for damages to paintings transported in a container from Hamburg, Germany to Toronto, Canada. The court found that the paintings had been improperly or inadequately packed. Judge Sheard said:[81]

> [D]amage resulting from improper or inadequate packing is an "inherent vice" in the goods which relieves the insurer from liability, even under an "all risks" policy, as here, unless expressly excluded. Authority for this proposition may be found in several cases, of which *Gee and Garnham Ltd. v. Whittall* (1955) 2 Lloyd's Rep. 562, is one. Accordingly, I dismiss the plaintiff's claim arising from the damage to the paintings.

---

80. Unreported, February 10, 1978 (Ont. Co. Ct.).
81. *Ibid.*

27

Total and Partial Losses

s. 57: (1) A loss may be either total or partial and any loss, other than a total loss as hereinafter defined is a partial loss.
(2) A total loss may be either an actual total loss or a constructive total loss.
(3) Unless a different intention appears from the terms of the policy, an insurance against total loss includes a constructive as well as an actual total loss.
(4) Where the assured brings an action for a total loss and the evidence proves only a partial loss, he may, unless the policy otherwise provides, recover for a partial loss.
(5) Where goods reach their destination *in specie*, but by reason of obliteration of marks, or otherwise, they are incapable of identification, the loss, if any, is partial and not total.

Most of the jurisprudence dealing with the issue of whether a loss was an actual total loss, a constructive total loss or a partial loss was generated prior to the codification of the common law. There are only a handful of Canadian decisions in which the characterization of the loss has been at issue. Even though the statute is relatively clear as to the definitions of partial and total losses, it is worthwhile to examine some of the earlier decisions.

Sir Barnes Peacock, of the Privy Council, commented on the meaning of "total loss" in *Cossman v. West:*[1]

> To constitute a total loss within the meaning of a policy of marine insurance, it is not necessary that a ship should be actually annihilated or destroyed; it may, as in the case of capture and sale upon condemnation, remain in its original state and condition; it may be capable of being repaired if damaged; it may be actually repaired by the purchaser, or it may not even require repairs. If it is lost to the owner by an adverse valid and legal transfer of his right of property and possession to a purchaser by a sale under a decree of a Court of competent jurisdiction in consequence of a peril insured against, it is as much a total loss as if it had been totally annihilated.

In *Phoenix Insurance Co. v. McGhee,*[2] Justice Strong of the Supreme Court of Canada observed:[3]

---

1. (1887), 13 App. Cas. 160 (J.C.P.C.).
2. (1890), 18 S.C.R. 61.
3. *Ibid.*, at 70-71.

Cases of high and unimpeachable authority have established that to constitute a total loss in the case of a ship the subject of insurance must be either such an entire wreck as to be reduced, as it is said, to a mere "congeries of planks," or if it still subsists *in specie* it must, as a result of perils insured against, be placed in such a situation that it is totally out of the power of the owner or the underwriter at any labor, and by means of any expenditure, to get it afloat and cause it to be repaired and used again as a ship. . . . In *Roux v. Salvador* (3 Bing. N.C. 386) . . . Lord Abinger says: "If in the progress of the voyage the thing insured becomes totally destroyed or annihilated, or if it be placed by the perils insured against in such a position that it is totally out of the power of the assured or the underwriter to procure its arrival, the latter is bound by the very terms of his contract to pay the whole sum assured."

As to the difference between total losses and partial losses, Justice Graham has said:[4]

> As to its being a total loss or a partial loss that is a question more applicable to the quantity of the damages than to the ground of the action. The ground of the action is the same whether the loss be partial or total, both are perils within the policy.

It is clear that an assured claiming for a total loss may recover for a partial loss if the policy permits it.[5] Justice Graham stated:[6]

> It has been the law for 150 years, at any rate, from the time of Lord Mansfield, that under a declaration claiming a total loss the plaintiff could recover for a partial loss.

Justice Tuck, in *O'Leary v. Pelican Insurance Co.*[7] stated:[8]

> A vessel may be driven ashore and liable to become a total loss, so that it would be competent for the owner to give notice of abandonment, and for the underwriters to refuse to accept it. If then a survey be held, and the vessel be condemned, but before action is brought the vessel is in safety, and capable of being repaired at a less cost than her value when repaired, and of being restored to her owner; in such case the insured is entitled to recover only for a partial loss.

Justice Wilson in *Harkley v. Provincial Insurance Co.*[9] observed:[10]

> [I]t has long been settled that, on a total loss alleged, a partial loss may be recovered for, because total or partial is not the ground of action: it is the estimate of damages merely.

---

4. *Hart v. Boston Marine Insurance Co.* (1894), 26 N.S.R. 427, at 448-49 (C.A.).
5. See *Troop v. Union Insurance Co.* (1893), 32 N.B.R. 135 (C.A.); *Merchants' Marine Insurance Co. v. Ross* (1884), 10 Q.L.R. 237 (C.A.).
6. *Supra* note 4, at 448.
7. (1889), 29 N.B.R. 510 (C.A.).
8. *Ibid.*, at 519.
9. (1868), 18 U.C.C.P. 335 (C.A.).
10. *Ibid.*, at 345.

Similarly Justice Strong in *Western Assurance Co. v. Scanlan & O'Connor*[11] said:[12]

> According to English practice however, a plaintiff suing on a marine policy for a constructive total loss, may, if it turns out that he is disentitled to recover for the loss suffered as a total loss, fall back on his right to recover as for a partial or average loss.

Where an insurance on goods was declared in the policy to be against "total loss" a constructive total loss is within the terms of the policy unless specifically excluded.[13]

---

11. (1886), 13 S.C.R. 207.
12. *Ibid.*, at 215.
13. *O'Leary v. Stymest* (1865), 11 N.B.R. 289 (C.A.).

28

Actual Total Losses

s. 58: (1) Where the subject-matter insured is destroyed or so damaged as to cease to be a thing of the kind insured, or where the assured is irretrievably deprived thereof, there is an actual total loss.
(2) In the case of an actual total loss no notice of abandonment need be given.

s. 59: Where the ship concerned in the adventure is missing and after the lapse of a reasonable time no news of her has been received, an actual total loss may be presumed.

s. 60: Where, by a peril insured against, the voyage is interrupted at an intermediate port or place under such circumstances as, apart from any special stipulation in the contract of affreightment, to justify the master in landing and reshipping the goods or other movables, or in transshipping them, and sending them on to their destination, the liability of the insurer continues notwithstanding the landing or transshipment.

An actual total loss has been described as a state whereby "the subject of the insurance from the effects of perils encountered be that, not of a vessel continuing to exist *in specie*, but of the *disjecta membra* of what once was a ship."[1]

A vessel is said to be an actual total loss when it is so "damaged as to be incapable of being repaired at all, or of being taken to a place where it could be repaired."[2]

Where a vessel is deserted by her master and crew in a sinking condition and is subsequently taken possession of by salvors and sold together with her cargo by order of the Admiralty Court for less than the actual cost of the salvage services, the sale by the court constitutes an actual total loss of the ship and cargo.[3]

In *Montreal Light, Heat & Power Co. v. Sedgwick et al.*,[4] a barge with cement settled down on a river bank and was submerged. The policy of insurance on the cargo specified that the cement was insured against total loss "by total loss of the vessel". The court found that

---

1. *Leslie et al. v. Taylor* (1876), 10 N.S.R. 352 at, 361-62 (C.A.).
2. *Phoenix Insurance Co. v. Anchor Insurance Co.* (1884), 4 O.R. 524, at 531 (C.P.).
3. *Cossman v. West* (1887), 13 App. Cas. 160 (J.C. P.C.)
4. [1910] A.C. 598 (P.C.).

there was an actual total loss of the cement even though there was not a total loss of the barge. Lord Atkinson concluded:[5]

> Cement being easily damaged by water, it is obvious that the defendants would naturally desire to protect themselves from liability for a partial or total loss of the cargo, caused by a slight injury to the barge, or by some casual incident of the voyage; but where a total loss of the cargo is brought about by such a wreckage of the barge as resulted in her sinking to the bottom of the river, becoming entirely flooded, and almost entirely submerged, the peril which the parties to the contract meant to guard against must, their Lordships think, be held to have supervened, and the total loss of the barge which they contemplated be held to have resulted.

In an actual total loss, notice of abandonment is not necessary.[6]

The difference between an actual total loss and a constructive total loss is a matter of degree. As new technologies are developed to raise ships or reconstruct ships there are fewer true "actual total losses". Justice Graham in *Churchill & Co. et al. v. Nova Scotia Marine Insurance Co.*[7] observed:[8]

> It is difficult to say how much the cost of repairs must exceed the value of the ship when repaired in order to constitute an actual total loss. I say this, because, nowadays, the expenditure of money will in most cases recover and restore vessels well within the definition of actual total loss. And there is a limit. Perhaps the frequently cited words of Mr. Justice Maule in *Moss v. Smith*, 9 C.B., 101, are helpful. He says: "If the ship is actually lost by a peril of the sea, or any other peril covered by the policy, the assured may call it a total loss. If she sustains damage to such an extent that she cannot be repaired at all, that also is a total loss. It may be that the injury sustained by the ship is irreparable with reference to the place where she is; for instance, the ship may have met with the disaster at a place where no workmen of requisite powers are to be met with, or where the necessary materials are not to be found, so that to repair her there is altogether impracticable; and in such a case the loss would also be a total loss. But, short of that, it may be that it may be physically possible to repair the vessel, but at an enormous cost, and then also the loss would be total; for in matters of business a thing is said to be impossible when it is not practicable, and a thing is impracticable when it can only be done at an excessive or unreasonable cost. A man may be said to have lost a shilling when he has dropped it into deep water, though it might be possible by some very expensive contrivance to recover it. So, if a ship sustains such extensive damage that it would not be reasonably practicable to repair her, seeing that the expense of repairs would be such that no man of common sense would incur the outlay, the ship is said to be totally lost. It is in that way alone that the questions as to what a prudent man would do arises."

In the *Churchill* decision the vessel had encountered heavy weather and was beached at an island to prevent her sinking. There was

---

5. *Ibid.*, at 604.
6. *Crawford v. St. Lawrence Insurance Co.* (1851), 8 U.C.Q.B. 135 (C.A.).
7. (1895), 28 N.S.R. 52 (C.A.); affd (1896), 26 S.C.R. 65.
8. *Ibid.*, at 69, 28 N.S.R.

no means of repairing the vessel at the island and the cost of repairing her there would have exceeded her value when repaired. The court held that the vessel was a constructive total loss.

Where it is found that a ship is an actual or constructive total loss, it will follow that there is an actual total loss of freight.[9]

Where the vessel can be repaired and there is not a constructive total loss, there will not be a total loss of freight.[10]

Where the ship is held to be not worth repairing, no notice of abandonment of freight is necessary.[11]

Where a vessel is disabled by a peril insured against and not able to carry her cargo to its destination without delay, and the cargo is one that is required to be carried forward without delay, the object of the voyage is wholly frustrated and there is a constructive loss of freight.[12]

---

9. *Troop et al. v. Merchants' Marine Insurance Co.* (1886), 13 S.C.R. 506.
10. *Wilson v. Merchants' Marine Insurance Co.* (1872), 9 N.S.R. 81 (S.C.).
11. *Patch v. Pitman* (1886), 19 N.S.R. 298, at 307 (C.A.); affd Cass. S.C. 389.
12. *Musgrave v. Mannheim Insurance Co.* (1899), 32 N.S.R. 405 (C.A.).

29

Constructive Total Losses

s. 61: (1) Subject to any express provision in the policy, there is a constructive total loss where the subject-matter insured is reasonably abandoned on account of its actual total loss appearing to be unavoidable or because it could not be preserved from actual total loss without an expenditure that would exceed its value when the expenditure had been incurred.
(2) In particular, there is a constructive total loss,
(a) where the assured is deprived of the possession of his ship or goods by a peril insured against; and
 (i) it is unlikely that he can recover the ship or goods, as the case may be, or
(ii) the cost of recovering the ship or goods, as the case may be, would exceed their value when recovered; or
(b) in the case of damage to a ship, where she is so damaged by a peril insured against that the cost of repairing the damage would exceed the value of the ship when repaired, and in estimating the cost of repairs, no deduction is to be made in respect of general average contributions to those repairs payable by other interests, but account is to be taken of the expense of future salvage operations and of any future general average contributions to which the ship would be liable if repaired; or
(c) in the case of damage to goods, where the cost of repairing the damage and forwarding the goods to their destination would exceed their value on arrival.

s. 62: Where there is a constructive total loss, the assured may either treat the loss as a partial loss or abandon the subject-matter insured to the insurer and treat the loss as if it were an actual total loss.

(1) Constructive Total Loss of Vessels-Generally

A constructive total loss has been described as follows:[1]

> Nor was there a constructive total loss. Taking the vessel's actual and not its policy value . . . I find as a fact on the evidence that it was worth much more than the cost of getting it off and repairing it.
> "The test by the law of England clearly is, whether a prudent man would think it worth his while to attempt to save and repair the vessel, and it is assumed that he would not do it unless he had the prospect of gaining something

---

1. *Phoenix Insurance Co. v. Anchor Insurance Co.*, (1884), 4 O.R. 524, at 532 (C.P.).

by the attempt; in other words, that he would not make the attempt unless it appeared probable that the vessel when got off and restored to the state she was in before the accident, would be worth as much as the operation would cost him."

The test as to whether an assured has a right to abandon property and claim for a constructive total loss has also been set out in *Gerow v. British American Assurance Co.*[2] as follows:[3]

> The test resorted to in English law . . . is well established to be that described in the case of *Irving v. Manning*, 1 H.L. Cas. 287, cited by Mr. Justice King, namely: "To consider the policy as altogether out of the question, and to enquire what a prudent, uninsured owner would have done in the state in which the vessel was placed by the perils insured against."

Thus, where a vessel sinks to the bottom of the sea it does not necessarily follow that she is a total loss. Where raising the vessel is easy and the costs of repairs are less than the repaired value, there is not a constructive total loss.[4]

Where an underwriter refuses to accept an abandonment and repairs a vessel at a cost less than the value of the vessel when repaired, there is not a constructive total loss.[5]

On the other hand, where an underwriter refuses to accept an abandonment and repairs a vessel at a cost greater than the value of the vessel restored, there is a constructive total loss.[6]

If at the time the action is brought the assured is only entitled to a partial loss, he will only be able to recover for a partial loss even if at the time of the loss it appeared to have been a total loss.[7]

In *Rose v. Weekes*,[8] a recent decision of the Federal Court of Canada, an assured claimed for a loss of a vessel on the basis of a constructive total loss. The vessel had been holed by ice, filled with water and abandoned by its crew. Some 10 days later, the abandoned vessel was sighted and towed to shore. The court found that, at the time the action was brought, the vessel could not be repaired for less than its repaired value. The court held that the vessel was a constructive total loss and not a partial loss. Justice McNair observed:[9]

---

2. (1889), 16 S.C.R. 524.
3. *Ibid.*, at 531-32.
4. *Cates Tug & Wharfage Co. Ltd. v. Franklin Fire Insurance Co.*, [1927] 3 D.L.R. 1025 (P.C.).
5. *Cunningham v. St. Paul Fire & Marine Insurance Co.* (1914), 19 B.C.R. 33, 5 W.W.R. 1098, 26 W.L.R. 870, 16 D.L.R. 39 (S.C.); see also *Taylor v. Smith* (1868), 12 N.B.R. 120 (C.A.).
6. *Troop et al. v. Jones* (1884), 17 N.S.R. 230 (C.A.).
7. *Meagher v. Home Insurance Co.* (1861), 11 U.C.C.P. 328 (C.A.).
8. (1984), 7 C.C.L.I. 287 (F.C. T.D.).
9. *Ibid.*, at 294-95.

A constructive total loss is one which entitles the assured to claim the whole amount of the insurance, on giving due notice of abandonment. A constructive total loss exists when the subject-matter insured is not in fact totally lost, but is likely to become so from the improbability of recovery or the impracticability of repair. The doctrine is peculiar to marine insurance. The assured must give notice of abandonment to justify constructive total loss recovery. But the notice of abandonment is not conclusive and the underwriters may refuse to accept it. It then becomes necessary to determine under the circumstances whether the abandonment should remain operative. One of these circumstances is whether the destruction or loss of the thing insured appears to be "unavoidable". Notice of abandonment must be justified by the facts as they exist at the time it is given and at the time of action brought. The first and basic test is: Is the recovery of the vessel unlikely? Another necessary test in the case of a vessel not totally destroyed is whether a prudent owner, who is uninsured, would have abandoned the vessel because of the probable likelihood of the cost of repair or restoration exceeding its value.

Section 60 of the *Marine Insurance Act*, 1906 (U.K.), c. 41, defines and circumscribes the definition of "constructive total loss". Subsections 60(1) and (2) contain different definitions which may apply to different sets of facts. The definitions are neither exhaustive nor exclusive and resort may be had to the common law to fill any lacuna left by the statutory provisions. There have been many cases on constructive total loss which go both ways. In most circumstances the matter falls to be determined on questions of fact.

A policy may by express provision specify when there is a constructive total loss. Thus, in *Western Assurance Co. v. Scanlan & O'Connor*,[10] a policy stipulated that "the insured shall not have a right to abandon the vessel in any case unless the amount the insurers would be liable to pay under an adjustment as of a partial loss shall exceed half the amount insured."

Similarly, in *Vaughan v. Providence Washington Insurance Co.*,[11] a policy specified that there would only be a constructive total loss if the cost of repairs exceeded the value of the hull specified in the policy. The policy value of the hull was $20,000 and the market value of the hull was less than the $14,280 it would cost to repair the vessel. The court found that there was not a constructive total loss.

In *Allarco Developments Ltd. v. Continental Insurance Co. et al.*,[12] a constructive total loss under a policy of insurance was only possible if the cost of recovery and repairing a vessel exceeded the value specified for hull insurance. The actual costs of repairs were in issue; the assured's estimate being greatly higher than the insurer's estimate. The court held that the estimate for the cost of repairs would be calculated in accordance with the vessel manufacturer's speci-

---

10. (1886), 13 S.C.R. 207.
11. (1887), 28 N.B.R. 133 (C.A.). See also *Slaughenwhite v. Western Assurance Co.* (1911), 11 E.L.R. 310 (N.S. S.C.).
12. [1980] I.L.R. 1-1281 (Alta. Q.B.).

fications or accepted repair practice. Using this method, the court found that the cost of the salvage and repair of the vessel was less than the hull value and therefore the assured could not recover for a constructive total loss.

(2) Constructive Total Loss of Vessels — Necessary Sale

A master may sell a vessel or cargo without notice of abandonment only in situations of stringent necessity. The necessity must be such that it leaves the master no alternative, as a prudent and skillful man acting *bona fide* for the best interests of all concerned. The master must examine the actual state of the ship or cargo, must exercise every means within his power to dispose of or extricate the ship or cargo from its peril or raise funds to do so.[13]

In *Providence Washington Insurance Co. v. Corbett*,[14] an assured claimed for a constructive total loss on a vessel. During a storm the vessel went ashore and notice of abandonment was given to the insurers but not accepted. The master sold the vessel the next day, three days after the vessel went ashore. The day after the sale, the purchaser used casks for floating the vessel and without much difficulty got her off the shore. The court held that the abandonment was not valid in that the evidence did not establish a constructive total loss. Similarly, the court found that the master was not justified in selling the vessel. Chief Justice Ritchie observed:[15]

> There must be a most stringent necessity to justify a captain in selling a vessel, and I think that it should not be tolerated that a sale should be made hastily without examination or without the captain having previously made every exertion in his power to get off his vessel.

In *Hart v. Boston Marine Insurance Co.*,[16] an assured sold a vessel after it was damaged in a storm. The assured claimed for a total loss of the vessel. A survey before the sale disclosed nothing which suggested a total loss or the necessity for the sale. The court found that there had been no actual or constructive total loss. Justice Graham observed:[17]

> There was not an actual total loss. The *"Sunbeam"* was still a ship. Her recovery and restoration were physically possible. There was not, as the result before action brought showed, a constructive total loss. She was extricated without trouble, kept afloat with the pumps, half of the cargo remaining in her, until

---

13. *Cobequid Marine Insurance Co. v. Barteaux* (1875), 6 L.R.P.C. 319 (J.C. P.C.).
14. (1884), 9 S.C.R. 256. See also *O'Leary v. Pelican Insurance Co.* (1889), 29 N.B.R. 510 (C.A.).
15. *Ibid.*, at 263, 9 S.C.R.
16. (1894), 26 N.S.R. 427 (C.A.).
17. *Ibid.*, at 441.

she reached Benoit's Cove, and there she was repaired to enable her to go on a voyage to Halifax in the spring. No one pretends that the cost of repairs exceeded her value when repaired. It could not be proved. She was not within any of the tests to be applied in determining a constructive total loss.

Justice Graham continued:[18]

[T]here must be a constructive total loss before a sale can be made, and that there must be an urgent necessity for the sale as well . . . Lord Esher said in *Kaltenbach v. McKenzie*, 3 C.P.D., p. 476: "A sale cannot make a total loss. Notice of abandonment cannot enable the assured to recover for a total loss unless the sale was justifiable by the circumstances, and the circumstances were such as to justify a person in claiming for a total loss. The constructive total loss, in other words, must exist before either the sale or the notice of abandonment, the circumstances must be such as justify it."

(3) Constructive Total Loss of Goods[19]

In *Rumsey v. Providence Washington Insurance Co.*,[20] a vessel was wrecked on the Labrador coast at a place where there was no means of saving the cargo. The master sold the cargo without notice of abandonment. In holding that the master was justified in doing so and that there had been a constructive total loss of the goods, the court stated:[21]

[I]t is perfectly true that to constitute a constructive total loss there must be a notice of abandonment if it is possible to give it and if it will avail anything when given. The object of the notice is to enable the insurers to take possession and save the cargo for themselves; but how could the cargo be saved at this outlandish place, at a time of the year when all the people, with the exception of three or four, had retired into the woods, and where there was no boat, no wharf, or anything to assist in landing and preserving the cargo. . . .What could the master of a vessel under such circumstances have done? To leave the cargo in the vessel all winter would have been exceedingly hazardous, and would certainly not have been for the benefit of the owners or insurers.

In order to succeed on a constructive total loss of cargo the assured must show that the cost of forwarding the goods to their destination would exceed their value on arrival. It is not enough to show that there were no vessels to which the goods could have been transhipped for their intended destination. The assured has to explore other means of transporting the goods to the destination.[22]

---

18. *Ibid.*, at 443.
19. See Rule 17 in the *Rules for Construction of Policy* in the Schedule to the *Marine Insurance Act*, R.S.O. 1980, c. 255. See also *Derksen v. Guardian Insurance Co. of Canada*, [1976] I.L.R. 1-773 (Alta. Dist. Ct.), where a container was held not to be "goods".
20. (1880), 13 N.S.R. 393 (C.A.).
21. *Ibid.*, at 395.
22. *Fairbanks et al. v. Union Marine Insurance Co.* (1854), 2 N.S.R. 271 (C.A.).

Where goods arrive at a destination *in specie* but valueless due to damage by a peril insured against, the insurers will be liable for a total loss.[23]

In a recent decision of the Federal Court of Canada, *Green Forest Lumber Ltd. v. General Security Insurance Co. of Canada*,[24] a shipper claimed for a constructive total loss of lumber. At the loading port the vessel was grounded and took on some water. The shipper abandoned the cargo. The insurer rejected the notice of abandonment. The lumber was not a total loss and all of it was later sold on the open market at the regular market price for lumber of the grade specified in the contract between the shipper and consignee. The court found that there had not been a constructive total loss. Justice Addy observed:[25]

> [C]onstructive total loss is a concept peculiar to marine insurance and the loss is considered as having occurred even where the subject-matter is not in fact totally lost, but likely to become so from the improbability, impracticability or expense of repair or recovery. . .
>
> Unlike actual total loss, which is a loss in law and in fact, constructive total loss is a total loss in law, although not a total loss in fact. A proper notice of abandonment given under conditions which warrant it, entitles the insured to claim a total loss against his insurer.
>
> It is clear, however, that the conditions must warrant the notice and if the circumstances are not such that it is unlikely that the assured can recover the goods, or if the property is not so badly damaged that the cost of repairing would exceed the value of the goods, or if the absolute destruction or irretrievable loss would not appear to be unavoidable, the insured cannot elect to turn what at the time of abandonment is only an average loss into a total loss merely by giving a notice of abandonment.
>
> Constructive total loss occurs where such circumstances exist, where a prudent uninsured owner, in the exercise of the soundest judgment, would have sold the cargo as she lay rather than try to save or repair it. The cost of saving and repairing must however exceed the full repaired value. There must be such a preponderating excess of expense that no reasonable man could hesitate as to the propriety of selling under the circumstances, rather than repairing.

---

23. *Almon v. British America Assurance Co.* (1882), 16 N.S.R. 43.
24. [1977] 2 F.C. 351, [1977] I.L.R. 1-849 (T.D.); affd [1978] 2 F.C. 773, [1978] I.L.R. 1-990 (C.A.); affd [1980] 1 S.C.R. 176, 34 N.R. 303, [1981] I.L.R. 1-332.
25. *Ibid.*, at 363-64, [1977] 2 F.C.

30

Notice of Abandonment

s. 63: (1) Subject to the provisions of the section, where the assured elects to abandon the subject-matter insured to the insurer, he must give notice of abandonment and if he fails to do so the loss can only be treated as a partial loss.

(2) Notice of abandonment may be given in writing or by word of mouth, or partly in writing and partly by word of mouth, and may be given in any terms that indicate the intention of the assured to abandon his insured interest in the subject-matter insured unconditionally to the insurer.

(3) Notice of abandonment must be given with reasonable diligence after the receipt of reliable information of the loss, but where the information is of a doubtful character, the assured is entitled to a reasonable time to make inquiry.

(4) Where notice of abandonment is properly given, the rights of the assured are not prejudiced by the fact that the insurer refuses to accept the abandonment.

(5) The acceptance of an abandonment may be either express or implied from the conduct of the insurer and the mere silence of the insurer after notice is not an acceptance.

(6) Where notice of abandonment is accepted, the abandonment is irrevocable and the acceptance of the notice conclusively admits liability for the loss and the sufficiency of the notice.

(7) Notice of abandonment is unnecessary where, at the time when the assured receives information of the loss, there would be no possibility of benefit to the insurer if notice were given to him.

(8) Notice of abandonment may be waived by the insurer.

(9) Where an insurer has reinsured his risk, no notice of abandonment need be given by him.

s. 64: (1) Where there is a valid abandonment, the insurer is entitled to take over the interest of the assured in whatever may remain of the subject-matter insured and all proprietary rights incidental thereto.

(2) Upon the abandonment of a ship, the insurer thereof is entitled to any freight in course of being earned and which is earned by her subsequent to the casualty causing the loss, less the expenses of earning it incurred after the casualty, and, where the ship is carrying the owner's goods, the insurer is entitled to a reasonable remuneration for the carriage of them subsequent to the casualty causing the loss.

Underwriters are not liable for constructive total losses where no notice of abandonment has been given.[1]

Where no notice of abandonment is given and there is no reason for it not having been given, the assured will not be able to recover for a constructive total loss.[2]

No abandonment can have any effectual operation unless the state of things is such as to justify it at the time it was made. Abandonment will not turn a partial loss into a constructive total loss.[3]

The reason that a notice of abandonment is necessary in a constructive total loss situation was explained by Justice Strong in *Phoenix Insurance Co. v. McGhee*:[4]

> The notice is required in order that the underwriters may have an option of doing that which the assured by the act of abandonment has announced his intention not to do, *viz.*, an opportunity of reclaiming and rescuing the insured property and (in the case of a ship) repairing it, and reinstating it in its original condition. Then it is manifest that if such restoration is a physical impossibility the reason for requiring notice is inapplicable, and the assured who fails to give it does not, in legal contemplation, by his omission, cause prejudice to the underwriters.

In *Baker et al. v. Brown*,[5] Chief Justice Young described what is required to be present in a notice of abandonment:[6]

> [T]he abandonment must be express and direct ... But whatever strictness of construction might have been applied to notices of abandonment in former times, it never could have been absolutely necessary to use the technical word 'abandon,' — any equivalent expressions which informed the underwriters that it was the intention of the insured to give up to them the property insured upon the ground of its having been totally lost must always have been sufficient.

Where an assured orally advises an underwriter of an abandonment and provides the underwriter with a letter from the master of the vessel advising that the expense of repairing the vessel is greater than the worth of the vessel, there is a valid notice of abandonment.[7]

What constitutes a reasonable time within which to give notice of abandonment depends in each case on the circumstances, and principally, on what steps the underwriters might take if they had notice. If there is nothing they can do, no notice is required.[8]

---

1. *Wood v. Stymest* (1862), 10 N.B.R. 309 (C.A.). See also *Nova Scotia Marine Insurance Co. v. Churchill & Co.* (1896), 26 S.C.R. 65.
2. *Gallagher v. Taylor* (1881), 5 S.C.R. 368.
3. *Troop et al. v. Jones* (1884), 17 N.S.R. 230 (C.A.).
4. (1890), 18 S.C.R. 61, at 72.
5. (1872), 9 N.S.R. 100 (S.C.).
6. *Ibid.*, at 104.
7. *Morton v. Patillo* (1872), 9 N.S.R. 17 (C.A.).
8. *Dickie v. Merchants' Marine Insurance Co.* (1883), 16 N.S.R. 244 (C.A.).

As methods of communication and travel have improved, so has the time decreased in which notice must be given to underwriters. What was once described as a very idle ceremony may be of great practical importance as the underwriters' orders might promptly reach the spot where the ship is in peril.[9]

In *Rose v. Weekes*,[10] a fishing vessel was abandoned after it had been holed by ice and was filling with water. The assured did not immediately give notice of abandonment to the insurer. The court held the lack of timely notice by the assured did not prevent recovery for the loss. The sufficiency and timeliness of a notice of abandonment are questions of fact which must be determined by the circumstances of each case.[11]

Where notice of abandonment is given to insurers and they say and do nothing, the conclusion is that they do not mean to accept the abandonment. But if they take a positive step with respect to the subject-matter of the abandonment, such as repairing a vessel, then there is a constructive acceptance of the abandonment of the subject-matter.[12]

The effect of a notice of abandonment has been described in *King et al. v. Western Assurance Co.*[13] by Justice Hagarty:[14]

> The effect of a notice of abandonment, if accepted or made on good grounds, is to vest the ownership of the property in the underwriters; from the moment of the loss the master will be considered the agent of the underwriters in all acts done by him from that time, within the scope of his authority, given to him by the policy, to sue, labour, and travel, for the defence, safeguard and recovery of the subject insured.

The receipt of a notice of abandonment by an agent of an insurer and his statement that he will forward the notice to his principal, and his belief that the loss will be paid, does not amount to acceptance of abandonment. The acceptance of the notice of abandonment must be by some unequivocal act.[15]

An agent of an assured has a right to give notice of abandonment to underwriters.[16]

In *Kenny et al. v. Halifax Marine Insurance Co.*,[17] the assured claimed for a total loss of a vessel which had been abandoned by the crew on the rocks of a shore. The underwriters had accepted

---

9. *Ibid.*, at 270.
10. (1984), 7 C.C.L.I. 287 (Fed. T.D.).
11. *Ibid.* See also chapter 29, note 9.
12. *Provincial Insurance Co. of Canada v. Leduc* (1874), 6 L.R.P.C. 224, 19 L.C Jur. 281 (P.C.).
13. (1858), 7 U.C.C.P. 300.
14. *Ibid.*, at 307.
15. *O'Leary v. Pelican Insurance Co.* (1889), 29 N.B.R. 510 (C.A.).
16. *Merchants' Marine Insurance Co. v. Barss* (1888), 15 S.C.R. 185.
17. (1840), 1 N.S.R. 141 (C.A.).

the notice of abandonment but subsequent to this acceptance, a gale
lifted the vessel off the rocks and she was brought safely into port.
The court held that although the notice of abandonment was made,
subsequent events made it so the assured could only recover for a
partial loss. To allow a total loss would be contrary to the principle
of indemnity. Chief Justice Halliburton observed:[18]

> As far as indemnity extends, the practice of insurance is most beneficial,
> not only to those immediately engaged in commerce but to society at large,
> as it divides among many those losses which would prove ruinous to one. Carried
> beyond mere indemnification, it would prove as pernicious as it is now beneficial.

Where an underwriter rejects an abandonment but takes possession of a ship and incompletely repairs her, and then allows her
to be sold for the costs of those repairs, this constitutes an acceptance
of the abandonment.[19]

In *Driscoll v. Millville Marine Insurance Co.*,[20] an owner claimed
for a constructive total loss of his vessel. The owner had given underwriters notice of abandonment after the loss. This was rejected and
thereafter the owner advised the master to "follow the best advice".
The master had a survey performed on the vessel and it was found
that it would cost more to repair her than she would be worth. The
master thereafter sold the vessel by auction. The court held that
the owner's instructions to the master did not constitute a waiver
of the notice of abandonment.

Where a ship is held to be not worth repairing no notice of abandonment of freight is necessary.[21]

---

18. *Ibid.*, at 146. See, however, s. 63 (6) of the *Marine Insurance Act*, R.S.O. 1980, c. 255.
19. *McLeod v. Insurance Co. of North America et al.* (1901), 34 N.S.R. 88 (C.A.).
20. (1883), 23 N.B.R. 160 (C.A.); revd 11 S.C.R. 183.
21. *Patch v. Pitman* (1886), 19 N.S.R. 298 (C.A.); affd Cass. S.C. 389.

31

Particular Average and Particular Charges

s. 65: (1) A particular average loss is a partial loss of the subject-matter insured, caused by a peril insured against, and which is not a general average loss.

(2) Expenses incurred by or on behalf of the assured for the safety or preservation of the subject-matter insured, other than general average and salvage charges, are called particular charges and particular charges are not included in particular average.

In commercial usage, the term "particular average" has come to be synonymous with partial loss. Particular average is a partial loss, fortuitously caused by a peril insured against, and which has to be borne by the party upon whom it falls. Particular average denotes actual damage done to, or loss of part of the subject-matter of insurance.[1] For example, if there is a collision at sea between a vessel and a submerged object whereby the vessel is damaged and seawater enters a hold and damages a cargo of wheat, these are particular average losses. The damage to the ship is borne by the shipowner and the damage to the cargo is borne by the cargo owner.

Particular average must be distinguished from general average. General average is a partial loss incurred in time of peril voluntarily for the purpose of preserving the property imperilled in the common adventure. The loss is made good proportionably by all parties concerned in the adventure. For example, where a cargo of tractors is jettisoned to lighten a vessel in a storm in order to prevent the sinking of the vessel, this is a general average act. The loss of the tractors will be made good proportionably by the shipowner and the owners of the other cargo saved by the act.

Particular charges, on the other hand, are those expenses which are incurred by the assured for the preservation of the subject-matter insured. For example, the cost of drying and repacking of goods are particular charges. Expenses incurred under the "sue and labour" clause of the policy are particular charges. Particular charges are recoverable in addition to the sum insured. For example, if a cargo of machinery insured for $20,000 is damaged by a peril insured against to the extent of $18,000 and the assured spends $3,000 to

---

1. *Glen Falls Insurance Co. v. Montreal Light, Heat & Power Consolidated* (1928), 45 Que. K.B. 304 (C.A.).

preserve the cargo from further damage, there is a partial loss or particular average loss of $18,000 and there is a particular charge of $3,000. The assured will be able to recover $21,000 even though the cargo is insured for only $20,000.[2]

2. See also *Western Assurance Co. v. Baden Marine Assurance Co.* (1902), 22 Q.R. 374 (S.C.).

32
Salvage Charges

s. 66: (1) Subject to any express provision in the policy, salvage charges incurred in preventing a loss by perils insured against may be recoverable as a loss by those perils.

(2) "Salvage charges" means the charges recoverable under maritime law by a salvor independently of contract but do not include the expenses of services in the nature of salvage rendered by the assured or his agents or any person employed for hire by them for the purpose of averting a peril insured against, and such expenses, where properly incurred, may be recovered as particular charges or as a general average loss according to the circumstances under which they were incurred.

The Act[1] distinguishes between salvage charges strictly so-called, *i.e.* charges recoverable under maritime law by a salvor who is not employed under any contract, and expenses of services in the nature of salvage, *i.e.* those rendered by the assured or his agents or any person employed by him for the purpose of avoiding a loss from a peril insured against.

The practical difference that results from this distinction is that, as salvage charges, strictly so-called, are recoverable under the policy, and not under the sue and labour clause, they cannot be recovered in addition to the sum insured.[2]

---

1. *Marine Insurance Act*, R.S.O. 1980, c. 255.
2. See *Montgomery v. Indemnity Mutual Marine Insurance Co. Ltd.* (1902), 1 K.B. 734 (C.A.). The distinction which has been embodied in the Act (*supra*, note 1) arises from the decision of *Aitchison v. Lohre* (1879), 4 App. Cas. 755, 28 W.R. 1 (H.L.) where an award paid to a salvor who was acting independently of contract could not be recoverable under the sue and labour clause. See also F.J. Laverty, *The Insurance Law of Canada*, Montreal: John Lovell & Son Ltd. 1911, at 621.

33

General Average

s. 67: (1) A general average loss is a loss caused by or directly consequential on a general average act and it includes a general average expenditure as well as a general average sacrifice.

(2) There is a general average act where any extraordinary sacrifice or expenditure is voluntarily and reasonably made or incurred in time of peril for the purpose of preserving the property imperilled in the common adventure.

(3) Where there is a general average loss, the party on whom it falls is entitled, subject to the conditions imposed by maritime law, to a rateable contribution from the other parties interested, and such contribution is called a general average contribution.

(4) Subject to any express provision in the policy, where the assured has incurred a general average expenditure, he may recover from the insurer in respect of the proportion of the loss that falls upon him; and, in the case of a general average sacrifice, he may recover from the insurer in respect of the whole loss without having enforced his right of contribution from the other parties liable to contribute.

(5) Subject to any express provision in the policy, where the assured has paid, or is liable to pay, a general average contribution in respect of the subject insured, he may recover therefor from the insurer.

(6) In the absence of express stipulation, the insurer is not liable for any general average loss or contribution where the loss was not incurred for the purpose of avoiding, or in connection with the avoidance of, a peril insured against.

(7) Where ship, freight, and cargo, or any two of those interests, are owned by the same assured, the liability of the insurer in respect of general average losses or contributions is to be determined as if those subjects were owned by different persons.

In *Kidd v. Thomson*,[1] Justice Lister outlined the general principles to be applied for general average:[2]

> Mr. Carver, in the 2nd edition of his work on the *Carriage of Goods by Sea*, at p. 392, states the rule thus: "Whenever under extraordinary circumstances of danger to both ship and cargo, a voluntary sacrifice of money is made in order to save both ship and cargo, by the expenditure of which both ship and cargo are saved, the person who made the voluntary sacrifice is entitled to call upon the others whose property has been saved by the voluntary sacrifice made on their behalf, as well as his own, for general average contribution....

---

1. (1899), 26 O.A.R. 220 (C.A.).
2. *Ibid.*, at 221-22.

Imminent peril must be impending over the whole adventure ... and the expenditure must be made for the immediate safety of the adventure and for no other purpose ... There can be no general average if the expenditure is made to avert a peril contemplated by the voyage, and thus within the scope of the shipowners' duty.

Thus, where a vessel is in a harbour lying in safety and a tug is employed for the purpose of releasing her from ice which has formed in the harbour, and which is normal for that time of year, to enable her to complete her voyage, this is not a general average expense.[3]

Justice Andrews, in *Singer Manufacturing Co. v. Western Assurance Co.*,[4] quoting Brett M.R. in *Svendsen v. Wallace Bros.*,[5] described what constitutes a proper general average act:[6]

> If there is a danger to the preservation of both ship and cargo from destruction, if the ship remains at sea, the act of putting into port to repair is an extraordinary act which may well be called a general average act. If in order to do that act, an expenditure is reasonably incurred, that expenditure is a general average expenditure. If in order to do that act, towage, pilotage or inward dues, must be paid, those expenditures are all and each general average expenditures.

Western Assurance Co. v. Ontario Coal Co. of Toronto[7] involved a general average claim by shipowners against cargo owners. The vessel was stranded in Humber Bay with a cargo of coal. In denying the claim of the owners of the vessel, the court found that "the coal which formed the schooner's cargo and the vessel herself were never in that common peril which is the very foundation of the right to claim for general average."[8] Justice Strong, citing the English decision of *Kemp v. Halliday*,[9] stated:[10]

> In that case Mr. Justice Blackburn says: "I do not mean to say that in every case where a ship with a cargo is submerged and the two are in fact raised together by one operation the expenditure must necessarily be for the common preservation of both. I think it is in every case a question of fact whether it was so; and if the cargo could be easily and cheaply taken out of the ship and saved by itself it would not be proper to charge it to any portion of the joint operation which in that case would not be incurred for the preservation of the cargo."

---

3. *Ibid.*
4. (1896), 10 Que. S.C. 379 (C.A.).
5. (1884), 13 Q.B.D. 69 (C.A.); affd (1885), 10 App. Cas. 404, 34 W.R. 369 (H.L.).
6. *Supra*, note 4, at 417.
7. (1892), 21 S.C.R. 383.
8. *Ibid.*, at 387.
9. (1865), 6 B. & S. 723, 122 E.R. 1361, 1 L.R.Q.B. 520 (Ex. Ct.).
10. *Supra*, note 7, at 388.

In *Grouselle v. Ferrie et al.*,[11] the owners of a cargo of wine carried on deck and thrown overboard to lighten a vessel during a storm, were entitled to a general average contribution from the shipowners.

In *Steinhoff v. Royal Canadian Insurance Co.*,[12] a steam barge was beached after throwing out part of her cargo. The master stated that the jettison was the only means of saving all concerned. The marine policy upon the vessel, described as a "steam barge" was warranted "to be free of any contribution for loss by jettison of property on deck of any sail vessel or barge." The court held that the "barge" mentioned in the policy did not mean "steam barge" and allowed the owner's claim for general average. The act of jettisoning part of the cargo was voluntary and it was a sacrifice made for the good of both the ship and the remaining cargo.

The mere steering of a vessel to a less dangerous place for stranding, when she is inevitably driving to the shore, is not a voluntary stranding.[13]

A vessel of Nova Scotian registry sailed from England to New York where she was the subject of general average.[14] The average was adjusted according to the usage of the port of New York, which amount was greater than if adjusted in Nova Scotia. The underwriters were bound to reimburse the assured for the general average charges as assessed by the foreign adjustment. Chief Justice Young stated:[15]

> Now it seems certain that the *English* underwriter must be bound by the very terms of his contract, to reimburse to the assured their proportion of all such general average charges as they, the assured have been compelled to pay by the law of *England*. If this be so, and it seems quite incontrovertible, then it follows, by necessary inference, that the underwriter is bound to reimburse all such general average charges as have been assessed on the insured by a foreign adjustment, if correctly settled, according to the law of the port of adjustment.... A foreign adjustment, to be binding, must be clearly proved to have been made in strict conformity with the laws and usages of the foreign port, and it would, doubtless, be set aside, or corrected, for fraud or gross error.

In *Northland Navigation Co. Ltd. et al. v. Patterson Boiler Works Ltd.*,[16] an owner of a barge claimed for a general average contribution from cargo owners. The barge was being towed by a tug when it had to be set adrift as the tug was having problems in heavy seas.

---

11. (1843), 6 O.S. 454 (C.A.).
12. (1877), 42 U.C.Q.B. 307 (C.A.). See also *Spooner et al. v. Western Assurance Co.* (1876), 38 U.C.Q.B. 62 (C.A.).
13. *Gibb v. McDonell* (1850), 7 U.C.Q.B. 356 (C.A.).
14. *Avon Marine Insurance Co. v. Barteaux* (1871), 8 N.S.R. 195 (C.A.).
15. *Ibid.*, at 196.
16. [1983] 2 F.C. 59 (T.D.).

The barge was stranded and the cargo was removed. The court held that the casting adrift of the barge was a general average sacrifice. Similarly, the expenses incurred in attempts to save the barge and cargo gave rise to general average. Justice Collier, stated:[17]

> There is little modern case law on general average. It is necessary, I think, to go back to certain basic principles. The words of Lawrence J., in *Birkley and others v. Presgrave* (1801), 1 East 220, at p. 228, have been cited many times: "All loss which arises in consequence of extraordinary sacrifices made or expenses incurred for the preservation of the ship and cargo comes within general average, and must be borne proportionably by all who are interested." It is to be noted general average can arise either where there has been an extraordinary sacrifice, or where there have been extraordinary expenses incurred, for the preservation of ship and cargo. Jettison of cargo is a well-known illustration of an extraordinary sacrifice. Other illustrations, where there have been sacrifice of parts of a vessel or her tackle, particularly in the sailing days, can be found in some older cases.

The danger which gives rise to the general average act must not have arisen through the fault of the person claiming contribution, where such fault would expose such person to legal liability for the damage done. This has been the law for a good number of years and was clearly enunciated by the court in *Dreyfus (Louis) & Co. v. Tempus Shipping Co. Ltd.*,[18] an English decision.

In *Western Canada Steamship Co. Ltd. v. Canadian Commercial Corp.*,[19] a shipowner claimed for general average contribution against the owners of the cargo carried on board the ship *Lake Chilco*. The ship's tail shaft broke while at sea on a return voyage as a result of what was later discovered to be a defect in the main propulsion machinery. The cargo owners denied liability on the ground that the ship was unseaworthy. Shortly before the beginning of the voyage, the ship propeller struck a fender log, but inspections showed that no damage had been done. The owner had been alerted to the high incidence of tail shaft failures on ships of that class (although the cause of this failure was still unknown at the time of the loss), and had the tail shaft carefully examined before the outward voyage even though her classification did not require this to be done at the time.

The trial judge found that the ship was unseaworthy, but that the carrier had exercised due diligence to make her seaworthy. This judgment was reversed by the Court of Appeal and again reversed by the Supreme Court of Canada.

---

17. *Ibid.*, at 64.
18. [1931] A.C. 726, [1931] All E.R. 577 (H.L.). See also Rule D of the York-Antwerp Rules, Appendix E.
19. [1960] S.C.R. 632, 24 D.L.R. (2d) 161.

In deciding for the shipowner, the Supreme Court stated that when unseaworthiness has been shown to be the cause of the loss, there is then a burden upon the shipowner to show that he exercised due diligence to make the ship seaworthy before and at the beginning of the voyage. This burden, however, does not require the shipowner to prove either the cause of the loss or the cause of the unseaworthiness and is also not to be treated as going so far as to make him prove all the circumstances which explain an obscure situation. The evidence disclosed that the shipowner had met the burden of proving due diligence to make the ship seaworthy before and at the beginning of the voyage which was to be taken as the period from at the least the beginning of loading of the cargo until the ship started on the contemplated voyage. The defect in the tail shaft was a latent one and due diligence did not require the shipowner to install torsiograph equipment and make numerous tests before the cause of the weakness could be determined.

The Supreme Court of Canada also had occasion to consider a general average situation in *Federal Commerce & Navigation Co. Ltd. & Halifax Overseas Freighters Ltd. v. Eisenerz G.m.b.H.*[20] In this case Halifax Overseas Freighters Ltd. owned a vessel which it time chartered to Federal Commerce and Navigation who in turn chartered it to Eisenerz G.m.b.H. under a voyage charter. Federal Commerce and Navigation issued two bills of lading covering Eisenerz G.m.b.H. cargoes of pig iron which incorporated the terms of the charter party. The two cargoes were loaded onto the vessel, in separate holds, as the two types of pig iron, which were uniform in size, length, shape and weight, differed in quality and in the purpose for which they were to be used. The cargo was loaded at Sorel and destined for Genoa. The vessel stranded near Lauzon and it was necessary to discharge the cargo pending repairs at Levis. In the course of reloading, the two cargoes were mixed to such an extent that they were lost and destroyed.

General average was declared and Eisenerz G.m.b.H. refused to contribute to the loss and alleged that the vessel was unseaworthy, *i.e.* the vessel was unseaworthy on departure from Sorel by reason of overloading and that this unseaworthiness directly contributed to the loss. The court found that the stranding was solely caused by a serious error in navigation on the part of the pilot who was in charge of the vessel at the time, and no causal connection was shown between unseaworthiness and stranding. The court further found that the stranding was the event which made it necessary for the cargo to be unloaded. This decision was made by the master for the benefit of the ship and cargo alike and could therefore be

---

20. [1974] S.C.R. 1225, 31 D.L.R. (3d) 209.

properly described as a "general average act" which was occasioned through negligent navigation, for which the owners were exempted from liability under the charter party.

However, it did not follow that the loss and damage to the respondent's cargo was a "general average loss". The expenses incurred in handling the cargo were a direct consequence of the general average act, but the combined negligence of the master and stevedores which occasioned the damage, was not attributable to the general average act; it constituted a separate and independent cause. Halifax Overseas and Federal Commerce and Navigation failed to show that the damage complained of was the direct consequence of the general average act. Similarly Eisenerz G.m.b.H.'s claim was one for damages for negligent performance of a contract of carriage and not a claim in general average. Halifax Overseas and Federal Commerce and Navigation were found to be jointly and severally liable for the damage to the cargo.

In *N.V. Bocimar S.A. v. Century Insurance Co. of Canada*,[21] a vessel was damaged by fire while carrying a cargo of grain from North America to Antwerp. The fire was put out and the vessel was temporarily repaired at Conception Bay enabling her to resume her voyage under her own power and to deliver her cargo, which was undamaged, to Europe. The shipowner's general average claim was for part of the cost of repairs, towage and other expenses incurred as a result of the firefighting efforts, *i.e.* expenses incurred for the preservation of the property committed to the common maritime adventure.

The trial judge dismissed the action on the ground that the vessel was unseaworthy in that the crew were not properly trained in firefighting. The trial judge concluded that most of the damage which was the subject of the general average claim had been caused by the unseaworthiness. The Federal Court of Appeal reviewed the evidence and reversed the finding of the trial judge. It found that the defendant failed to establish, on a balance of probabilities, that the vessel was unseaworthy and therefore allowed the general average claim. Justice Hugessen, in respect of the burdens of proof on the defendant, stated:[22]

> The claim for general average being contested solely on the grounds of the ship's being unseaworthy, the defendant bore and bears the burden of proving that fact as well as demonstrating that the proven unseaworthiness caused or contributed to the damage. If unseaworthiness and causality are established, the plaintiff bears the burden of proving that he had exercised due diligence to make the vessel seaworthy. In each case these are simply the normal civil

---

21. (1984), 7 C.C.L.I. 165, 53 N.R. 383 (Fed. C.A.); leave to appeal to S.C.C. granted 57 N.R. 80*n* (S.C.C.).

22. *Ibid.*, at 169, 7 C.C.L.I.

burdens of bringing evidence which makes the facts sought to be proved more probable than not.

In rejecting the trial judge's finding that the crew was so poorly trained as to make the ship unseaworthy, Justice Hugessen stated:[23]

> Some mistakes are bound to occur in an emergency situation such as a fire at sea. Even the most highly trained crew of firefighters are not going to do everything perfectly. The trial Judge recognized this and it is for this reason that he emphasizes the great number of errors which he thought had been committed. For my own part, I can only say that I am not persuaded that the relatively few well founded criticisms of the ship's firefighting efforts are of such number and gravity as to indicate that the crew was so poorly trained as to make the ship unseaworthy. The mistakes that were made seem to me to be at least as consistent with simple human error committed in a situation of great stress.

The case of *St. Lawrence Construction Ltd. v. Federal Commerce and Navigation Co. Ltd.*[24] was heard by Justices Urie, Mahoney and Stone in the Federal Court of Appeal. It concerned a barge which had been driven onto a sandbar by wind during towage into a river. Evidence was introduced that the carrier failed to examine available information concerning weather in the area that would have shown that the tug had insufficient horsepower to control the barge in weather conditions that could reasonably be expected to be found in James Bay. The shipper alleged that as such the tug was therefore unseaworthy. The court agreed.

Justice Arthur Stone wrote the decision of the court. In holding that the carrier could not recover a general average contribution from the shipper, Justice Stone said:[25]

> [T]he law is also clear that a carrier is not entitled to recover from a shipper a contribution in general average where the general average situation was brought about by his own actionable fault.... [T]he appellant [carrier] was obliged to exercise due diligence to make the tug and barge seaworthy. Its failure to do so was due entirely to its own negligence and it was that negligence that caused the stranding and the resulting loss. Had due diligence been exercised, as it ought to have been, the stranding would not have occurred and declaration of general average would have been unnecessary. As the appellant was itself at fault it cannot expect the respondent to contribute anything in general average.

Where an insurer pays for a loss and becomes the owner of cargo and thereafter a general average expense is incurred, he will be held liable to contribute to the general average.[26]

---

23. *Ibid.*, at 176, 7 C.C.L.I.
24. [1985] 1 F.C. 767, 56 N.R. 174, 32 C.C.L.T. 19 (C.A.); leave to appeal to S.C.C. refused 58 N.R. 236 (S.C.C.).
25. *Ibid.*, at 51, 32 C.C.L.T.
26. *Insurance Co. of North America v. Colonial S.S. Ltd.*, [1942] S.C.R. 357, [1942] 3 D.L.R. 225.

34

Measure of Indemnity

s. 68: (1) The sum that the assured can recover in respect of a loss on a policy by which he is insured, in the case of an unvalued policy to the full extent of the insurable value, or in the case of a valued policy to the full extent of the value fixed by the policy, is called the measure of indemnity.

(2) Where there is a loss recoverable under the policy, the insurer, or each insurer if there is more than one, is liable for such proportion of the measure of indemnity as the amount of his subscription bears to the value fixed by the policy in the case of a valued policy or to the insurable value in the case of an unvalued policy.

s. 69: Subject to the provisions of this Act and to any express provision in the policy, where there is a total loss of the subject-matter insured,
(*a*) if the policy is a valued policy, the measure of indemnity is the sum fixed by the policy;
(*b*) if the policy is an unvalued policy, the measure of indemnity is the insurable value of the subject-matter insured.

s. 70: Where a ship is damaged but is not totally lost, the measure of indemnity, subject to any express provision in the policy, is as follows:
1. Where the ship has been repaired, the assured is entitled to the reasonable cost of the repairs, less the customary deduction, but not exceeding the sum insured in respect of any one casualty.
2. Where the ship has been only partially repaired, the assured is entitled to the reasonable cost of such repairs, computed as above, and also to be indemnified for the reasonable depreciation, if any, arising from the unrepaired damage, provided that the aggregate amount shall not exceed the cost of repairing the whole damage, computed as above.
3. Where the ship has not been repaired and has not been sold in her damaged state during the risk, the assured is entitled to be indemnified for the reasonable depreciation arising from the unrepaired damage, but not exceeding the reasonable cost of repairing such damage, computed as above.

s. 71: Subject to any express provision in the policy, where there is a partial loss of freight, the measure of indemnity is such proportion of the sum fixed by the policy in the case of a valued policy, or of the insurable value in the case of an unvalued policy, as the proportion of freight lost by the assured bears to the whole freight at the risk of the assured under the policy.

s. 72: Where there is a partial loss of goods, merchandise, or other movables, the measure of indemnity, subject to any express provision in the policy, is as follows:

1. Where part of the goods, merchandise, or other movables insured by a valued policy is totally lost, the measure of indemnity is such proportion of the sum fixed by the policy as the insurable value of the part lost bears to the insurable value of the whole, ascertained as in the case of an unvalued policy.

2. Where part of the goods, merchandise, or other movables insured by an unvalued policy is totally lost, the measure of indemnity is the insurable value of the part lost, ascertained as in case of total loss.

3. Where the whole or any part of the goods or merchandise insured has been delivered damaged at its destination, the measure of indemnity is such proportion of the sum fixed by the policy in the case of a valued policy, or of the insurable value in the case of an unvalued policy, as the difference between the gross sound and damaged values at the place of arrival bears to the gross sound value.

4. "Gross value" means the wholesale price or, if there be no such price, the estimated value, with, in either case, freight, landing charges, and duty paid beforehand; provided that, in the case of goods or merchandise customarily sold in bond, the bonded price is deemed to be the gross value.

5. "Gross proceeds" means the actual price obtained at a sale where all charges on sale are paid by the sellers.

s. 73: (1) Where different species of property are insured under a single valuation, the valuation must be apportioned over the different species in proportion to their respective insurable values, as in the case of an unvalued policy. The insured value of any part of a species is such proportion of the total insured value of the same as the insurable value of the part bears to the insurable value of the whole, ascertained in both cases as provided by this Act.

(2) Where a valuation has to be apportioned and particulars of the prime cost of each separate species, quality, or description of goods cannot be ascertained, the division of the valuation may be made over the net arrived sound values of the different species, qualities, or description of goods.

s. 74: (1) Subject to any express provision in the policy, where the assured has paid, or is liable for, any general average contribution, the measure of indemnity is the full amount of such contribution, if the subject-matter liable to contribution is insured for its full contributory value; but if such subject-matter is not insured for its full contributory value, or if only part of it is insured, the indemnity payable by the insurer must be reduced in proportion to the under-insurance, and where there has been a particular average loss that constitutes a deduction from the contributory value, and for which the insurer

is liable, that amount must be deducted from the insured value in order to ascertain what the insurer is liable to contribute.
(2) Where the insurer is liable for salvage charges, the extent of his liability must be determined on the like principle.

s. 75: Where the assured has effected an insurance in express terms against any liability to a third party, the measure of indemnity, subject to any express provision in the policy, is the amount paid or payable by him to such third party in respect of such liability.

s. 76: (1) Where there has been a loss in respect of any subject-matter not expressly provided for in the foregoing provisions of this Act, the measure of indemnity shall be ascertained, as nearly as may be, in accordance with those provisions, in so far as applicable to the particular case.
(2) Nothing in the provisions of this Act relating to the measure of indemnity affects the rules relating to double insurance, or prohibits the insurer from disproving interest wholly or in part, or from showing that at the time of the loss the whole or any part of the subject-matter insured was not at risk under the policy.

Marine insurance is a contract of indemnity. Sections 68 to 76 specify what that indemnity is for the particular situation and how it is measured or calculated.

Section 69 deals with total losses, (both actual and constructive), for loss of ship, goods and freight. Unless there is fraud, the value of the subject-matter stated in a policy is conclusive as between the insurer and the assured.[1]

Section 70 deals with partial loss of a ship. If the ship is insured only against total losses, the assured will not be able to recover for a partial loss. Similarly, if the Memorandum[2] forms part of the policy the underwriters will only be liable if the loss amounts to the percentage specified therein.

Section 71 deals with partial loss of freight.

Section 72 deals with partial loss of goods and merchandise.[3]

---

1. See *Kenny v. Union Marine Insurance Co.* (1880), 13 N.S.R. 313, at 318 (C.A.).
2. See the Schedule to the *Marine Insurance Act*, R.S.O. 1980, c. 255. The Memorandum states: "... the ship ... [is] warranted free from average under three pounds per cent., unless general, or the ship be stranded."
3. See *Richardson (James) & Sons Ltd. v. Standard Marine Insurance Co.*, [1936] S.C.R. 573, [1936] 3 D.L.R. 513, at 519, 3 I.L.R. 494, where the partial loss of a cargo of wheat was calculated as the difference between the damaged and sound values, ascertained by comparing the gross produce of the damaged sales and applying the percentage difference to the value of the goods specified in the policy. See also *Singer Manufacturing Co. v. Western Assurance Co.* (1896), 10 Que. S.C. 379 (C.A.), where the insurers, of sewing machines insured under one policy but separately valued, were liable for such machines as were totally lost.

The loss may also be subject to the terms of the Memorandum[4] if included in the policy of insurance.[5]

Section 73 deals with the apportionment of valuation of different species of property.[6]

Section 74 deals with the calculation of general average contribution and salvage charges that the insurer must reimburse the assured for.

Section 75 deals with the measure of other liabilities the assured has to third parties. Section 76 is a catch all provision for calculating the measure of indemnity.

---

4. *Supra*, note 2.

5. See *Mowat v. Boston Marine Insurance Company* (1896), 26 S.C.R. 47, at 51-52, where three types of situations are outlined by Chief Justice Strong:

> "The law applicable to the case is stated in the judgment of the Court of Exchequer Chamber in the case of *Ralli v. Janson*, 6 E. & B. 422, as follows: 'Where memorandum goods of the same species are shipped, whether in bulk or packages, not expressed by distinct valuation or otherwise in the policy to be separately insured, and there is no general average and no stranding, the ordinary memorandum exempts the underwriters from liability for a total loss or destruction of part only, though consisting of one or more entire package or packages, and although such package or packages be entirely destroyed or otherwise lost by the specified perils.' In Arnould on *Marine Insurance*, 6 ed., p. 1016, it is said: 'There are three cases frequently occurring in practice, touching the insurance of memorandum articles: (1) where a cargo or quantity of memorandum articles of the same species is shipped in bulk, valued in bulk, and insured in bulk; (2) where it is shipped in separate packages but not expressed in the policy, by distinct valuation or otherwise, to be separately insured; (3) where, being shipped in separate packages it is expressed by distinct valuation or otherwise to be separately insured.' Then, it is further said by the same writer that the first case is one which never admitted of any reasonable doubt, and the case of *Hills v. The London Assurance Co.* (5 M. & M. 569) is referred to. In that case wheat was shipped and insured in bulk by one entire insurance and there was a loss of a quantity which was pumped up out of the hold during a storm and totally lost; it was held that this was an average and not a total loss. The case of *Ralli v. Janson*, (6 E. & B. 422), settled the law in the second case in favour of the underwriters."

6. See *Gilmour v. Dyde* (1861), 12 Low. Can. R. 337, 11 R.J.R.Q. 96.

35

Particular Average Warranties

s. 77: (1) Where the subject-matter insured is warranted free from particular average, the assured cannot recover for a loss of part, other than a loss incurred by a general average sacrifice, unless the contract contained in the policy is apportionable, but, if the contract is apportionable, the assured may recover for a total loss of any apportionable part.

(2) Where the subject-matter insured is warranted free from particular average, either wholly or under a certain percentage, the insurer is nevertheless liable for salvage charges, and for particular charges and other expenses properly incurred pursuant to the provisions of the suing and labouring clause in order to avert a loss insured against.

(3) Unless the policy otherwise provides, where the subject-matter insured is warranted free from particular average under a specified percentage, a general average loss cannot be added to a particular average loss to make up the specified percentage.

(4) For the purpose of ascertaining whether the specified percentage has been reached regard shall be had only to the actual loss suffered by the subject-matter insured, and particular charges and the expenses of and incidental to ascertaining and proving the loss must be excluded.

The Memorandum[1] is in effect a particular average warranty. It was introduced in 1749 to prevent underwriters from being harrassed by trifling demands on account of the perishable nature of the cargo. Other clauses such as the Institute Clauses[2] are often included in policies of insurance on perishable goods. For example, the W.A. Clause (Warranted Free of Average) clause limits the assured's right of recovery to claims for total loss. The F.P.A. (Free of Particular Average) cargo clause, on the other hand is a variation of the Memorandum but adds sinking and burning to the stranding exception.

In *Berry v. Columbian Insurance Co.*,[3] a vessel was insured under a policy which provided that no partial loss or particular average would be paid unless amounting to five per cent. The assured demonstrated that the damage, by grounding on a reef, was in excess of five per cent of the value of the vessel and was able to recover for the entire loss.

---

1. See the Schedule to the *Marine Insurance Act*, R.S.O. 1980, c. 255; Chapter 47.
2. See chapter 48 and Appendices A to D.
3. (1866), 12 Gr. 418.

In *Moore et al. v. Provincial Insurance Co.*,[4] an assured claimed for a loss of some packages of tin. The tin shipment was insured free from average unless general. The court held that where it is not expressed that packages are separately insured, the ordinary memorandum exempts the underwriters from liability for a total loss or destruction of a part only. Justice Galt reasoned that if the policy were not so construed, there would be nothing to prevent the average clause from being frittered away to nothing, "for if the cargo was fruit, the value of each orange might be declared."[5]

In *Watson v. Mercantile Marine Insurance Co.*,[6] an assured shipped a cargo of goods under a policy of insurance that would not pay for partial losses or particular average unless amounting to five per cent. Some of the goods were insured "free from average unless general." The vessel encountered heavy weather and put in at an intermediate port for repairs whereupon the master sold the goods. The court found, that on the evidence presented, the assured failed to show the percentage of the goods damaged by the storm, or that the cost of forwarding the goods was more than the value of the goods at its final destination. The assured could not recover for his loss.

Where goods are separately valued, a condition in a policy that it is "free of particular average" will not prevent an assured from recovering for a total loss or destruction of individual units.[7]

---

4. (1873), 23 U.C.C.P. 383 (C.A.).
5. *Ibid.*, at 392.
6. (1873), 9 N.S.R. 396 (C.A.).
7. *Singer Manufacturing Co. v. Western Assurance Co.* (1896), 10 Que. S.C. 379 (C.A.).

36

Successive Losses

s. 78: (1) Unless the policy otherwise provides and subject to the provisions of this Act, the insurer is liable for successive losses even though the total amount of such losses may exceed the sum insured.

(2) Where, under the same policy, a partial loss that has not been repaired or otherwise made good is followed by a total loss, the assured can only recover in respect of the total loss.

(3) Nothing in this section affects the liability of the insurer under the suing and labouring clause.

37
Suing and Labouring

s. 79: (1) Where the policy contains a suing and labouring clause, the engagement thereby entered into is deemed to be supplementary to the contract of insurance and the assured may recover from the insurer any expenses properly incurred pursuant to the clause, notwithstanding that the insurer may have paid for a total loss or that the subject-matter may have been warranted free from particular average, either wholly or under a certain percentage.

(2) General average losses and contributions and salvage charges as defined by this Act are not recoverable under the suing and labouring clause.

(3) Expenses incurred for the purpose of averting or diminishing any loss not covered by the policy are not recoverable under the suing and labouring clause.

(4) It is the duty of the assured and his agents to take such measures as may be reasonable for the purpose of averting or minimizing a loss.

The standard Lloyd's policy, the form of which is in the Schedule to the Act,[1] contains a suing and labouring clause. It states:

> And in the case of any loss or misfortune it shall be lawful to the assured, their factors, servants, and assigns, to sue, labour, and travel for, in and about the defence, safeguards, and recovery of the said goods and merchandises, and ship, etc., or any part thereof, without prejudice to this insurance; to the charges whereof we, the assurers, will contribute each one according to the rate and quantity of his sum herein assured.

The principle behind the sue and labour clause is that a person entitled to an indemnity must do everything in his power to minimize the loss. The clause benefits the insurer in that his liability may be substantially reduced if the assured or his servants or agents take prompt action for the preservation of the subject-matter of insurance. The clause takes the form of a separate or supplementary contract with the insurer over and above the sum insured proper. The assured can thus recover the money spent in order to minimize the loss in spite of the fact that such efforts may have been fruitless and that he received payment under the policy for the whole sum insured for a total loss.[2]

---

1. *Marine Insurance Act*, R.S.O. 1980, c. 255.
2. See chapter 31 and s. 65 re particular charges. See also *Glen Falls Insurance Co. v. Montreal Light, Heat and Power Consolidated* (1928), 45 Que. K.B. 304, and also *McLeod v. Insurance Co. of North America* (1901), 34 N.S.R. 88.

In *Porter (J.P.) & Sons Ltd. v. Western Assurance Co.*,[3] an assured claimed for expenses and repairs to a steel dredge scow. The scow, which was taking on water, was beached to prevent her from sinking. At the time she was carrying a cargo of buckets. The claim related to expenses incurred after the beaching of the vessel. The defendants argued that the expenses were general average expenses, *i.e.* incurred for the benefit of scow and cargo.

The court found that at the time the expenses were incurred, the cargo was safe. The scow, on the other hand, was still in danger, in that the tide together with the weather conditions would cause it to break up. The expenses were all incurred to prevent the loss of the scow and were therefore sue and labour expenses. Justice Archibald stated:[4]

It was the duty of the assured and his agents to avert or minimize the impending loss to the property insured by exercising such measures as were reasonable and necessary. I think the expenses incurred were clearly expenses contemplated by the Sue and Labour clause of the policy.

Eldridge on *Marine Policies*, 2nd ed., p. 113 states: "It (the Sue and Labour clause) is strictly confined to the cost of efforts made to save the thing insured from damage by the perils insured against in the policy."

Again at p. 116: "Expenses payable under the sue and labour clause must have been incurred to prevent an impending loss when the subject of the insurance is actually in peril."

In Halsbury Laws of England (2nd ed.), vol. 18, p. 336, (ss. 469 & 471) there are the following statements with reference to the Sue and Labour clause in marine insurance policies: "The clause covers particular charges and not a general average loss, because by its very terms it is confined to expenses incurred for the safety and preservation of the particular property insured, and does not comprise expenses incurred for the safety of the whole adventure."

"Although the provision in the suing and labouring clause is of a permissive character, it is nevertheless the duty of the assured and his agents, in all cases, to take such measures as may be reasonable for the purpose of averting or minimising a loss."

Particular charges incurred under the sue and labour clause are recoverable over and above the amount insured. Justice Doherty, in *Western Assurance Co. v. Baden Marine Assurance Co.*[5] has observed:[6]

[T]hose [particular charges] incurred under the "sue and labour clause" are treated as being expenditures made in the interest of the insurer and under the authorization by him given by the terms of that clause, and are recoverable by the insured over and above the amount insured.

---

3. [1938] 1 D.L.R. 619, 12 M.P.R. 469, 5 I.L.R. 142 (N.S. C.A.).
4. *Ibid.*, at 624-25, [1938] 1 D.L.R.
5. (1902), 22 Que. S.C. 374 (S.C.).
6. *Ibid.*, at 381.

The duty of the assured to minimize the loss has been the subject of a number of recent decisions.

In *Stad et al. v. Firemans Fund Insurance Co. et al.*,[7] an assured claimed for a total loss of his vessel the *Gofer*. The assured and his wife were travelling in the *Gofer* towing another vessel, the *Tornado*, when the *Gofer* began taking on water and was partially submerged. The assured and his wife abandoned the *Gofer* and went home in the other vessel. The next morning, the *Gofer* had disappeared. Justice MacDonald, in denying the assured recovery, stated:[8]

> There is another factor which bears on the question whether the proximate cause of the loss of the *"Gofer"* was an insured peril. The policy permitted the assured to sue and labour. S. 80(4) of the *Marine Insurance Act.*, which is in the following words, required it....
>
> In my judgment there was a failure in the duty to take reasonable measures for the purpose of averting or minimizing the loss. Captain Slater criticized the cutting of the tow line, thus separating the *"Gofer"* and *"Tornado"*. But one must be slow to criticize the action of the man faced with the situation who may have feared that the towed vessel was in imminent danger of sinking and dragging him down with it. And, in the anxiety of the moment, even if he thought of it, he might have feared that there was not even time to attach a buoy or light. Then there is the question as to what the plaintiff should have done when he saw the *"Gofer"* apparently riding comfortably with three or four feet of its bow above water. With the lines floating about the *"Gofer"*, I cannot say that he could reasonably have been expected to approach closely enough to secure another tow line or attach a buoy or light. But Mr. Stad left for shelter aware that he had not obtained a reasonably accurate fix on the location. The *"Tornado"* was not in danger. The plaintiff left the scene for the sake of personal comfort. He should have remained with the spotlights shining on the *"Gofer"*. If it remained afloat until daylight, it would be available for towing to the beach or other salvage efforts. If it sank, the location would be known. If the *"Tornado"* had stayed, it would have been located by Mr. Lotoski in the aircraft just as readily as it was in the place where Mr. Stad anchored. Having gone to a shelter, Mr. Stad should have returned to the *"Gofer"* at daylight. But some four hours, which might have been critical, were lost while he waited for Mr. Lotoski to arrive by aircraft.

In *Suo v. Openshaw Simmons Ltd. et al.*[9] an assured claimed for the total loss of his vessel, the *Sea-Ment*. The assured was travelling alone on board the vessel when he felt a bump. Shortly thereafter the vessel began to take on water. Another vessel, the *Karem* came to assist and began towing the *Sea-Ment* to a shipyard. The tow line had to be cut, however, as the *Sea-Ment* was taking on water and the list was so great that the assured feared that the *Karem* would be pulled over.

---

7. [1979] I.L.R. 1-1070 (B.C. S.C.).
8. *Ibid.*, at 66.
9. 5 B.C.L.R. 370, [1978] I.L.R. 1-982 (S.C.).

The court held that there was no breach of s. 80(4) of the *Marine Insurance Act*[10] as the assured had done everything possible to either minimize or avert the loss. The court also commented on the relationship between s. 80(4) and s. 57(2)(*a*) and whether an assured who had breached s. 80(4) was entitled to recover by way of s. 57(2)(*a*). Justice Proudfoot observed:[11]

> It seems to me that s. 80(4) and s. 57(2)(*a*) are not in conflict because suing and labouring clauses are, in the words of s. 80(1), "supplementary to the contract of insurance" or, in effect, contracts within contracts. The duty imposed by s. 80(4) only arises in relation to suing and labouring and only once an actual peril has created a potential loss. Hence, s. 80(4) has no effect on the general provisions of s. 57(2)(*a*).

The comments of Justice Proudfoot on this point are *obiter*. He may be correct that in terms of liability, s. 80(4) and s. 57(2)(*a*) are independent, but in terms of the quantum of the loss, certainly, s. 80(4) will play a large role on what the assured can recover.

In *Oswald v. Anglo-Scottish Insurance Co. Ltd.*[12] an assured claimed for a loss on his vessel. The assured had moored his boat on the north side of Vancouver Harbour at a moorage known as Kanata Wharfage. The boat was stolen by some person or persons unknown and it was eventually found on fire on the beach at Spanish Banks. The boat was then high and dry. The assured examined the boat at that time and found that not too much damage had been done to the hull.

The assured was told by the police officer who had contacted him that he would have to look after supervision of his boat as the police would not undertake that responsibility. The officer also advised the assured that a storm could come up very quickly in that area which could damage the boat and that there was a high tide that evening which would enable the assured to float the boat out of the area. The assured took no steps and a severe storm did come up that night which damaged the boat beyond repair. The insurer denied coverage for the loss caused by the storm on the basis that the assured had breached the sue and labour clause.

The court held that the assured did not take such measures as might be reasonable for the purpose of averting or minimizing a loss to his boat and was "not entitled to recover any greater sum than would be required to repay him for the loss suffered prior to the [storm]."[13]

---

10. *Marine Insurance Act*, R.S.B.C. 1960, c. 231. See now *Insurance (Marine) Act*, R.S.B.C. 1979, c. 203.

11. *Ibid.*, note 9, at 1064, [1978] I.L.R.

12. [1961] I.L.R. 1-020 (B.C. S.C.).

13. *Ibid.*, at 93.

38

Subrogation

s. 80: (1) Where the insurer pays for a total loss, either of the whole or, in the case of goods, of any apportionable part of the subject-matter insured, he thereupon becomes entitled to take over the interest of the assured in whatever may remain of the subject-matter so paid for, and he is thereby subrogated to all the rights and remedies of the assured in and in respect of that subject-matter as from the time of the casualty causing the loss.

(2) Subject to the foregoing provisions, where the insurer pays for a partial loss, he acquires no title to the subject-matter insured or such part of it as may remain, but he is thereupon subrogated to all rights and remedies of the assured in and in respect of the subject-matter insured as from the time of the casualty causing the loss in so far as the assured has been indemnified according to this Act by such payment for the loss.

The doctrine of subrogation is derived from the doctrine of indemnification. Upon settling the loss, the insurer may sue, in the assured's name, any person through whose default, negligence or other unlawful act the loss or damage may have occurred. Accordingly, the assured has a duty to protect those rights he may have against third parties.

An assured must therefore protect the insurer's right to commence suit against the third party. If the assured allows prescription to occur, he may thereafter be unable to recover under a policy of insurance.[1]

The assured cannot enter into any contract with a third party that will impair the insurer's right of subrogation.[2] To do so, without the express authority of the insurer, will relieve the underwriter of any liability. Thus, a bill of lading with a clause giving the carrier the full benefit of any insurance that may be effected on the goods, may entitle the insurer to avoid any liability under the policy, for they would be "deprived of the fruit of subrogation."[3]

---

1. *Moryoussef v. Maritime Insurance Co.*, [1982] C.P. 22 (Que. Prov. Ct.).
2. See *Rose et al. v. Borisko Brothers Ltd.*, 41 O.R. (2d) 606, 147 D.L.R. (3d) 191, [1983] I.L.R. 1-1704 (C.A.); and see also *Canadian National Railway Co. v. Canadian Industries Ltd.*, [1941] S.C.R. 591, [1941] 4 D.L.R. 561, 53 C.R.T.C. 162.
3. *Ibid.*, at 599, [1941] S.C.R.

39

Contribution

s. 81: (1) Where the assured is over-insured by double insurance, each insurer is bound, as between himself and the other insurers to contribute rateably to the loss in proportion to the amount for which he is liable under his contract.
(2) If any insurer pays more than his proportion of the loss, he is entitled to maintain an action for contribution against the other insurers, and is entitled to the like remedies as a surety who has paid more than his proportion of the debt.

The law in Canada is the same as that in England, that in case of a double insurance the insured may sue any of the insurers, leaving them to recover contribution from the others.[1]

---

1. *Bank of British North America v. Western Assurance Co.* (1884), 7 O.R. 166 (Ch. Div.). See also chapter 14 and s. 33 of the *Marine Insurance Act*, R.S.O. 1980, c. 255.

40

Under-Insurance

s. 82: Where the assured is insured for an amount less than the insurable value or, in the case of a valued policy, for an amount less than the policy valuation, he is deemed to be his own insurer in respect of the uninsured balance.

Where the subject-matter insured is damaged or lost and it is under-insured, the assured is his own insurer in respect of the uninsured balance. Thus, if a ship valued at $10,000 is insured with an insurer for $5,000 and is damaged by perils of the seas to the extent of $2,000, the insurer is liable for $1,000.

41

Return of Premium[1]

s. 83: Where the premium, or a proportionate part thereof, is declared by this Act to be returnable,
(a) if already paid, it may be recovered by the assured from the insurer; and
(b) if unpaid, it may be retained by the assured or his agent.

s. 84: Where the policy contains a stipulation for the return of the premium, or a proportionate part thereof, on the happening of a certain event and that event happens, the premium, or, as the case may be, the proportionate part thereof, is thereupon returnable to the assured.

s. 85: (1) Where the consideration for the payment of the premium totally fails and there has been no fraud or illegality on the part of the assured or his agents, the premium is thereupon returnable to the assured.
(2) Where the consideration for the payment of the premium is apportionable and there is a total failure of any apportionable part of the consideration, a proportionate part of the premium is, under the like conditions, thereupon returnable to the assured.
(3) In particular,
(a) where the policy is void, or is avoided by the insurer as from the commencement of the risk, the premium is returnable, provided that there has been no fraud or illegality on the part of the assured; but if the risk is not apportionable, and has once attached, the premium is not returnable.
(b) where the subject-matter insured, or part thereof, has never been imperilled, the premium, or, as the case may be, a proportionate part thereof, is returnable; provided that where the subject-matter has been insured "lost or not lost" and has arrived in safety at the time when the contract is concluded, the premium is not returnable unless at such time the insurer knew of the safe arrival;
(c) where the assured has no insurable interest throughout the currency of the risk, the premium is returnable, provided that this rule does not apply to a policy effected by way of gaming or wagering;
(d) where the assured has a defeasible interest that is terminated during the currency of the risk, the premium is not returnable;
(e) where the assured has over-insured under an unvalued policy, a proportionate part of the premium is returnable;
(f) subject to the foregoing provisions, where the assured has over-insured by double insurance, a proportionate part of the several pre-

---

1. See also ss. 53-55 and 83-85 of the *Marine Insurance Act*, R.S.O. 1980, c. 255.

miums is returnable; provided that, if the policies are effected at different times, and any earlier policy has at any time borne the entire risk, or if a claim has been paid on the policy in respect of the full sum insured thereby, no premium is returnable in respect of that policy, and when the double insurance is effected knowingly by the assured no premium is returnable.

In *Berner and Bradley Finance Ltd. v. Sun Insurance Office Ltd.*,[2] the insurer alleged that a policy was void by reason of the lack of good faith and because of failure by the assured to disclose material circumstances, *i.e.* the installation of an auxilliary motor on the boat. The court found that the assured had acted in good faith and had not failed to disclose all material circumstances. Justice Kelly added:[3]

> It follows that if the policy were void from the date of its issue by reason of lack of good faith or because of failure to disclose material circumstances, then the premium paid by the plaintiff should have been returned, pursuant to sec. 85 of *The Marine Insurance Act*, as I find that there was no fraud or illegality on the part of the plaintiff or his agents. Failure to return the premium on receiving the report of their adjuster is further evidence that the defendant did not rely on their rights, if any, under sections 18 and 19 of *The Marine Insurance Act* and elect to avoid the contract of insurance.

Where there is fraud in respect of a contract of marine insurance, the premium need not be returned.[4]

---

2. [1952] I.L.R. 1-069 (Ont. H.C.).
3. *Ibid.*, at 293.
4. *Intermunicipal Realty & Development v. Gore Mutual Insurance Co. et al.*, [1981] 1 F.C. 151, 112 D.L.R. (3d) 432, [1981] I.L.R. 1-1350 (T.D.).

42

Mutual Insurance[1]

s. 86: (1) Where two or more persons mutually agree to insure each other against marine losses, there is said to be a mutual insurance.

(2) The provisions of this Act relating to the premium do not apply to mutual insurance, but a guarantee, or such other arrangement as may be agreed upon, may be substituted for the premium.

(3) The provisions of the Act, in so far as they may be modified by the agreement of the parties, may in the case of mutual insurance be modified by the terms of the policies issued by the association or by the rules and regulations of the association.

(4) Subject to the exceptions mentioned in this section, the provisions of this Act apply to mutual insurance.

---

1. In *Pickles v. China Mutual Insurance Co.* (1913), 47 S.C.R. 429, Justice Idington described the position of an individual member of a mutual insurance company, at 435:

> By the law constituting the company each person insured became a member of the company and entitled during the currency of his policy to take part in its management.
> He became at once insurer and insured. He has no more right to escape from this position than a partner with limited liability in any other venture where the fundamental principle is that what he has given or promised shall stand good for losses though he may when all losses and liabilities are satisfied be entitled to rank upon any fund left for distribution when these are satisfied.

Justice Duff, at 438, described it as thus:

> By virtue of the contract of insurance the insured stands in a two-fold relation to the company and the other policy holders. To the extent of his own policy he is insured; to the extent of his own premium note he is an insurer in the sense that he is a holder of unpaid capital in respect of which he is entitled to share in the profits of the company, and to the extent of that capital he is liable to contribute to the discharge of the obligations of the company.

43

Ratification

s. 87: Where a contract of marine insurance is in good faith effected by one person on behalf of another, the person on whose behalf it is effected, may ratify the contract even after he is aware of a loss.

44

Implied Obligations Varied by Agreement or Usage

s. 88: (1) Where any right, duty, or liability would arise under a contract of marine insurance by implication of law, it may be negatived or varied by express agreement, or by usage, if the usage is such as to bind both parties to the contract.

(2) The provisions of this section extend to any right, duty or liability declared by this Act which may be lawfully modified by agreement.

This section reiterates the fact that marine insurance is a contract reached by consensus. The parties may, as long as it is not prohibited by law, enter into any agreement they so choose regarding the insurance of the subject-matter.

45

Reasonable Time, etc.

s. 89: Where by this Act any reference is made to reasonable time, reasonable premium, or reasonable diligence, the question of what is reasonable is a question of fact.

46

Rules of Common Law Saved

s. 90: The rules of the common law, including the law merchant, save in so far as they are inconsistent with the express provisions of this Act, continue to apply to contracts of marine insurance.

Justice McNair in *Rose v. Weekes*[1] has observed:[2]

> Section 60 of the *Marine Insurance Act* 1906 (U.K.), c. 41 defines and circumscribes the definition of "constructive total loss". Subsections 60(1) and (2) contain different definitions which may apply to different sets of fact. The definitions are neither exhaustive nor exclusive and *resort may be had to the common law to fill any lacuna left by the statutory provisions.*

---

1. (1984), 7 C.C.L.I. 287 (F.C. T.D.).
2. *Ibid.*, at 295. Emphasis added.

47

The Schedule

SCHEDULE

(Section 31)

FORM OF POLICY

Be it known that .... as well in .... own name as for and in the name and names of all and every other person or persons to whom the same doth, may, or shall appertain, in part or in all doth make assurance and cause .... and them, and every of them, to be insured lost or not lost, at and from .... Upon any kind of goods and merchandises, and also upon the body, tackle, apparel, ordnance, munition, artillery, boat, and other furniture, of and in the good ship or vessel called the .... whereof is master under God, for this present voyage .... or whosoever else shall go for master in the said ship, or by whatsoever other name or names the said ship, or the master thereof, is or shall be named or called: beginning the adventure upon the said goods and merchandises from the loading thereof aboard the said ship .... upon the said ship, etc .... and so shall continue and endure, during her abode there, upon the said ship, etc. And further, until the said ship, with all her ordnance, tackle, apparel, etc., and goods and merchandises whatsoever shall be arrived at .... upon the said ship, etc., until she hath moored at anchor twenty-four hours in good safety; and upon the goods and merchandises, until the same be there discharged and safely landed. And it shall be lawful for the said ship, etc., in this voyage, to proceed and sail to and touch and stay at any ports or places whatsoever .... without prejudice to this insurance. The said ship, etc., goods and merchandises, etc., for so much as concerns the assured by agreement between the assured and assurers in this policy, are and shall be valued at ....

(Sue and labour clause)
(Waiver clause)

Touching the adventures and perils which we, the assurers, are contented to bear and do take upon us in this voyage: they are of the seas, men-of-war, fire, enemies, pirates, rovers, thieves, jettisons, letters of mart and countermart, surprisals, takings at sea, arrests, restraints, and detainments of all kings, princes, and people, of what nation, condition, or quality soever, barratry of the master and mariners, and of all other perils, losses, and misfortunes, that have or shall come to the hurt, detriment, or damage of the said goods and merchandises, and ship, etc., or any part thereof. And in case of any loss or misfortune it shall be lawful to the assured, their factors, servants, and assigns, to sue, labour, and travel for, in and about the defence, safeguards, and recovery of the said goods and merchandises, and ship, etc., or any part thereof, without prejudice to this insurance; to the charges whereof we, the assurers, will contribute each one according to the rate and quantity of his sum herein assured. And it is especially declared and agreed that no acts of the insurer or insured in recovering, saving, or preserving the property insured shall be considered as a waiver, or acceptance of abandonment. And it is agreed by us, the insurers, that this writing or policy of assurance shall be of as much force and effect as the surest writing or policy of assurance heretofore made in Lombard Street, or in the Royal Exchange, or elsewhere in London. And so we, the assurers, are contented, and do hereby promise and bind ourselves, each one for his own part, our heirs, executors, and goods to the assured, their executors, administrators, and assigns, for the true performance of the premises, confessing ourselves paid the consideration due unto us for this assurance by the assured, at and after the rate of

In witness whereof we, the assurers, have subscribed our names and sums assured in

(Memorandum)

N.B. — Corn, fish, salt, fruit, flour, and seed are warranted free from average, unless general, or the ship be stranded; sugar tobacco, hemp, flax, hides and skins are warranted free from average, under five pounds per cent: and all other goods, also the ship and freight, are warranted free from average, under three pounds per cent, unless general, or the ship be stranded.

RULES FOR CONSTRUCTION OF POLICY

The following are the rules referred to by this Act for the construction of a policy in the above or other like form, where the context does not otherwise require:

Lost or not lost

1. Where the subject-matter is insured "lost or not lost" and the loss has occurred before the contract is concluded, the risk attaches, unless at such time the assured was aware of the loss, and the insurer was not.

From

2. Where the subject-matter is insured "from" a particular place, the risk does not attach until the ship starts on the voyage insured.

At and from

3. (a) Where a ship is insured "at and from" a particular place, and she is at that place in good safety when the contract is concluded, the risk attaches immediately.

(Ship)

(b) If she be not at that place when the contract is concluded, the risk attaches as soon as she arrives there in good safety, and, unless the policy otherwise provides, it is immaterial that she is covered by another policy for a specified time after arrival.

(Freight)

(c) Where chartered freight is insured "at and from" a particular place, and the ship is at that place in good safety when the contract is concluded, the risk attaches immediately. If she be not there when the contract is concluded, the risk attaches as soon as she arrives there in good safety.

Idem

(d) Where freight, other than chartered freight, is payable without special conditions and is insured "at and from" a particular place, the risk attaches pro rata as the goods or merchandise are shipped; provided that if there be cargo in readiness which belongs to the ship-owner, or which some other person has contracted with him to ship, the risk attaches as soon as the ship is ready to receive such cargo.

From the loading thereof

4. Where goods or other movables are insured "from the loading thereof", the risk does not attach until such goods or movables are actually on board, and the insurer is not liable for them while in transit from the shore to the ship.

Safely landed

5. Where the risk on goods or other movables continues until they are "safely landed", they must be landed in the customary

manner and within a reasonable time after arrival at the port of discharge, and if they are not so landed the risk ceases.

Touch and stay

6. In the absence of any further licence or usage, the liberty to touch and stay "at any port or place whatsoever" does not authorize the ship to depart from the course of her voyage from the port of departure to the port of destination.

Perils of the seas

7. The term "perils of the sea" refers only to fortuitous accidents or casualties of the seas. It does not include the ordinary action of the winds and waves.

Pirates

8. The term "pirates" includes passengers who mutiny and rioters who attack the ship from the shore.

Thieves

9. The term "thieves" does not cover clandestine theft or a theft committed by any one of the ship's company, whether crew or passengers.

Restraint of princes

10. The term "arrests, etc., of kings, princes, and people" refers to political or executive acts, and does not include a loss caused by riot or by ordinary judicial process.

Barratry

11. The term "barratry" includes every wrongful act wilfully committed by the master or crew to the prejudice of the owner, or, as the case may be, the charterer.

All other perils

12. The term "all other perils" includes only perils similar in kind to the perils specifically mentioned in the policy.

Average unless general

13. The term "average unless general" means a partial loss of the subject-matter insured other than a general average loss, and does not include "particular charges."

Stranded

14. Where the ship has stranded, the insurer is liable for the excepted losses, although the loss is not attributable to the stranding, provided that when the stranding takes place the risk has attached and, if the policy be on goods, that the damaged goods are on board.

Ship

15. The term "ship" includes the hull, materials and outfit, stores and provisions for the officers and crew, and, in the case of vessels engaged in a special trade, the ordinary fittings requisite for the trade, and also, in the case of a steamship, the machinery, boilers, and coals, oils, and engine stores, if owned by the assured.

Freight

16. The term "freight" includes the profit derivable by a ship-owner from the employment of his ship to carry his own goods or movables, as well as freight payable by a third party, but does not include passage-money.

Goods

17. The term "goods" means goods in the nature of merchandise, and does not include personal effects or provisions and stores for use on board.

In the absence of any usage to the contrary, deck cargo and living animals must be insured specifically, and not under the general denomination of goods.

48

Institute Clauses

There are no restrictions as to the form of a marine insurance policy. The policy may be in the form as provided for in the Schedule to the Act.[1] It is usual for a number of clauses to be added to the ordinary form. These are usually the Institute Clauses.[2]

Some of these clauses, such as the Inchmaree Clause found in the Institute Time Clauses (Hulls), were introduced as a result of litigation.[3] Some, such as the Inchmaree Clause, have in themselves been the subject of litigation.

(1) Decisions involving the Inchmaree Clause

The clause[4] provides that:

This insurance includes loss of or damage to the subject-matter insured directly caused by:
(a) Accidents in loading, discharging or shifting cargo or fuel.
Explosions on shipboard or elsewhere.
Breakdown of or accident to nuclear installations or reactors on shipboard or elsewhere.
Bursting of boilers breakage of shafts or any latent defect in the machinery or hull.
Negligence of Master Officers Crew or Pilots.
Negligence of repairers provided such repairers are not Assured(s) hereunder.
(b) Contact with aircraft.
Contact with any land conveyance, dock or harbour equipment or installation.
Earthquake, volcanic eruption or lightning
provided such loss or damage has not resulted from want of due diligence by the Assured, Owners or Managers.

The litigation has been generated by the issue of due diligence. The courts have been asked to determine in each case if the loss or damage resulted from the want of due diligence by the assured. The onus is on the assured to show that the loss falls within the Inchmaree Clause.[5]

---

1. *Marine Insurance Act*, R.S.O. 1980, c. 255.
2. These are issued by the Institute of London Underwriters. See Appendices A to D.
3. See chapter 26, note 14.
4. See Appendix D, Institute Time Clauses (Hulls), clause 7.
5. See *Russell v. Aetna Insurance Co.*, [1975] I.L.R. 1-699 (Ont. C.A.).

In *Atlantic Freighting Co. Ltd. v. Provincial Insurance Co. Ltd.*,[6] an assured claimed for damage to a hull of a vessel caused by a latent defect in the hull; the internal fastenings of the keelsons had been weakened by launching. The plaintiff relied upon the Inchmaree clause in the hull policy of insurance. Justice Parker, of the Nova Scotia Supreme Court, stated what was required of the assured in order to succeed:[7]

> [T]he plaintiff must prove by a preponderance of evidence, first, that the loss or damage to the hull, for which recovery is sought, occurred during the term of the policy sued on and that such loss or damage was directly caused by a latent defect; and second, that such loss or damage did not result from want of due diligence by the owners, or any of them or by the manager. If the evidence shows that there is some equally or more reasonable and probable cause of the loss or damage, the plaintiff cannot succeed.

The court found that the damage which occurred during the currency of the policy was nothing more than a development of the latent defect through ordinary wear and tear. As such, it was not a matter for which indemnity is provided in the Inchmaree clause.[8] Justice Parker added:[9]

> If there were a latent defect in the hull which came into existence at the time of the launching, of the nature contended for by the plaintiff, I am of the opinion that the evidence shows a "want of due diligence" on the part of the owners or some of them and the manager in not becoming aware of it and in not rectifying it before the vessel put to sea with the cargo of salt. There is ample evidence to prove that the vessel for some reason was hogged or bent to the extent of 7 ins. and was in a weakened condition generally before the cargo of salt was loaded, and that condition was known to the master, to the vessel's husband and to the owners, and it was also known to them that salt in bulk in the holds is one of the worst possible cargoes for a weakened vessel to carry. In my opinion the evidence shows great want of due diligence on the part of the owners, or some of them, and the manager in loading the salt without first having a thorough inspection or survey of the hull made.

In *J.L. Fisheries Ltd. v. Boston Insurance Co. et al.*,[10] the assured claimed for damage to the vessel's main driving machinery which resulted from the breaking of a pinion shaft in the reduction gearbox. The assured relied upon the Inchmaree Clause but the insurers denied liability on the ground that the loss had been caused by the inherent weakness in design of the machinery. In allowing the assured recovery, Justice Dubinsky stated:[11]

---

6. 5 D.L.R. (2d) 164, [1956] I.L.R. 1-245 (N.S. S.C.).
7. *Ibid.*, at 167, 5 D.L.R. (2d).
8. *Supra.*, note 6, 5 D.L.R. (2d) 164 at 171.
9. *Supra.*, note 6, 5 D.L.R. (2d) 164 at 172.
10. 69 D.L.R. (2d) 18, [1969] I.L.R. 1-227 (N.S. S.C.).
11. *Ibid.*, at 29-30, 69 D.L.R. (2d).

I am satisfied here and so do find that the resulting damage flowed from the broken pinion shaft to other parts of the machinery and to the hull itself. This in itself would be sufficient to establish the plaintiff's case. . . .Mr. Jost pleaded the defence of weakness in design and properly raised the suggestion of fatigue resulting from usage. Kennedy, J., in *Jackson v. Mumford* (1902), 19 T.L.R. 18, would not regard "latent defect in the machinery" as covering a weakness of design. The phrase "defect in machinery", in his opinion is a defect of material, in respect either of its original composition or in respect of its original or its after-acquired condition. It did not cover the erroneous judgment of the designer as to the effect of the strain which his machinery would have to resist. . . . Morris Evans, a consultant engineer with many years' experience in mechanical engineering, was qualified as an expert witness. A close reading of his testimony leaves no doubt in one's mind that a latent defect existed in the pinion shaft causing it to break. . . . Clearly the case is quite different from the situation obtained in *Jackson v. Mumford.*

In *Coast Ferries Ltd. v. Century Insurance Co. of Canada et al.,*[12] a master's negligence in overloading a vessel led to its loss. The assured relied upon the Inchmaree Clause. The court denied the assured recovery as he was wanting in due diligence in seeing that the vessel was properly loaded. When an owner leaves full responsibility for loading with the master of the vessel, the owner has a duty to provide the master with sufficient information regarding freeboard and trim to enable the master to exercise sound judgment in loading. Having failed to do so, the assured owner was not entitled to the protection of the Inchmaree Clause. Justice de Grandpré, of the Supreme Court of Canada, observed:[13]

> The duty of due diligence imposed upon the owner is not satisfied if for years he closes his eyes and does nothing. His obligation is to act reasonably in the circumstances and the evidence in the present case discloses that the appellant's main competitor maintains a much better procedure.

In *Holm v. T.W. Rice & Co. Inc., Underwriters et al.,*[14] an assured owner was also the master of the vessel. The vessel, a pleasure craft, sank at its moorings after two weeks because the owner had removed an exhaust hose leaving a port open to the sea. The court found that a reasonable owner would have inspected the vessel within a few days. The assured claimed for the loss under the Inchmaree Clause, in that the loss resulted from his negligence as a master. The court held that where an owner is negligent not only as a master but in his capacity as owner, he cannot avail himself of the Inchmaree Clause.

In *Hatfield v. The Queen,*[15] the assured was also an owner-operator. The assured's fishing vessel sank and the insurer alleged

---

12. 48 D.L.R. (3d) 310, [1974] I.L.R. 1-612 (S.C.C.).
13. *Ibid.,* at 935, [1974] I.L.R.
14. 29 B.C.L.R. 141, 124 D.L.R. (3d) 463, [1981] I.L.R. 1-1438 (S.C.).
15. (1984), 5 C.C.L.I 276 (F.C. T.D.); supplementary reasons at, 5 C.C.L.I. 276, at 283; affd 10 C.C.L.I. 280, [1984] I.L.R. 1-1838 (Fed. C.A.).

that the sinking was caused by the assured's negligence in failing to open a hatch cover when carrying a load of wet lobster traps. The open hatch cover would allow water from the traps which came aboard to travel to the bilge. The insurer argued that the assured as owner had failed to exercise due diligence. Justice Collier found due diligence to be "equivalent to reasonable diligence, having regard to the circumstances known, or fairly to be expected, and to the nature of the voyage, and the cargo to be carried."[16] He indicated that the onus was on the defendant insurer to prove want of due diligence. Justice Collier was not safisfied that the practice of travelling with the hatch cover closed amounted to want of due diligence and the insurer had failed to satisfy its onus on a balance of probabilities.

In *Case Existological Laboratories Ltd. v. Foremost Insurance Co. et al.*[17] a vessel sank as a result of the negligence of the crew in the operation of an air valve.[18] The assured claimed for a loss under the "perils of the sea" clause in the insurance policy and not under the Inchmaree Clause, which also formed part of the policy. The court found that the sinking caused by the negligence of the crew was a fortuitous event and fell under the "perils of the sea" coverage of the policy. Presumably, the assured was not prepared to put the question of his due diligence in issue before the court.

In *Atwood v. The Queen*,[19] an assured claimed for the loss of a vessel destroyed by fire which started from a spark when the assured tried to start the vessel's engine by bridging the points on the solenoid starter with a screwdriver. The court found that the loss by fire was a loss by "perils of the sea". As such, the defence of "want of due diligence" was not available to the insurer. This defence is only available where the assured invokes coverage under the Inchmaree Clause.[20]

(2) Decisions involving the Institute Cargo Clauses (F.P.A.)

In *Savroche Enterprises Inc. v. Great Atlantic Insurance Co. of Delaware*,[21] an assured shipped certain goods in a container. The

---

16. *Ibid.*, at 282, 5 C.C.L.I.
17. 133 D.L.R. (3d) 727, [1982] I.L.R. 1-1567 (B.C. C.A.); affd [1983] 2 S.C.R. 47 (*sub nom. Century Insurance Co. of Canada v. Case Existological Laboratories Ltd.*), 48 B.C.L.R. 273, [1984] 1 W.W.R. 97, 150 D.L.R. (3d) 9, 49 N.R. 19, [1983] I.L.R. 1-1698.
18. See chapter 26 (3.2).
19. (1985), 10 C.C.L.I. 63 (F.C. T.D.).
20. *Ibid.*, at 68.
21. Unreported, January 10, 1984 (Federal Court of Canada, Trial Division). This decision of Decary J. was reversed on appeal. The Court of Appeal held that the onus was on the insurer who invokes the exclusionary clause to prove that the loss occurred after interruption in transit due to circumstances which were within the control of the insured. The court found that the insurer failed to meet the onus. See (1985), 31 A.C.W.S. (2d) 365 (Fed. C.A.); leave to appeal to S.C.C. refused. See (1985), 33 A.C.W.S. (2d) 208.

assured claimed for the loss of the container which disappeared and the insurer alleged the goods were not covered when the container disappeared. The insurer relied upon the Warehouse to Warehouse Clause[22] in the policy of insurance. Under this clause the insurance terminates when the goods cease to be in transit.

The container was delivered to the assured's yard on the day that the Yom Kippur holidays began. The container was left outside during these religious holidays. The container disappeared from the assured's yard.

The court noted that the question of whether a loss occurs within the period of the coverage agreement, is a question of fact. In denying the assured coverage, it observed:[23]

A policy which insures against loss of goods while in transit or while being transported ordinarily insures loss which occurs during the movement of the goods on a transporting conveyance from starting point to point of delivery, including stops along the way incidental to carriage and minor deviations from customary route and temporary stops, even overnight, for convenience of operator of the conveyance and for other purposes connected with the carriage, will not remove the goods from transportation within the meaning of the policy. Accordingly, in view of the evidence before me, the movement of transit has stopped for the Yom Kippur holidays for a period of time too long to be appreciated as only incidental to carriage. The delay in the transportation of the goods to their final destination was, from the evidence, due to wrong timing and did not fit in the tight schedule of that particular week.

One phone call from the plaintiff, had he been ready to receive the goods, would have permitted the completion of the journey. Only the plaintiff then had control on the duration of suspension of transit. On his behest, the movement of the transit stopped.

Plaintiff's goods were no longer in the ordinary course of transit when, to his convenience, the movement of the goods was interrupted or suspended. The said interruption or suspension of transit was the result of circumstances contrived solely for the benefit and at the express request of the plaintiff, and nothing in the evidence points out that it is the result of circumstances beyond the control of the plaintiff.

There is no rational basis for the contention that plaintiff's goods were in transit within the intendment . . . of the policy. In my view, they were in storage at the moment of the loss and therefore not covered by the said policy.

---

22. See Appendix A.
23. *Supra*, note 21.

49

Agents and Brokers[1]

(1) The Nature of the Broker/Agent's Role[2]

In marine insurance, as in other forms of insurance, it is clear that an agent can be an agent of both the assured and the underwriter.[3] Whether acting for one or the other, the agent must use reasonable care in carrying out his duties. The standard of care required will be that which an agent in a like position, holding himself out to have expertise in marine insurance, is expected to have.[4] The role of the insurance agent has been defined as follows:[5]

> The main ground of appeal from the judgment of the learned trial Judge is that he put far too broad and sweeping a duty on insurance agents. They are not insurers. It is not part of their duty to know everything about their clients' businesses so as to be in a position to anticipate every conceivable form of loss to which they might be subject. The agent's duty, counsel submits, is "to exercise a reasonable degree of skill and care to obtain policies in the terms bargained for and to service those policies as circumstances might require." I take no issue with counsel's statement of the scope of the insurance agent's duty except to add that the agent also has duty to advise his principal if he is unable to obtain the policies bargained for so that his principal may take such further steps to protect himself as he deems desirable. The operative words, however, in counsel's definition of the scope of the agent's duty are "policies in the terms bargained for." In many instances, an insurance agent will be asked to obtain a specific type of coverage and his duty in those circumstances will be to use a reasonable degree of skill and care in doing so or, if he is unable to do so, "to inform the principal promptly in order to prevent him from suffering loss through relying upon the successful completion of the transaction by the agent"; Ivamy, *General Principles of Insurance Law* (2nd Edition) (1970), at p. 464. But there are other cases, and in my view this is one of them,

---

1. As to the payment of premium and the relationship amongst assured, broker and underwriter, see ss. 53-55 of the *Marine Insurance Act*, R.S.O. 1980, c. 255.
2. The term insurance broker is used throughout this chapter interchangeably with the term insurance agent.
3. See for example *Dickie v. Merchants' Marine Insurance Co.* (1883), 16 N.S.R. 244 (C.A.); *New Forty Mines Ltd. v. St. Paul Fire and Marine Insurance Co. et al.*, 34 Alta. L.R. (2d) 28, 56 A.R. 335, [1985] I.L.R. 1-1872 (Alta. Q.B.); *Fallas v. Continental Insurance Co.*, [1973] 6 W.W.R. 379, [1973] I.L.R. 1-558 (B.C. S.C.) where an agent held out to an assured that he represented the insurer, the insurer was estopped from denying the agent did not have authority to waive a warranty in a policy of insurance.
4. *Hedley Byrne Co. Ltd. v. Heller & Partners Ltd.*, [1964] A.C. 465 (H.L.).
5. *Fine's Flowers Ltd. et al. v. General Accident Assurance Co. of Canada et al.*, 17 O.R. (2d) 529, 81 D.L.R. (3d) 139, 2 B.L.R. 257 (C.A.), *per* Madame Justice Wilson (as she then was), at 538.

in which the client gives no such specific instructions but rather relies upon his agent to see that he is protected and, if the agent agrees to do business with him on those terms, then he cannot afterwards, when an uninsured loss arises, shrug off the responsibility he has assumed. If this requires him to inform himself about his client's business in order to assess the foreseeable risks and insure his client against them, then this he must do. It goes without saying that an agent who does not have the requisite skills to understand the nature of his client's business and assess the risks that should be insured against should not be offering this kind of service. As Mr. Justice Haines said in *Lahey v. Hartford Fire Insurance Co.*, (1968) 1 O.R. 727: "The solution lies in the intelligent insurance agent who inspects the risks when he insures them, knows what his insurer is providing, discovers the areas that may give rise to dispute and either arranges for the coverage or makes certain the purchaser is aware of the exclusion." I do not think this is too high a standard to impose upon an agent who knows that his client is relying upon him to see that he is protected against all foreseeable, insurable risks.

(2) Liability of the Agent or Broker for Negligence or Breach of Contract

The liability of an agent or broker arising from his failure to discharge his duties can be said to arise in contract and in tort. It is also a duty that arises in equity based upon the fiduciary relationship existing between the agent and his principal.[6] Whatever way this duty is characterized, it is one which the courts have been quick to demand be carried out with reasonable care. There are a number of categories of cases in which liability will be imposed for failure to meet this duty. The categories of cases are not closed. The following are illustrative of the situations in which liability was imposed or considered.

(2.1) Liability for failure to obtain coverage or the coverage requested

In the *Fine's Flowers* case,[7] the assured claimed against his insurance agent for failure to obtain proper coverage on his greenhouse. The assured operated a greenhouse which had a water heating system. The heating system shut down due to a pump breakdown. The pump failure was due to wear and tear which was not covered under the insurance policy in place. Mr. Fine gave evidence that he relied upon the agent for all of his insurance needs and that he left it to the agent to obtain the insurance necessary for his business. The trial judge found against the agent on the basis of breach of contract. On appeal, Justice Estey found that there was no contract but held

---

6. See *Norlympia Seafoods Ltd. et al. v. Dale & Co. Ltd.*, [1983] I.L.R. 1-1688 (B.C. S.C.) and *Fine's Flowers, supra*, note 5.

7. *Supra*, note 5.

the agent liable based on negligence. Madam Justice Wilson (as she then was), on the other hand, found that there was a breach of contract.[8] In finding the agent liable, Chief Justice Estey observed:[9]

> [I]t was the duty of the defendant agent to either procure such coverage, or draw to the attention of the plaintiff his failure or inability to do so and the consequent gap in coverage. Having done neither, the defendant agent is liable in negligence, whether or not the instructions were to insure all "insurable" risks or to see that the plaintiff was "adequately covered with insurance" . . . [T]he onus on the defendant agent is to carry out the instructions according to the common usage of the words in the industry, unless the evidence indicates otherwise. There is no evidence, as I have said before, that any insurance would be available to cover failure of the pumps by reason of "wear and tear". The problem here, however, is that the defendant agent did not obtain any insurance coverage in respect of the equipment which gave rise to the failure. Furthermore, he failed to obtain insurance coverage against the most obvious and fundamental of all risks which would face a nursery, at least in one-half of the year, namely, a failure of the heat supply by reason of mechanical or water difficulties. Finally, when the defendant, knew that complete insurance against a failure of the heating system for any reason would not be available, as the evidence in part infers, he failed to report this fact to the plaintiff.

In *Desgagnés v. Antonin Belleau Inc.*,[10] an assured claimed against his agent for failure to obtain insurance on a vessel which would cover a constructive total loss situation. The agent had obtained insurance against absolute total loss only. In finding against the agent, Justice Montgomery of the Quebec Court of Appeal stated:[11]

> The insurance agent who accepts a mandate to place insurance is, in my opinion, obliged either to place such insurance within a reasonable delay or to notify his client that he is unable to do so. The client is, at least up to a certain point, entitled to rely on the superior knowledge and experience of the agent.

In *Eedy v. Stephens*,[12] an owner of a vessel brought suit against his insurance agent for damages for negligence for failure to insure his vessel as requested or alternatively for failing to advise him that insurance had not been procured. There was a period of about three days between the request to obtain insurance and the date the vessel was lost. The court found that the agent had warned the plaintiff of the difficulty of obtaining insurance for the vessel. Justice Spencer of the British Columbia Supreme Court stated:[13]

---

8. *Supra.*
9. *Supra*, at 533-34.
10. [1970] I.L.R. 1-348 (Que. C.A.).
11. *Ibid.*, at 996.
12. [1976] I.L.R. 1-735 (B.C. S.C.).
13. *Ibid.*, at 92-93.

The warning of difficulty, even if not indicating impossibility, was at least sufficient to have put the Plaintiff on guard that the obtaining of coverage might be delayed. . . . The Plaintiff, as an experienced real estate salesman working for a company which also owned an insurance agency, must have been of sufficient business awareness to realize the importance of being insured and to realize the difference between the Defendant . . . telling him he was covered on the one hand or telling him that he would decide the next day whether to cover him or not. In my judgment it was the Plaintiff's responsibility to ensure whether or not he had coverage.

In *Centre Sportif de Caraquet Ltée v. Edmond E. Landry Assurance Ltd. et al.,*[14] a boat owner called his agent to arrange insurance for his boat. The agent did not have the necessary application forms but ordered some. The forms arrived two days later. The agent attempted for three days to contact the plaintiff to complete the application form, without success. The vessel was lost on the weekend. Justice Stratton, in dismissing the plaintiff's claim stated:[15]

> The duty of an insurance agent to his principal is defined in *Halsbury's Laws of England*, 3rd edition, at page 48, as follows: "All agents, whether paid or unpaid, skilled or unskilled, are under a legal obligation to exercise due care and skill in performance of the duties which they have undertaken, a greater degree of care being required from a paid than from an unpaid, and from a skilled than from an unskilled, agent. The question in all such cases is whether the act or omission complained of is inconsistent with that reasonable degree of care and skill which persons of ordinary prudence and ability might be expected to show in the situation and profession of the agent."
>
> The question whether an insurance agent has exercised reasonable care and skill is a question of fact. . . . On the facts of this case, I am not prepared to say that the conduct of [the agent] was inconsistent with that reasonable degree of care and skill required of an insurance agent of ordinary prudence and ability.

In *Norlympia Seafoods Ltd. et al. v. Dale & Co. Ltd.,*[16] the owner of a vessel instructed his broker to persuade an insurer to omit a warranty from the policy, that a tug was to stand by the vessel. The broker negotiated with the insurer regarding the warranty but did not advise the plaintiff of the condition that there would have to be another survey of the vessel before the underwriters agreed to remove the warranty. The plaintiff assumed that the matter had been taken care of and breached the warranty before the provision was deleted. In holding the defendant broker liable for breach of contract, Justice McLachlin, of the British Columbia Supreme Court stated:[17]

---

14. (1977), 16 N.B.R. (2d) 489 (N.B. Q.B.).
15. *Ibid.*, at 494-95.
16. *Supra*, note 6.
17. *Supra*, at 6489-90.

In my view, insurance brokers must be expected to know the basic principles of contract law that affect the formation and termination of contracts of insurance. They must further be expected to apply these principles in dealing with their clients' affairs. A reading of the *Marine Insurance Act* of British Columbia and application of basic principles of insurance law would have led the defendant to the conclusion that there was no insurance in effect after the tug had left the barge, notwithstanding the fact that the underwriters, after being advised of this breach of warranty, had not immediately given notice that the insurance was at an end. Application of basic contract principles would have further led the defendant to the conclusion that the subsequent offer by the underwriters to hold cover on condition that the assured cooperate with a further survey by the London Salvage Association, was of no legal effect until accepted. The defendant having told the underwriter that it would not comply with the condition, it should have been aware that there was no insurance in effect. It should further have been aware that rejection of that offer terminated it.

(2.2) Liability for improper selection of underwriter

Having regard to the fact that a number of insurers have become insolvent in the last couple of years, a broker or agent may be liable if he places coverage with an insurer that is in financial trouble. The broker or agent must select the insurer with the same skill and care expected of a reasonably competent broker or agent.

In the *Norlympia* decision,[18] the plaintiffs had obtained judgment in England against "loss of profits" insurers on the policy placed through the defendant Dale & Co. Some of those insurers were insolvent and the plaintiff was unable to collect on the judgment. The plaintiff claimed against Dale & Co. for placing the "loss of profits" coverage with companies of inferior security. The court found the brokers liable for failing to advise the plaintiff that it had placed the coverage with these companies. Justice McLachlin observed:[19]

> The evidence is clear that Dale & Company represented to the plaintiffs that all their insurance, including loss of profits coverage, was with Lloyds of London and Institute Companies, the best marine security in the world. ...The certificate of insurance for the loss of profits coverage subsequently issued by Dale & Company showed that 100% of the $3 million dollars of coverage was placed with Lloyd's of London and I.L.U. (Institute) companies. The defendant admits that this representation was untrue. 24.5% of the coverage had not been placed at the time the certificate was issued. Later this 24.5% was placed with companies offering inferior security. The plaintiffs were never told that not all the loss of profits coverage had been placed with Lloyd's and Institute companies.
>
> I am satisfied that the plaintiffs relied on the representations contained in the certificate of insurance as to the companies with which the security was placed.

---

18. *Supra.*
19. *Supra*, at 6493.

(2.3) Liability for failure to give underwriters correct information

The agent or broker has a duty to exercise reasonable skill and care in providing information to the underwriter when the policy is being negotiated. Failure by an agent to disclose information material to the risk to the underwriter can result in denial of liability when a loss occurs. If the information has been given by the assured to the broker but not passed on to the insurer, the broker will be liable for any loss which results. On the other hand, if the information supplied by the assured is incorrect or false, the broker will not be liable if he acted on the information presented to him as a "reasonable" broker would.[20]

(2.4) Liability for failure to renew

An agent will be liable in negligence in failing to give his client notice when a policy expires and in certain cases will be liable for failing to renew the coverage automatically.[21]

20. *De Groot v. J.T. O'Bryan & Co. et al.*, 15 B.C.L.R. 271, [1979] I.L.R. 1-1152 (C.A.).
21. See *Lewis v. C.M. & M. Insurance Services Ltd. et al*, (1983), 4 C.C.L.I. (N.B.Q.B.); *Grove Service Ltd. v. Lenhart Agencies Ltd.* (1979), 10 C.C.L.T. 101 (B.C. S.C.); *Roy v. Atlantic Underwriters Ltd.* (1984), 9 C.C.L.I. 77 (N.B. Q.B.); revd [1986] I.L.R. 1-2006 (*sub nom. Edmond Vienneau Ltée v. Roy*), 67 N.B.R. (2d) 16, 35 C.C.L.T 249, 17 C.C.L.I. 266 (N.B. C.A.).

50

The New Clauses[1]

In January 1982 a new policy form and a new set of Institute Cargo Clauses was introduced to the London marine insurance market. The "new clauses", drafted in plain English, were to be in use by 1983. On March 31st, 1983, the "old" clauses were withdrawn from the London market. On the 1st day of October, 1983, the new Institute Hull Clauses were introduced to the market. The new clauses were introduced to the London market after many years of study of new wordings. They received impetus from the United Nations body UNCTAD which produced a report calling for a re-appraisal of the approach to marine insurance.[2]

Although available, the clauses are not in widespread use in Canada.[3]

---

1. See Appendix G.
2. Report by the UNCTAD Secretariat, "*Legal and Documentary Aspects of the Marine Insurance Contract*," TD/B/C.4/ISL/27, 20 November 1978. See also, *Report of the Working Group on International Shipping Legislation on its Seventh Session*, Trade and Development Board, Committee on Shipping, Tenth Session, UNCTAD, TD/B/C.4/219, TD/B/C.4/ISL/32, 26 January 1981.
3. There are no reported cases, yet, dealing with the new clauses. See, however, the following articles:
   Samir Mankabody, "*The New Lloyd's Policy and Cargo Clauses*" (1982), 13 *Journal of Maritime Law and Commerce* 527; Alex L. Parks, "Recent Developments in Marine Insurance Law" (1983), 14 *Journal of Maritime Law and Commerce* 159; Neville Gough, "Plain English Moves into Marine Market" January 28, 1982, *The Post Magazine* 222; Neville Gough, "Plain English Moves into Marine Market (2)" February 4, 1982, *The Post Magazine* 286; F.J.J. Cadwallader, "The Recalcitrant Insurer", *Third International Maritime Law Conference Papers*, The Continuing Legal Education Society of British Columbia, Vancouver, 1986

Institute Cargo Clauses (F.P.A.)

1.1.63 INSTITUTE CARGO CLAUSES (F.P.A.)

Transit Clause (incorporating Warehouse to Warehouse Clause).

1. This insurance attaches from the time the goods leave the warehouse or place of storage at the place named in the policy for the commencement of the transit, continues during the ordinary course of transit and terminates either on delivery

(a) to the Consignees' or other final warehouse or place of storage at the destination named in the policy,

(b) to any other warehouse or place of storage, whether prior to or at the destination named in the policy, which the Assured elect to use either

(i) for storage other than in the ordinary course of transit

or

(ii) for allocation or distribution, or

(c) on the expiry of 60 days after completion of discharge overside of the goods hereby insured from the oversea vessel at the final port of discharge,

whichever shall first occur.

If, after discharge overside from the oversea vessel at the final port of discharge, but prior to termination of this insurance, the goods are to be forwarded to a destination other than that to which they are insured hereunder, this insurance whilst remaining subject to termination as provided for above, shall not extend beyond the commencement of transit to such other destination.

This insurance shall remain in force (subject to termination as provided for above and to the provisions of Clause 2 below) during delay beyond the control of the Assured, any deviation, forced discharge, reshipment or transhipment and during any variation of the adventure arising from the exercise of a liberty granted to shipowners or charterers under the contract of affreightment, but shall in no case be deemed to extend to cover loss damage or expense proximately caused by delay or inherent vice or nature of the subject matter insured.

Termination of Adventure Clause.

2. If owing to circumstances beyond the control of the assured either the contract of affreightment is terminated at a port or place

other than the destination named therein or the adventure is otherwise terminated before delivery of the goods as provided for in Clause 1 above, then, subject to prompt notice being given to Underwriters and to an additional premium if required, this insurance shall remain in force until either

    (i) the goods are sold and delivered at such port or place, or, unless otherwise specially agreed, until the expiry of 60 days after completion of discharge overside of the goods hereby insured from the oversea vessel at such port or place, whichever shall first occur, or

    (ii) if the goods are forwarded within the said period of 60 days (or any agreed extension thereof) to the destination named in the policy or to any other destination, until terminated in accordance with the provisions of Clause 1 above.

Craft, & c. Clause.

3. Including transit by craft, raft or lighter to or from the vessel. Each craft, raft or lighter to be deemed a separate insurance. The Assured are not to be prejudiced by any agreement exempting lightermen from liability.

Change of Voyage Clause.

4. Held covered at a premium to be arranged in case of change of voyage, or of any omission or error in the description of the interest vessel or voyage.

F.P.A. Clause.

5. Warranted free from Particular Average unless the vessel or craft be stranded, sunk, or burnt, but notwithstanding this warranty the Underwriters are to pay the insured value of any package or packages which may be totally lost in loading, transhipment or discharge, also for any loss of or damage to the interest insured which may reasonably be attributed to fire, explosion, collision or contact of the vessel and/or craft and/or conveyance with any external substance (ice included) other than water, or to discharge of cargo at a port of distress, also to pay special charges for landing, warehousing and forwarding if incurred at an intermediate port of call or refuge for which Underwriters would be liable under the standard form of English Marine Policy with the Institute Cargo Clauses (W.A.) attached. This clause shall operate during the whole period covered by the policy.

Constructive Total Loss Clause.

6. No claim for Constructive Total Loss shall be recoverable hereunder unless the goods are reasonably abandoned either on account of their actual total loss appearing to be unavoidable or because the cost of recovering, reconditioning and forwarding the

goods to the destination to which they are insured would exceed their value on arrival.

G/A Clause.

7. General average and salvage charges payable according to Foreign Statement or to York-Antwerp Rules if in accordance with the contract of affreightment.

Seaworthiness Admitted Clause.

8. The seaworthiness of the vessel as between the Assured and Underwriters is hereby admitted.

In the event of loss the Assured's right of recovery hereunder shall not be prejudiced by the fact that the loss may have been attributable to the wrongful act or misconduct of the shipowners or their servants, committed without the privity of the Assured.

Bailee Clause.

9. It is the duty of the Assured and their Agents, in all cases, to take such measures as may be reasonable for the purpose of averting or minimising a loss and to ensure that all rights against carriers, bailees or other third parties are properly preserved and exercised.

Not to Inure Clause.

10. This insurance shall not inure to the benefit of the carrier or other bailee.

"Both to Blame Collision" Clause.

11. This insurance is extended to indemnify the Assured against such proportion of liability under the Contract of Affreightment "Both to Blame Collision" Clause as is in respect of a loss recoverable hereunder.

In the event of any claim by shipowners under the said Clause the Assured agree to notify the Underwriters who shall have the right, at their own cost and expense, to defend the Assured against such claim.

F. C. & S. Clause.

12. Warranted free of capture, seizure, arrest, restraint or detainment, and the consequences thereof or of any attempt thereat; also from the consequences of hostilities or warlike operations, whether there be a declaration of war or not; but this warranty shall not exclude collision, contact with any fixed or floating object (other than a mine or torpedo), stranding, heavy weather or fire unless caused directly (and independently of the nature of the voyage or service which the vessel concerned or, in the case of a collision, any other vessel involved therein, is performing) by a hostile act by or against a belligerent power; and for the purpose of this warranty "power" includes any authority maintaining naval, military or air forces in association with a power.

Further warranted free from the consequences of civil war, revolution, rebellion, insurrection, or civil strife arising therefrom, or piracy.

Should Clause No. 12 be deleted, the relevant current Institute War Clauses shall be deemed to form part of this Insurance.

Strikes, riots and civil commotions.

13. Warranted free of loss or damage
   (a) caused by strikers locked-out workmen or persons taking part in labour disturbances riots or civil commotions;
   (b) resulting from strikes, lock-outs, labour disturbances, riots or civil commotions.

Should Clause No. 13 be deleted, the relevant current Institute Strikes, Riots and Civil Commotions Clauses shall be deemed to form part of this Insurance.

Reasonable Despatch Clause.

14. It is a condition of this insurance that the Assured shall act with reasonable despatch in all circumstances within their control.

NOTE. — It is necessary for the Assured when they become aware of an event which is "held covered" under this insurance to give prompt notice to Underwriters and the right to such cover is dependent on compliance with this obligation.

Appendix B

Institute Cargo Clauses (W.A.)

1.1.63   INSTITUTE CARGO CLAUSES (W.A.)

These are the same as the Institute Cargo Clauses (F.P.A.) except for Clause 5, which reads as follows: —

Average Clause.

5. Warranted free from average under the percentage specified in the policy, unless general, or the vessel or craft be stranded, sunk or burnt, but notwithstanding this warranty the Underwriters are to pay the insured value of any package which may be totally lost in loading, transhipment or discharge, also for any loss of or damage to the interest insured which may reasonably be attributed to fire, explosion, collision or contact of the vessel and/or craft and/or conveyance with any external substance (ice included) other than water, or to discharge of cargo at a port of distress. This clause shall operate during the whole period covered by the policy.

Appendix C

Institute Cargo Clauses (All Risks)

1.1.63 INSTITUTE CARGO CLAUSES (ALL RISKS)

These clauses were first introduced on January 1, 1951, and are the same as the Institute Cargo Clauses (W.A.) except for Clause 5.

All Risks Clause.

5. This insurance is against all risks of loss of or damage to the subject-matter insured but shall in no case be deemed to extend to cover loss damage or expense proximately caused by delay or inherent vice or nature of the subject-matter insured. Claims recoverable hereunder shall be payable irrespective of percentage.

Appendix D
Institute Time Clauses (Hulls)

1.10.70 INSTITUTE TIME CLAUSES
HULLS

1. It is further agreed that if the Vessel hereby insured shall come into collision with any other vessel and the Assured shall in consequence thereof become liable to pay and shall pay by way of damages to any other person or persons any sum or sums in respect of such collision for

(i) loss of or damage to any other vessel or property or any other vessel,

(ii) delay to or loss of use of any such other vessel or property thereon, or

(iii) general average of, or salvage of, or salvage under contract of, any such other vessel or property thereon,

the Underwriters will pay the Assured such proportion of three-fourths of such sum or sums so paid as their respective subscriptions hereto bear to the value of the Vessel hereby insured, provided always that their liability in respect of any one such collision shall not exceed their proportionate part of three-fourths of the value of the vessel hereby insured, and in the cases in which, with the prior consent in writing of the Underwriters, the liability of the Vessel has been contested or proceedings have been taken to limit liability, they will also pay a like proportion of three-fourths of the costs which the Assured shall thereby incur or be compelled to pay; but when both vessels are to blame, then unless the liability of the Owners of one or both of such vessels becomes limited by law, claims under this clause shall be settled on the principle of cross-liabilities as if the Owners of each vessel had been compelled to pay to the Owners of the other of such vessels such one-half or other proportion of the latter's damages as may have been properly allowed in ascertaining the balance or sum payable by or to the Assured in consequence of such collision.

Provided always that this clause shall in no case extend or be deemed to extend to any sum which the Assured may become liable to pay or shall pay for or in respect of: —

(a) removal or disposal, under statutory powers or otherwise, of obstructions, wrecks, cargoes or any other thing whatsoever,

(b) *any real or personal property or thing whatsoever except other vessels or property on other vessels,*

(c) *the cargo or other property on or the engagements of the insured Vessel,*

(d) *loss of life, personal injury or illness.*

2. Should the Vessel hereby insured come into collision with or receive salvage services from another vessel belonging wholly or in part to the same Owners or under the same management, the Assured shall have the same rights under this Policy as they would have were the other vessel entirely the property of Owners not interested in the Vessel hereby insured; but in such cases the liability for the collision or the amount payable for the services rendered shall be referred to a sole arbitrator to be agreed upon between the Underwriters and the Assured.

3. (a) The Vessel is covered subject to the provisions of this Policy at all times and has leave to sail or navigate with or without pilots, to go on trial trips and to assist and tow vessels or craft in distress, but it is warranted that the Vessel shall not be towed, except as is customary or to the first safe port or place when in need of assistance, or undertake towage or salvage services under a contract previously arranged by the Assured and/or Owners and/or Managers and/or Charterers. This clause shall not exclude customary towage in connection with loading and discharging.

(b) In the event of the Vessel being employed in trading operations which entail cargo loading or discharging at sea from or into another vessel (not being a barge, lighter or similar harbour or inshore craft) no claim shall be recoverable under this insurance for loss of or damage to the Vessel or any other vessel arising from such loading or discharging operations, including whilst approaching, lying alongside and leaving, unless previous notice that the Vessel is to be employed in such operations has been given to the Underwriters and any amended terms of cover and any additional premium required by them have been agreed.

4. Should the Vessel at the expiration of this Policy be at sea or in distress or at a port of refuge or of call, she shall, provided previous notice be given to the Underwriters, be held covered at a *pro rata* monthly premium to her port of destination.

5. Held covered in case of any breach of warranty as to cargo, trade, locality, towage, salvage services or date of sailing, provided notice be given to the Underwriters immediately after receipt of advices and any amended terms of cover and any additional premium required by them be agreed.

6. If the Vessel is sold or transferred to new management then unless the Underwriters agree in writing to continue the insurance this Policy shall become cancelled from the time of sale or transfer, unless the Vessel has cargo on board and has already sailed from her loading port or is at sea in ballast, in either of which cases such cancellation shall, if required, be suspended until arrival at final port of discharge if with cargo, or at port of destination if in ballast. A *pro rata* daily return of premium shall be made.

This clause shall prevail notwithstanding any provision whether written, typed or printed in the Policy inconsistent therewith.

7. This insurance includes loss of or damage to the subject-matter insured directly caused by: —

    (a) Accidents in loading discharging or shifting cargo or fuel

        Explosions on shipboard or elsewhere

        Breakdown of or accident to nuclear installations or reactors on shipboard or elsewhere

        Bursting of boilers breakage of shafts or any latent defect in the machinery or hull

        Negligence of Master Officers Crew or Pilots

        Negligence of repairers provided such repairers are not Assured(s) hereunder

    (b) Contact with aircraft.

        Contact with any land conveyance, dock or harbour equipment or installation.

        Earthquake, volcanic eruption or lightning

provided such loss or damage has not resulted from want of due diligence by the Assured, Owners or Managers.

Masters Officers Crew or Pilots not to be considered as part Owners within the meaning of this clause should they hold shares in the Vessel.

8. General average and salvage to be adjusted according to the law and practice obtaining at the place where the adventure ends, as if the contract of affreightment contained no special terms upon the subject; but where the contract of affreightment so provides the adjustment shall be according to York-Antwerp Rules.

When the Vessel sails in ballast, not under charter, the provisions of the York-Antwerp Rules, 1950 (excluding Rules XX and XXI) shall be applicable, and the voyage for this purpose shall be deemed to continue from the port or place of departure until the arrival of the Vessel at the first port or place thereafter other than a port or place of refuge or a port or place of call for bunkering only. If at any such intermediate port or place there is an abandonment of the adventure originally contemplated the voyage shall thereupon be deemed to be terminated.

9. (a) In the event of expenses being incurred pursuant to the Suing and Labouring Clause, the liability under this Policy shall not exceed the proportion of such expenses that the amount insured hereunder bears to the value of the Vessel as stated herein, or to the sound value of the Vessel at the time of the occurrence giving rise to the expenditure if the sound value exceeds that value. Where the Underwriters have admitted a claim for total loss and property insured by this Policy is saved, the foregoing provisions shall not apply unless the expenses of suing and labouring exceed the value of such property saved and then shall apply only to the amount of the expenses which is in excess of such value.

(b) Where a claim for total loss of the Vessel is admitted under this Policy and expenses have been reasonably incurred in salving or attempting to salve the Vessel and other property and there are no proceeds, or the expenses exceed the proceeds, then this Policy shall bear its *pro rata* share of such proportion of the expenses, or of the expenses in excess of the proceeds, as the case may be, as may reasonably be regarded as having been incurred in respect of the Vessel; but if the Vessel be insured for less than its sound value at the time of the occurrence giving rise to the expenditure, the amount recoverable under this clause shall be reduced in proportion to the under-insurance.

10. Average payable without deduction new for old, whether the average be particular or general.

11. In the event of a claim for loss of or damage to any boiler, shaft, machinery or associated equipment, arising from any of the causes enumerated in Clause 7 (a), attributable in part or in whole to negligence of Master Officers or Crew and recoverable under this insurance only by reason of Clause 7, then the Assured shall, in addition to the deductible, also bear in respect of each accident or occurrence an amount equal to 10 per cent. of the balance of such claim. This clause shall not apply to a claim for total or constructive total loss of the Vessel.

12. No claim arising from a peril insured against shall be payable under this insurance unless the aggregate of all such claims arising out of each separate accident or occurrence (including claims under the Running Down and Suing and Labouring Clauses) exceeds .... in which case this sum shall be deducted. Nevertheless the expense of sighting the bottom after stranding, if reasonably incurred specially for that purpose, shall be paid even if no damage be found. This paragraph shall not apply to a claim for total or constructive total loss of the Vessel.

Claims for damage by heavy weather occurring during a single sea passage between two successive ports shall be treated as being due to one accident. In the case of such heavy weather extending over a period not wholly covered by this insurance, the deductible to be applied to the claim recoverable hereunder shall be the proportion of the above deductible that the number of days of such heavy weather falling within the period of this insurance bears to the number of days of heavy weather during the single sea passage.

The expression "heavy weather" in the preceding paragraph shall be deemed to include contact with floating ice.

Excluding any interest comprised therein, recoveries against any claim which is subject to the above deductible shall be credited to the Underwriters in full to the extent of the sum by which the aggregate of the claim unreduced by any recoveries exceeds the above deductible.

Interest comprised in recoveries shall be apportioned between the Assured and the Underwriters, taking into account the sums paid by Underwriters and the dates when such payments were made, notwithstanding that by the addition of interest the Underwriters may receive a larger sum than they have paid.

13. Grounding in the Panama Canal, Suez Canal, Manchester Ship Canal or its connections, River Mersey above Rock Ferry Slip, River Plate (above a line drawn from the North Basin Buenos Aires to the mouth of the San Pedro River) or its tributaries, Danube or Demerara Rivers or on the Yenikale Bar, shall not be deemed to be a stranding.

14. No claim shall in any case be allowed in respect of scraping or painting the Vessel's bottom.

15. No claim shall be allowed in particular average for wages and maintenance of the Master, Officers and Crew, or any member thereof, except when incurred solely for the necessary removal of the Vessel from one port to another for repairs, or for trial trips for average repairs, and then only for such wages and maintenance as are incurred whilst the Vessel is under way.

However, this Policy shall bear only that proportion of such wages and maintenance that the cost of repairs at the repair port recoverable under this Policy bears to the total cost of work done at the repair port.

16. In no case shall the Underwriters be liable for unrepaired damage in addition to a subsequent total loss sustained during the period covered by this policy or any extension thereof under Clause 4.

17. In ascertaining whether the Vessel is a constructive total loss the insured value shall be taken as the repaired value and nothing in respect of the damaged or break-up value of the Vessel or wreck shall be taken into account.

No claim for constructive total loss based upon the cost of recovery and/or repair of the Vessel shall be recoverable hereunder unless such cost would exceed the insured value.

18. In the event of total or constructive total loss no claim to be made by the Underwriters for freight whether notice of abandonment has been given or not.

19. In the event of accident whereby loss or damage may result in a claim under this Policy, notice shall be given to the Underwriters prior to survey and also, if the Vessel is abroad, to the nearest Lloyd's Agent so that a surveyor may be appointed to represent the Underwriters should they so desire. The Underwriters shall be entitled to decide the port to which the Vessel shall proceed for docking or repair (the actual additional expense of the voyage arising from compliance with the Underwriters' requirements being refunded to the Assured) and shall have a right of veto concerning a place of repair or a repairing firm. The Underwriters may also take tenders or may require further tenders to be taken for the repair of the Vessel. Where a tender so taken is accepted with the approval of the Underwriters an allowance shall be made at the rate of 30 per cent. per annum on the insured value for time lost between the despatch of the invitations to tender and the acceptance of a tender to the extent that such time is lost solely as the result of tenders having been taken and provided that the tender is accepted without delay after receipt of the Underwriters' approval.

Due credit shall be given against the allowance as above for any amount recovered: —

(a) in respect of fuel and stores and wages and maintenance of the Master Officers and Crew or any member thereof allowed in general or particular average,

(b) from third parties in respect of damages for detention and/or loss of profit and/or running expenses,

for the period covered by the tender allowance or any part thereof.

Where a part of the cost of average repairs other than a fixed deductible is not recoverable from the Underwriters the allowance shall be reduced by a similar proportion.

In the event of failure to comply with the conditions of this clause, 15 per cent. shall be deducted from the amount of the ascertained claim.

20. Additional insurances as follows are permitted: —

(a) *Disbursements, Managers' Commissions, Profits or Excess or Increased Value of Hull and Machinery.* A sum not exceeding 10 per cent. of the value stated herein.

(b) *Freight, Chartered Freight or Anticipated Freight, insured for time.* A sum not exceeding 10 per cent. of the value as stated herein less any sum insured, however described, under Section (a).

(c) *Freight or Hire, under contracts for voyage.* A sum not exceeding the gross freight or hire for the current cargo passage and next succeeding cargo passage (such insurance to include, if required, a preliminary and an intermediate ballast passage) plus the charges of insurance. In the case of a voyage charter where payment is made on a time basis, the sum permitted for insurance shall be calculated on the estimated duration of the voyage, subject to the limitation of two cargo passages as laid down herein. Any sum insured under Section (b) to be taken into account and only the excess thereof may be insured, which excess shall be reduced as the freight or hire is advanced or earned by the gross amount so advanced or earned.

(d) *Anticipated Freight if the Vessel sails in ballast and not under Charter.* A sum not exceeding the anticipated gross freight on next cargo passage, such sum to be reasonably estimated on the basis of the current rate of freight at time of insurance plus the charges of insurance. Any sum insured under Section (b) to be taken into account and only the excess thereof may be insured.

(e) *Time Charter Hire or Charter Hire for series of Voyages.* A sum not exceeding 50 per cent. of the gross hire which is to be earned under the charter in a period not exceeding 18 months. Any sum insured under Section (b) to be taken into account and only the excess thereof may be insured, which excess shall be reduced as the hire is advanced or earned under the charter by 50 per cent. of the gross amount so advanced or earned but the sum insured need not be reduced while the total of the sums insured under Sections (b) and (e) does not exceed 50 per cent. of the gross hire still to be earned under the charter. An insurance under this Section may begin on the signing of the charter.

(f) *Premiums.* A sum not exceeding the actual premiums of all interests insured for a period not exceeding 12 months (excluding premiums insured under the foregoing sections but including, if required, the premium or estimated calls on any Club or War, etc., Risk insurance) reducing *pro rata* monthly.

(g) *Returns of Premium.* A sum not exceeding the actual returns which are recoverable subject to "and arrival" under any policy of insurance.

(*h*) *Insurance irrespective of amount against:* —
Risks excluded by the Free of Capture, etc. Clause and risks enumerated in the Institute War and Strike Clauses.

Warranted that no insurance on any interests enumerated in the foregoing Sections (*a*) to (*g*) in excess of the amounts permitted therein and no other insurance P.P.I., F.I.A., or subject to any other like term, is or shall be effected to operate during the currency of this Policy by or for account of the Assured, Owners, Managers or Mortgagees. Provided always that a breach of this warranty shall not afford the Underwriters any defence to a claim by a Mortgagee who has accepted this Policy without knowledge of such breach.

21. To return as follows:
... per cent. net for each uncommenced month if this Policy be cancelled by agreement,
and, for each period of 30 consecutive days the Vessel may be laid up in port or in a lay-up area approved by the Underwriters (with special liberties as hereinafter allowed): —

(*a*) ... per cent. net not under repair

(*b*) ... per cent. net under repair

If the Vessel is under repair during part only of a period for which a return is claimable, the return payable shall be calculated pro-rata to the number of days under (*a*) and (*b*) respectively.

Provided always that

(i) in no case shall a return be allowed when the within named Vessel is lying in exposed or unprotected waters, or in a port or lay-up area not approved by the Underwriters, but, provided the Underwriters agree that such nonapproved lay-up area is deemed to be within the vicinity of the approved port or lay-up area, days during which the Vessel is laid up in such non-approved lay-up area may be added to days in the approved port or lay-up area to calculate a period of 30 consecutive days and a return shall be allowed for the proportion of such period during which the Vessel is actually laid up in the approved port or lay-up area

(ii) loading or discharging operations or the presence of cargo on board shall not debar returns but no return shall be allowed for any period during which the Vessel is being used for the storage of cargo

(iii) in the event of a return for special trade or any other reason being recoverable, the above rates of return of premium shall be reduced accordingly.

In the event of any return recoverable under this clause being based on 30 consecutive days which fall on successive policies, effected for the same Assured, this Policy shall only be liable for an amount calculated at pro-rata of the period rates (a) and/or (b) above for the number of days which come within the period of this Policy and to which a return is actually applicable. Such overlapping period shall run, at the option of the Assured, either from the first day on which the Vessel is laid up or the first day of a period of 30 consecutive days as provided under (a) or (b) or (i) above.

22. No assignment of or interest in this Policy or in any moneys which may be or become payable thereunder is to be binding on or recognised by the Underwriters unless a dated notice of such assignment of interest signed by the Assured, and by the assignor in the case of subsequent assignment, is endorsed on this Policy and the Policy with such endorsement is produced before payment of any claim or return of premium thereunder; but nothing in this clause is to have effect as an agreement by the Underwriters to a sale or transfer to new management.

Unless deleted by the Underwriters the following clauses shall be paramount and shall override anything contained in this insurance inconsistent therewith.

23. Warranted free of capture, seizure, arrest, restraint or detainment, and the consequences thereof or of any attempt thereat; also from the consequences of hostilities or warlike operations, whether there be a declaration of war or not; but this warranty shall not exclude collision, contact with any fixed or floating object (other than a mine or torpedo), stranding, heavy weather or fire unless caused directly (and independently of the nature of the voyage or service which the Vessel concerned or, in the case of a collision, any other vessel involved therein is performing) by a hostile act by or against a belligerent power; and for the purpose of this warranty "power" includes any authority maintaining naval, military or air forces in association with a power.

Further warranted free from the consequences of civil war, revolution, rebellion, insurrection, or civil strife arising therefrom, or piracy.

24. Warranted free from loss damage liability or expense arising from: —

(a) the detonation of an explosive

(b) any weapon of war

and caused by any person acting maliciously or from a political motive.

25. Warranted free from loss damage liability or expense arising from any weapon of war employing atomic or nuclear fission &/ or fusion or other like reaction or radioactive force or matter.

Appendix E

The York-Antwerp Rules 1974

Rule of Interpretation. — In the adjustment of general average the following lettered and numbered Rules shall apply to the exclusion of any Law and Practice inconsistent therewith.

Except as provided by the numbered Rules, general average shall be adjusted according to the lettered Rules.

Rule A. — There is a general average act, when, and only when, any extraordinary sacrifice or expenditure is intentionally and reasonably made or incurred for the common safety for the purpose of preserving from peril the property involved in a common maritime adventure.

Rule B. — General average sacrifices and expenses shall be borne by the different contributing interests on the basis hereinafter provided.

Rule C. — Only such losses, damages or expenses which are the direct consequence of the general average act shall be allowed as general average.

Loss or damage sustained by the ship or cargo through delay, whether on the voyage or subsequently, such as demurrage, and any indirect loss whatsoever, such as loss of market, shall not be admitted as general average.

Rule D. — Rights to contribution in general average shall not be affected, though the event which gave rise to the sacrifice or expenditure may have been due to the fault of one of the parties to the adventure, but this shall not prejudice any remedies or defences which may be open against or to that party in respect of such fault.

Rule E. — The onus of proof is upon the party claiming in general average to show that the loss or expense claimed is properly allowable as general average.

Rule F. — Any extra expense incurred in place of another expense which would have been allowable as general average shall be deemed to be general average and so allowed without regard to the saving, if any, to other interests, but only up to the amount of the general average expense avoided.

Rule G. — General average shall be adjusted as regards both loss and contribution upon the basis of values at the time and place when and where the adventure ends.

This rule shall not affect the determination of the place at which the average statement is to be made up.

Rule I. Jettison of Cargo. — No jettison of cargo shall be made good as general average unless such cargo is carried in accordance with the recognised custom of the trade.

Rule II. Damage by Jettison and Sacrifice for the Common Safety. — Damage done to a ship and cargo, or either of them, by or in consequence of a sacrifice made for the common safety, and by water which goes down a ship's hatches opened or other opening made for the purpose of making a jettison for the common safety, shall be made good as general average.

Rule III. Extinguishing Fire on Shipboard. — Damage done to a ship and cargo, or either of them, by water or otherwise, including damage by beaching or scuttling a burning ship, in extinguishing a fire on board the ship, shall be made good as general average; except that no compensation shall be made for damage by smoke or heat however caused.

Rule IV. Cutting away Wreck. — Loss or damage sustained by cutting away wreck or parts of the ship which have been previously carried away or are effectively lost by accident shall not be made good as general average.

Rule V. Voluntary Stranding. — When a ship is intentionally run on shore for the common safety, whether or not she might have been driven on shore, the consequent loss or damage shall be allowed in general average.

Rule VI. Salvage Remuneration. — Expenditure incurred by the parties to the adventure on account of salvage, whether under contract or otherwise, shall be allowed in general average to the extent that the salvage operations were undertaken for the purpose of preserving from peril the property involved in the common maritime adventure.

Rule VII. Damage to Machinery and Boilers. — Damage caused to any machinery and boilers of a ship which is ashore and in a position of peril, in endeavouring to refloat, shall be allowed in general average when shown to have arisen from an actual intention to float the ship for the common safety at the risk of such damage; but where a ship is afloat no loss or damage caused by working the propelling machinery and boilers shall in any circumstances be made good as general average.

Rule VIII. Expenses Lightening a Ship when Ashore, and Consequent Damage. — When a ship is ashore and cargo and ship's fuel and stores or any of them are discharged as a general average act, the extra cost of lightening, lighter hire and reshipping if incurred and the loss or damage sustained thereby, shall be admitted as general average.

Rule IX. Ship's Materials and Stores Burnt for Fuel. — Ship's materials and stores, or any of them, necessarily burnt for fuel for the common safety at a time of peril, shall be admitted as general average, when and only when an ample supply of fuel had been provided; but the estimated quantity of fuel that would have been consumed, calculated at the price current at the ship's last port of departure at the date of her leaving, shall be credited to the general average.

Rule X. Expenses at Port of Refuge, etc. — (*a*) When a ship shall have entered a port or place of refuge or shall have returned to her port or place of loading in consequence of accident, sacrifice or other extraordinary circumstances, which render that necessary for the common safety, the expenses of entering such port or place shall be admitted as general average; and when she shall have sailed thence with her original cargo, or part of it, the corresponding expenses of leaving such port or place consequent upon such entry or return shall likewise be admitted as general average.

When a ship is at any port or place of refuge and is necessarily removed to another port or place because repairs cannot be carried out in the first port or place, the provisions of this Rule shall be applied to the second port or place as if it were a port or place of refuge and the cost of such removal including temporary repairs and towage shall be admitted as general average. The provisions of Rule XI shall be applied to the prolongation of the voyage occasioned by such removal.

(*b*) The cost of handling on board or discharging cargo, fuel or stores whether at a port or place of loading, call or refuge, shall be admitted as general average, when the handling or discharge was necessary for the common safety or to enable damage to the ship caused by sacrifice or accident to be repaired if the repairs were necessary for the safe prosecution of the voyage, except in cases where the damage to the ship is discovered at a port or place of loading or call without any accident or other extraordinary circumstance connected with such damage having taken place during the voyage.

The cost of handling on board or discharging cargo, fuel or stores shall not be admissible as general average when incurred solely for the purpose of restowage due to shifting during the voyage unless such restowage is necessary for the common safety.

(c) Whenever the cost of handling or discharging cargo, fuel or stores is admissible as general average, the costs of storage, including insurance if reasonably incurred, reloading and stowing of such cargo, fuel or stores shall likewise be admitted as general average.

But when the ship is condemned or does not proceed on her original voyage storage expenses shall be admitted as general average only up to the date of the ship's condemnation or of the abandonment of the voyage or up to the date of completion of discharge of cargo if the condemnation or abandonment takes place before that date.

Rule XI. Wages and Maintenance of Crew and other expenses Bearing up for and in a port of Refuge, etc. — (a) Wages and maintenance of master, officers and crew reasonably incurred and fuel and stores consumed during the prolongation of the voyage occasioned by a ship entering a port or place of refuge or returning to her port or place of loading shall be admitted as general average when the expenses of entering such port or place are allowable in general average in accordance with Rule X (a).

(b) When a ship shall have entered or been detained in any port or place in consequence of accident, sacrifice or other extraordinary circumstances which render that necessary for the common safety, or to enable damage to the ship caused by sacrifice or accident to be repaired, if the repairs were necessary for the safe prosecution of the voyage, the wages and maintenance of the master, officers, and crew reasonably incurred during the extra period of detention in such port or place until the ship shall or should have been made ready to proceed upon her voyage, shall be admitted in general average.

Provided that when damage to the ship is discovered at a port or place of loading or call without any accident or other extraordinary circumstance connected with such damage having taken place during the voyage, then the wages and maintenance of master, officers and crew and fuel and stores consumed during the extra detention for repairs to damage so discovered shall not be admissible as general average, even if the repairs are necessary for the safe prosecution of the voyage.

When the ship is condemned or does not proceed on her original voyage, wages and maintenance of the master, officers and crew and fuel and stores consumed shall be admitted as general average only up to the date of the ship's condemnation or of the abandonment of the voyage or up to the date of completion of discharge of cargo if the condemnation or abandonment takes place before that date.

Fuel and stores consumed during the extra period of detention shall be admitted as general average, except such fuel and stores as are consumed in effecting repairs not allowable in general average.

Port charges incurred during the extra period of detention shall likewise be admitted as general average except such charges as are incurred solely by reason of repairs not allowable in general average.

(c) For the purpose of this and the other Rules wages shall include all payments made to or for the benefit of the master, officers and crew, whether such payments be imposed by law upon the shipowners or be made under the terms or articles of employment.

(d) When overtime is paid to the master, officers or crew for maintenance of the ship or repairs, the cost of which is not allowable in general average, such overtime shall be allowed in general average only up to the saving in expense which would have been incurred and admitted as general average, had such overtime not been incurred.

Rule XII. Damage to Cargo in discharging, etc. — Damage to or loss of cargo, fuel or stores caused in the act of handling, discharging, storing, reloading and stowing shall be made good as general average, when and only when the cost of those measures respectively is admitted as general average.

Rule XIII. Deductions from Cost of Repairs. — Repairs to be allowed in general average shall not be subject to deductions in respect of "new for old" where old material or parts are replaced by new unless the ship is over fifteen years old in which case there shall be a deduction of one third. The deductions shall be regulated by the age of the ship from the 31st December of the year of completion of construction to the date of the general average act, except for insulation, life and similar boats, communications and navigational apparatus and equipment, machinery and boilers for which the deductions shall be regulated by the age of the particular parts to which they apply.

The deductions shall be made only from the cost of the new material or parts when finished and ready to be installed in the ship.

No deduction shall be made in respect of provisions, stores, anchors and chain cables.

Drydock and slipway dues and costs of shifting the ship shall be allowed in full.

The costs of cleaning, painting or coating of bottom shall not be allowed in general average unless the bottom has been painted or coated within the twelve months preceding the date of the general average act in which case one half of such costs shall be allowed.

Rule XIV. Temporary Repairs. — Where temporary repairs are effected to a ship at a port of loading, call or refuge, for the common safety, or of damage caused by general average sacrifice, the cost of such repairs shall be admitted as general average.

Where temporary repairs of accidental damage are effected in order to enable the adventure to be completed, the cost of such repairs shall be admitted as general average without regard to the saving, if any, to other interest, but only up to the saving in expense which would have been incurred and allowed in general average if such repairs had not been effected there.

No deductions "new for old" shall be made from the cost of temporary repairs allowable as general average.

Rule XV. Loss of Freight. — Loss of freight arising from damage to or loss of cargo shall be made good as general average, either when caused by a general average act, or when the damage to or loss of cargo is so made good.

Deduction shall be made from the amount of gross freight lost, of the charges which the owner thereof would have incurred to earn such freight, but has, in consequence of the sacrifice, not incurred.

Rule XVI. Amount to be made good for Cargo lost or Damaged by Sacrifice. — The amount to be made good as general average for damage to or loss of cargo sacrificed shall be the loss which has been sustained thereby based on the value at the time of discharge, ascertained from the commercial invoice rendered to the receiver or if there is no such invoice from the shipped value. The value at the time of discharge shall include the cost of insurance and freight except insofar as such freight is at the risk of interests other than the cargo.

When cargo so damaged is sold and the amount of the damage has not been otherwise agreed, the loss to be made good in general average shall be the difference between the net proceeds of sale and the net sound value as computed in the first paragraph of this Rule.

Rule XVII. Contributory Values. — The contribution to a general average shall be made upon the actual net value of the property at the termination of the adventure except that the value of cargo shall be the value at the time of discharge, ascertained from the commercial invoice rendered to the receiver or if there is no such invoice from the shipped value. The value of the cargo shall include the cost of insurance and freight unless and insofar as such freight is at the risk of interests other than the cargo, deducting therefrom any loss or damage suffered by the cargo prior to or at the time of discharge. The value of the ship shall be assessed without taking into account the beneficial or detrimental effect of any demise or time charter-party to which the ship may be committed.

To these values shall be added the amount made good as general average for property sacrificed, if not already included, deduction being made from the freight and passage money at risk of such charges and crew's wages as would not have been incurred in earning the freight had the ship and cargo been totally lost at the date of the general average act and have not been allowed as general average; deduction being also made from the value of the property of all extra charges incurred in respect thereof subsequently to the general average act, except such charges as are allowed in general average.

Where cargo is sold short of destination, however, it shall contribute upon the actual net proceeds of sale, with the addition of any amount made good as general average.

Passenger's luggage and personal effects not shipped under Bill of Lading shall not contribute in general average.

Rule XVIII. Damage to Ship. — The amount to be allowed as general average for damage or loss to the ship, her machinery and/or gear caused by a general average act shall be as follows:

(*a*) When repaired or replaced,

The actual reasonable cost of repairing or replacing such damage or loss subject to deduction in accordance with Rule XIII;

(*b*) When not repaired or replaced,

The reasonable depreciation arising from such damage or loss, but not exceeding the estimated cost of repairs. But where the ship is an actual total loss or when the cost of repairs of the damage would exceed the value of the ship when repaired, the amount to be allowed as general average shall be the difference between the estimated sound value of the ship after deducting therefrom the estimated cost of repairing damage which is not general average and the value of the ship in her damaged state which may be measured by the net proceeds of sale, if any.

Rule XIX. Undeclared or Wrongfully declared Cargo. — Damage or loss caused to goods loaded without the knowledge of the shipowner or his agent or to goods wilfully misdescribed at time of shipment shall not be allowed as general average but such goods shall remain liable to contribute, if saved.

Damage or loss caused to goods which have been wrongfully declared on shipment at a value which is lower than their real value shall be contributed for at the declared value, but such goods shall contribute upon their actual value.

Rule XX. Provision of Funds. — A commission of two per cent. of general average disbursements, other than the wages and maintenance of master, officers and crew and fuel and stores not replaced during the voyage, shall be allowed in general average, but when the funds are not provided by any of the contributing interests the necessary cost of obtaining the funds required by means of a bottomry bond or otherwise, or the loss sustained by owners of goods sold for the purpose, shall be allowed in general average.

The cost of insuring money advanced to pay for general average disbursements shall also be allowed in general average.

Rule XXI. Interest on Losses made good in general average. — Interest shall be allowed on expenditure, sacrifices and allowances charged to general average at the rate of seven per cent. per annum, until the date of the general average statement, due allowance being made for any interim reimbursement from the contributory interests or from the general average deposit fund.

Rule XXII. Treatment of Cash Deposits. — Where cash deposits have been collected in respect of cargo's liability for general average, salvage or special charges such deposits shall be paid without any delay into a special account in the joint names of a representative nominated on behalf of the shipowner and a representative nominated on behalf of the depositors in a bank to be approved by both. The sum so deposited together with accrued interest, if any, shall be held as security for payment to the parties entitled thereto of the general average, salvage or special charges payable by cargo in respect to which the deposits have been collected. Payments on account of refund of deposits may be made if certified to in writing by the average adjuster. Such deposits and payments or refunds shall be without prejudice to the ultimate liability of the parties.

Federal Court Act

R.S.C. 1970, c. 10 (2nd Supp.)

Section 22.

Navigation and Shipping

(1) The Trial Division has concurrent original jurisdiction as well between subject and subject as otherwise, in all cases in which a claim for relief is made or a remedy is sought under or by virtue of Canadian maritime law or any other law of Canada relating to any matter coming within the class of subject of navigation and shipping, except to the extent that jurisdiction has been otherwise specially assigned.

Maritime jurisdiction —

(2) Without limiting the generality of subsection (1), it is hereby declared for greater certainty that the Trial Division has jurisdiction with respect to any claim or question arising out of one or more of the following:

(a) any claim as to title, possession or ownership of a ship or any part interest therein or with respect to the proceeds of sale of a ship or any part interest therein;

(b) any question arising between co-owners of a ship as to possession, employment or earnings of a ship;

(c) any claim in respect of a mortgage or hypothecation of, or charge on a ship or any part interest therein or any charge in the nature of bottomry or *respondentia* for which a ship or part interest therein of cargo was made security;

(d) any claim for damage or for loss of life or personal injury caused by a ship either in collision or otherwise;

(e) any claim for damage sustained by, or for loss of, a ship including, without restricting the generality of the foregoing, damage to or loss of the cargo or equipment of or any property in or on or being loaded on or off a ship;

(f) any claim arising out of an agreement relating to the carriage of goods on a ship under a rough bill of lading or in respect of which a through bill of lading is intended to be issued, for loss or damage to goods occurring at any time or place during transit;

(g) any claim for loss of life or personal injury occurring in connection with the operation of a ship including, without restricting the generality of the foregoing, any claim for loss of life or personal injury sustained in consequence of any defect in a ship or in her apparel or equipment, or of the wrongful act, neglect or default of the owners, charterers or persons in possession or control of a ship or of the master or crew thereof or of any other person for whose wrongful acts, neglects or defaults the owners, charterers or persons in possession or control of the ship are responsible, being an act, neglect or default in the management of the ship, in the loading, carriage or discharge of goods on, in or from the ship or in the embarkation, carriage or disembarkation of persons on, in or from the ship;

(h) any claim for loss of or damage to goods carried in or on a ship including, without restricting the generality of the foregoing, loss of or damage to passengers' baggage or personal effects;

(i) any claim arising out of any agreement relating to the carriage of goods in or on a ship or to the use or hire of a ship whether by charter party or otherwise;

(j) any claim for salvage including, without restricting the generality of the foregoing, claims for salvage of life, cargo, equipment or other property of, from or by an aircraft to the same extent and in the same manner as if such aircraft were a ship;

(k) any claim for towage in respect of a ship or of an aircraft while such aircraft is waterborne;

(l) any claim for pilotage in respect of a ship or of an aircraft while such aircraft is waterborne;

(m) any claim in respect of goods, materials or services wherever supplied to a ship for her operation or maintenance including, without restricting the generality of the foregoing, claims in respect of stevedoring and lighterage;

(n) any claim arising out of a contract relating to the construction, repair or equipping of a ship;

(o) any claim by a master, officer or member of the crew of a ship for wages, money, property or other remuneration or benefits arising out of his employment;

(p) any claim by a master, charterer or agent of a ship or shipowner in respect of disbursements or by a shipper in respect of advances, made on account of a ship;

(q) any claim in respect of general average contribution;

(r) any claim arising out of or in connection with a contract of marine insurance; and

(s) any claim for dock charges, harbour dues or canal tolls including, without restricting the generality of the foregoing, charges for the use of facilities supplied in connection therewith.

Jurisdiction applicable

(3) For greater certainty it is hereby declared that the jurisdiction conferred on the Court by this section is applicable

(*a*) in relation to all ships whether Canadian or not and wherever the residence or domicile of the owners may be;

(*b*) in relation to all aircraft where the cause of action arises out of paragraphs 2(*j*), (*k*), and (*l*) whether those aircraft are Canadian or not and wherever the residence or domicile of the owners may be :

(*c*) in relation to all claims whether arising on the high seas or within the limits of the territorial, internal or other waters of Canada or elsewhere and whether such waters are naturally navigable or artificially made so, incuding, without restricting the generality of the foregoing, in the case of salvage, claims in respect of cargo or wreck found on the shore of such waters; and

(*d*) in relation to all mortgages or hypothecations of or charges by way of security on a ship, whether registered or not, or whether legal or equitable, and whether created under foreign law or not.

Appendix G

The New Clauses

1 The New Marine Policy Form

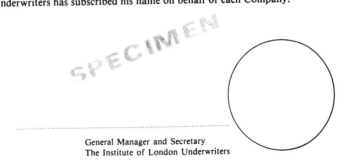

The Institute of London Underwriters

Companies Marine Policy

WE, THE COMPANIES, hereby agree, in consideration of the payment to us by or on behalf of the Assured of the premium specified in the Schedule, to insure against loss damage liability or expense in the proportions and manner hereinafter provided. Each Company shall be liable only for its own respective proportion.

IN WITNESS whereof the General Manager and Secretary of The Institute of London Underwriters has subscribed his name on behalf of each Company.

....

General Manager and Secretary
The Institute of London Underwriters

This Policy is not valid unless it bears the embossment of the Policy Department of The Institute of London Underwriters.

This insurance is subject to English jurisdiction.

2   <u>SCHEDULE</u>

POLICY NUMBER

NAME OF ASSURED

VESSEL

VOYAGE OR PERIOD OF INSURANCE

SUBJECT-MATTER INSURED

AGREED VALUE
   (if any)

AMOUNT INSURED HEREUNDER

PREMIUM

CLAUSES, ENDORSEMENTS, SPECIAL CONDITIONS AND WARRANTIES

THE ATTACHED CLAUSES AND ENDORSEMENTS FORM PART OF THIS POLICY

COMPANIES' PROPORTIONS

For use by the Policy Department

of

The Institute of London Underwriters

In all communications please quote the following reference	

The Institute of London Underwriters
Companies Marine Policy

This Policy is subscribed by Insurance Companies
Members of The Institute of London Underwriters
40, Lime Street,
London, EC3M 5DA

2 Institute Cargo Clauses (A)

1/1/82   (FOR USE ONLY WITH THE NEW MARINE POLICY FORM)

INSTITUTE CARGO CLAUSES (A)

RISKS COVERED

1   This insurance covers all risks of loss of or damage to the subject-matter insured except as provided in Clauses 4, 5, 6 and 7 below.
    Risks Clause

2   This insurance covers general average and salvage charges, adjusted or determined according to the contract of affreightment and/or the governing law and practice, incurred to avoid or in connection with the avoidance of loss from any cause except those excluded in Clauses 4, 5, 6 and 7 or elsewhere in this insurance.
    General Average Clause

3   This insurance is extended to indemnify the Assured against such proportion of liability under the contract of affreightment "Both to Blame Collision" Clause as is in respect of a loss recoverable hereunder. In the event of any claim by shipowners under the said Clause the Assured agree to notify the Underwriters who shall have the right, at their own cost and expense, to defend the Assured against such claim.
    "Both to Blame Collision" Clause

EXCLUSIONS

4   In no case shall this insurance cover
    General Exclusions Clause

    4.1   loss damage or expense attributable to wilful misconduct of the Assured

    4.2   ordinary leakage, ordinary loss in weight or volume, or ordinary wear and tear of the subject-matter insured

    4.3   loss damage or expense caused by insufficiency or unsuitability of packing or preparation of the subject-matter insured (for the purpose of this Clause 4.3 "packing" shall be deemed to include stowage in a container or liftvan but only when such stowage is carried out prior to attachment of this insurance or by the Assured or their servants)

    4.4   loss damage or expense caused by inherent vice or nature of the subject-matter insured

    4.5   loss damage or expense proximately caused by delay, even though the delay be caused by a risk insured against (except expenses payable under Clause 2 above)

    4.6   loss damage or expense arising from insolvency or financial default of the owners managers charterers or operators of the vessel

    4.7   loss damage or expense arising from the use of any weapon of war employing atomic or nuclear fission and/or fusion or other like reaction or radioactive force or matter.

5   5.1   In no case shall this insurance cover loss damage or expense arising from
    Unseaworthiness and Unfitness Exclusion Clause

        unseaworthiness of vessel or craft,

        unfitness of vessel craft conveyance container or liftvan for the safe carriage of the subject-matter insured,

        where the Assured or their servants are privy to such unseaworthiness or unfitness, at the time the subject-matter insured is loaded therein.

    5.2   The Underwriters waive any breach of the implied warranties of seaworthiness of the ship and fitness of the ship to carry the subject-matter insured to destination, unless the Assured or their servants are privy to such unseaworthiness or unfitness.

6   In no case shall this insurance cover loss damage or expense caused by
    War Exclusion Clause

    6.1   war civil war revolution rebellion insurrection, or civil strife arising therefrom, or any hostile act by or against a belligerent power

    6.2   capture seizure arrest restraint or detainment (piracy excepted), and the consequences thereof or any attempt thereat

    6.3   derelict mines torpedoes bombs or other derelict weapons of war.

7   In no case shall this insurance cover loss damage or expense
    Strikes Exclusion Clause

    7.1   caused by strikers, locked-out workmen, or persons taking part in labour disturbances, riots or civil commotions

    7.2   resulting from strikes, lock-outs, labour disturbances, riots or civil commotions

    7.3   caused by any terrorist or any person acting from a political motive.

DURATION

8   8.1   This insurance attaches from the time the goods leave the warehouse or place of storage at the place named herein for the commencement of the transit, continues during the ordinary course of transit and terminates either
    Transit Clause

    8.1.1   on delivery to the Consignees' or other final warehouse or place of storage at the destination named herein,

    8.1.2   on delivery to any other warehouse or place of storage, whether prior to or at the destination named herein, which the Assured elect to use either

    8.1.2.1   for storage other than in the ordinary course of transit or

    8.1.2.2   for allocation or distribution,

        or

    8.1.3   on the expiry of 60 days after completion of discharge overside of the goods hereby insured from the oversea vessel at the final port of discharge,

    whichever shall first occur.

    8.2   If, after discharge overside from the oversea vessel at the final port of discharge, but prior to termination of this insurance, the goods are to be forwarded to a destination other than that to which they are insured hereunder, this insurance, whilst remaining subject to termination as provided for above, shall not extend beyond the commencement of transit to such other destination.

    8.3   This insurance shall remain in force (subject to termination as provided for above and to the provisions of Clause 9 below) during delay beyond the control of the Assured, any deviation, forced discharge, reshipment or transhipment and during any variation of the adventure arising from the exercise of a liberty granted to shipowners or charterers under the contract of affreightment.

(Continued)

9 If owing to circumstances beyond the control of the Assured either the contract of carriage is terminated at a port or place other than the destination named therein or the transit is otherwise terminated before delivery of the goods as provided for in Clause 8 above, then this insurance shall also terminate *unless prompt notice is given to the Underwriters and continuation of cover is requested when the insurance shall remain in force, subject to an additional premium if required by the Underwriters,* either *(Termination of Contract of Carriage Clause)*

    9.1 until the goods are sold and delivered at such port or place, or, unless otherwise specially agreed, until the expiry of 60 days after arrival of the goods hereby insured at such port or place, whichever shall first occur,

        or

    9.2 if the goods are forwarded within the said period of 60 days (or any agreed extension thereof) to the destination named herein or to any other destination, until terminated in accordance with the provisions of Clause 8 above.

10 Where, after attachment of this insurance, the destination is changed by the Assured, *held covered at a premium and on conditions to be arranged subject to prompt notice being given to the Underwriters.* *(Change of Voyage Clause)*

CLAIMS

11 11.1 In order to recover under this insurance the Assured must have an insurable interest in the subject-matter insured at the time of the loss. *(Insurable Interest Clause)*

    11.2 Subject to 11.1 above, the Assured shall be entitled to recover for insured loss occurring during the period covered by this insurance, notwithstanding that the loss occurred before the contract of insurance was concluded, unless the Assured were aware of the loss and the Underwriters were not.

12 Where, as a result of the operation of a risk covered by this insurance, the insured transit is terminated at a port or place other than that to which the subject-matter is covered under this insurance, the Underwriters will reimburse the Assured for any extra charges properly and reasonably incurred in unloading storing and forwarding the subject-matter to the destination to which it is insured hereunder. *(Forwarding Charges Clause)*

This Clause 12, which does not apply to general average or salvage charges, shall be subject to the exclusions contained in Clauses 4, 5, 6 and 7 above, and shall not include charges arising from the fault negligence insolvency or financial default of the Assured or their servants.

13 No claim for Constructive Total Loss shall be recoverable hereunder unless the subject-matter insured is reasonably abandoned either on account of its actual total loss appearing to be unavoidable or because the cost of recovering, reconditioning and forwarding the subject-matter to the destination to which it is insured would exceed its value on arrival. *(Constructive Total Loss Clause)*

14 14.1 If any Increased Value insurance is effected by the Assured on the cargo insured herein the agreed value of the cargo shall be deemed to be increased to the total amount insured under this insurance and all Increased Value insurances covering the loss, and liability under this insurance shall be in such proportion as the sum insured herein bears to such total amount insured. *(Increased Value Clause)*

        In the event of claim the Assured shall provide the Underwriters with evidence of the amounts insured under all other insurances.

    14.2 **Where this insurance is on Increased Value the following clause shall apply:**
        The agreed value of the cargo shall be deemed to be equal to the total amount insured under the primary insurance and all Increased Value insurances covering the loss and effected on the cargo by the Assured, and liability under this insurance shall be in such proportion as the sum insured herein bears to such total amount insured.

        In the event of claim the Assured shall provide the Underwriters with evidence of the amounts insured under all other insurances.

BENEFIT OF INSURANCE

15 This insurance shall not inure to the benefit of the carrier or other bailee. *(Not to Inure Clause)*

MINIMISING LOSSES

16 It is the duty of the Assured and their servants and agents in respect of loss recoverable hereunder *(Duty of Assured Clause)*

    16.1 to take such measures as may be reasonable for the purpose of averting or minimising such loss,

        and

    16.2 to ensure that all rights against carriers, bailees or other third parties are properly preserved and exercised

    and the Underwriters will, in addition to any loss recoverable hereunder, reimburse the Assured for any charges properly and reasonably incurred in pursuance of these duties.

17 Measures taken by the Assured or the Underwriters with the object of saving, protecting or recovering the subject-matter insured shall not be considered as a waiver or acceptance of abandonment or otherwise prejudice the rights of either party. *(Waiver Clause)*

AVOIDANCE OF DELAY

18 It is a condition of this insurance that the Assured shall act with reasonable despatch in all circumstances within their control. *(Reasonable Despatch Clause)*

LAW AND PRACTICE

19 This insurance is subject to English law and practice. *(English Law and Practice Clause)*

NOTE:— *It is necessary for the Assured when they become aware of an event which is "held covered" under this insurance to give prompt notice to the Underwriters and the right to such cover is dependent upon compliance with this obligation.*

---

3 Institute Cargo Clauses (B)

1/1/82 **(FOR USE ONLY WITH THE NEW MARINE POLICY FORM)**

INSTITUTE CARGO CLAUSES (B)

RISKS COVERED

1 This insurance covers, except as provided in Clauses 4, 5, 6 and 7 below,   *Risks*
   Clause

  1.1   loss of or damage to the subject-matter insured reasonably attributable to

  1.1.1   fire or explosion

  1.1.2   vessel or craft being stranded grounded sunk or capsized

  1.1.3   overturning or derailment of land conveyance

  1.1.4   collision or contact of vessel craft or conveyance with any external object other than water

  1.1.5   discharge of cargo at a port of distress

  1.1.6   earthquake volcanic eruption or lightning,

  1.2   loss of or damage to the subject-matter insured caused by

  1.2.1   general average sacrifice

  1.2.2   jettison or washing overboard

  1.2.3   entry of sea lake or river water into vessel craft hold conveyance container liftvan or place of storage,

  1.3   total loss of any package lost overboard or dropped whilst loading on to, or unloading from, vessel or craft.

2 This insurance covers general average and salvage charges, adjusted or determined according to the contract of   *General*
affreightment and/or the governing law and practice, incurred to avoid or in connection with the avoidance of   *Average*
loss from any cause except those excluded in Clauses 4, 5, 6 and 7 or elsewhere in this insurance.   *Clause*

3 This insurance is extended to indemnify the Assured against such proportion of liability under the   *"Both to*
contract of affreightment "Both to Blame Collision" Clause as is in respect of a loss recoverable hereunder.   *Blame*
In the event of any claim by shipowners under the said Clause the Assured agree to notify the Under-   *Collision"*
writers who shall have the right, at their own cost and expense, to defend the Assured against such claim.   *Clause*

EXCLUSIONS

4 In no case shall this insurance cover   *General*
   Exclusions
   Clause

  4.1   loss damage or expense attributable to wilful misconduct of the Assured

  4.2   ordinary leakage, ordinary loss in weight or volume, or ordinary wear and tear of the subject-matter insured

  4.3   loss damage or expense caused by insufficiency or unsuitability of packing or preparation of the subject-matter insured (for the purpose of this Clause 4.3 "packing" shall be deemed to include stowage in a container or liftvan but only when such stowage is carried out prior to attachment of this insurance or by the Assured or their servants)

  4.4   loss damage or expense caused by inherent vice or nature of the subject-matter insured

  4.5   loss damage or expense proximately caused by delay, even though the delay be caused by a risk insured against (except expenses payable under Clause 2 above)

  4.6   loss damage or expense arising from insolvency or financial default of the owners managers charterers or operators of the vessel

  4.7   deliberate damage to or deliberate destruction of the subject-matter insured or any part thereof by the wrongful act of any person or persons

  4.8   loss damage or expense arising from the use of any weapon of war employing atomic or nuclear fission and/or fusion or other like reaction or radioactive force or matter.

5   5.1   In no case shall this insurance cover loss damage or expense arising from   *Unseaworthiness*
   and Unfitness

         unseaworthiness of vessel or craft,   *Exclusion*

         unfitness of vessel craft conveyance container or liftvan for the safe carriage of the subject-matter   *Clause*
         insured,

         where the Assured or their servants are privy to such unseaworthiness or unfitness, at the time the subject-matter insured is loaded therein.

  5.2   The Underwriters waive any breach of the implied warranties of seaworthiness of the ship and fitness of the ship to carry the subject-matter insured to destination, unless the Assured or their servants are privy to such unseaworthiness or unfitness.

6 In no case shall this insurance cover loss damage or expense caused by   *War*
   Exclusion
   Clause

  6.1   war civil war revolution rebellion insurrection, or civil strife arising therefrom, or any hostile act by or against a belligerent power

  6.2   capture seizure arrest restraint or detainment, and the consequences thereof or any attempt thereat

  6.3   derelict mines torpedoes bombs or other derelict weapons of war.

7 In no case shall this insurance cover loss damage or expense   *Strikes*
   Exclusion
   Clause

  7.1   caused by strikers, locked-out workmen, or persons taking part in labour disturbances, riots or civil commotions

  7.2   resulting from strikes, lock-outs, labour disturbances, riots or civil commotions

  7.3   caused by any terrorist or any person acting from a political motive.

DURATION

8   8.1   This insurance attaches from the time the goods leave the warehouse or place of storage at the   *Transit*
place named herein for the commencement of the transit, continues during the ordinary course of   *Clause*
transit and terminates either

  8.1.1   on delivery to the Consignees' or other final warehouse or place of storage at the destination named herein,

  8.1.2   on delivery to any other warehouse or place of storage, whether prior to or at the destination named herein, which the Assured elect to use either

  8.1.2.1   for storage other than in the ordinary course of transit or

  8.1.2.2   for allocation or distribution,

         or

  8.1.3   on the expiry of 60 days after completion of discharge overside of the goods hereby insured from the oversea vessel at the final port of discharge,

       whichever shall first occur.

Continued

8.2 If, after discharge overside from the oversea vessel at the final port of discharge, but prior to termination of this insurance, the goods are to be forwarded to a destination other than that to which they are insured hereunder, this insurance, whilst remaining subject to termination as provided for above, shall not extend beyond the commencement of transit to such other destination.

8.3 This insurance shall remain in force (subject to termination as provided for above and to the provisions of Clause 9 below) during delay beyond the control of the Assured, any deviation, forced discharge, reshipment or transhipment and during any variation of the adventure arising from the exercise of a liberty granted to shipowners or charterers under the contract of affreightment.

9 If owing to circumstances beyond the control of the Assured either the contract of carriage is terminated at a port or place other than the destination named therein or the transit is otherwise terminated before delivery of the goods as provided for in Clause 8 above, then this insurance shall also terminate *unless prompt notice is given to the Underwriters and continuation of cover is requested when the insurance shall remain in force, subject to an additional premium if required by the Underwriters,* either
Termination of Contract of Carriage Clause

9.1 until the goods are sold and delivered at such port or place, or, unless otherwise specially agreed, until the expiry of 60 days after arrival of the goods hereby insured at such port or place, whichever shall first occur,

or

9.2 if the goods are forwarded within the said period of 60 days (or any agreed extension thereof) to the destination named herein or to any other destination, until terminated in accordance with the provisions of Clause 8 above.

10 Where, after attachment of this insurance, the destination is changed by the Assured, *held covered at a premium and on conditions to be arranged subject to prompt notice being given to the Underwriters.*
Change of Voyage Clause

CLAIMS

11 11.1 In order to recover under this insurance the Assured must have an insurable interest in the subject-matter insured at the time of the loss.
Insurable Interest Clause

11.2 Subject to 11.1 above, the Assured shall be entitled to recover for insured loss occurring during the period covered by this insurance, notwithstanding that the loss occurred before the contract of insurance was concluded, unless the Assured were aware of the loss and the Underwriters were not.

12 Where, as a result of the operation of a risk covered by this insurance, the insured transit is terminated at a port or place other than that to which the subject-matter is covered under this insurance, the Underwriters will reimburse the Assured for any extra charges properly and reasonably incurred in unloading storing and forwarding the subject-matter to the destination to which it is insured hereunder.
Forwarding Charges Clause

This Clause 12, which does not apply to general average or salvage charges, shall be subject to the exclusions contained in Clauses 4, 5, 6 and 7 above, and shall not include charges arising from the fault negligence insolvency or financial default of the Assured or their servants.

13 No claim for Constructive Total Loss shall be recoverable hereunder unless the subject-matter insured is reasonably abandoned either on account of its actual total loss appearing to be unavoidable or because the cost of recovering, reconditioning and forwarding the subject-matter to the destination to which it is insured would exceed its value on arrival.
Constructive Total Loss Clause

14 14.1 If any Increased Value insurance is effected by the Assured on the cargo insured herein the agreed value of the cargo shall be deemed to be increased to the total amount insured under this insurance and all Increased Value insurances covering the loss, and liability under this insurance shall be in such proportion as the sum insured herein bears to such total amount insured.
Increased Value Clause

In the event of claim the Assured shall provide the Underwriters with evidence of the amounts insured under all other insurances.

14.2 **Where this insurance is on Increased Value the following clause shall apply:**
The agreed value of the cargo shall be deemed to be equal to the total amount insured under the primary insurance and all Increased Value insurances covering the loss and effected on the cargo by the Assured, and liability under this insurance shall be in such proportion as the sum insured herein bears to such total amount insured.

In the event of claim the Assured shall provide the Underwriters with evidence of the amounts insured under all other insurances.

BENEFIT OF INSURANCE

15 This insurance shall not inure to the benefit of the carrier or other bailee.
Not to Inure Clause

MINIMISING LOSSES

16 It is the duty of the Assured and their servants and agents in respect of loss recoverable hereunder
Duty of Assured Clause

16.1 to take such measures as may be reasonable for the purpose of averting or minimising such loss, and

16.2 to ensure that all rights against carriers, bailees or other third parties are properly preserved and exercised

and the Underwriters will, in addition to any loss recoverable hereunder, reimburse the Assured for any charges properly and reasonably incurred in pursuance of these duties.

17 Measures taken by the Assured or the Underwriters with the object of saving, protecting or recovering the subject-matter insured shall not be considered as a waiver or acceptance of abandonment or otherwise prejudice the rights of either party.
Waiver Clause

AVOIDANCE OF DELAY

18 It is a condition of this insurance that the Assured shall act with reasonable despatch in all circumstances within their control.
Reasonable Despatch Clause

LAW AND PRACTICE

19 This insurance is subject to English law and practice.
English Law and Practice Clause

NOTE:— It is necessary for the Assured when they become aware of an event which is "held covered" under this insurance to give prompt notice to the Underwriters and the right to such cover is dependent upon compliance with this obligation.

CL. 253.   *Sold by Witherby & Co. Ltd., London.*

4   Institute Cargo Clauses (C)

1/1/82   **(FOR USE ONLY WITH THE NEW MARINE POLICY FORM)**

INSTITUTE CARGO CLAUSES (C)

RISKS COVERED

1   This insurance covers, except as provided in Clauses 4, 5, 6 and 7 below,   Risks
                                                                                        Clause
    1.1   loss of or damage to the subject-matter insured reasonably attributable to

    1.1.1   fire or explosion

    1.1.2   vessel or craft being stranded grounded sunk or capsized

    1.1.3   overturning or derailment of land conveyance

    1.1.4   collision or contact of vessel craft or conveyance with any external object other than water

    1.1.5   discharge of cargo at a port of distress,

    1.2   loss of or damage to the subject-matter insured caused by

    1.2.1   general average sacrifice

    1.2.2   jettison.

2   This insurance covers general average and salvage charges, adjusted or determined according to the contract of   General
affreightment and/or the governing law and practice, incurred to avoid or in connection with the avoidance of   Average
loss from any cause except those excluded in Clauses 4, 5, 6 and 7 or elsewhere in this insurance.   Clause

3   This insurance is extended to indemnify the Assured against such proportion of liability under the   "Both to
contract of affreightment "Both to Blame Collision" Clause as is in respect of a loss recoverable hereunder.   Blame
In the event of any claim by shipowners under the said Clause the Assured agree to notify the Under-   Collision"
writers who shall have the right, at their own cost and expense, to defend the Assured against such claim.   Clause

EXCLUSIONS

4   In no case shall this insurance cover   General
                                                  Exclusions
    4.1   loss damage or expense attributable to wilful misconduct of the Assured   Clause

    4.2   ordinary leakage, ordinary loss in weight or volume, or ordinary wear and tear of the subject-matter
insured

    4.3   loss damage or expense caused by insufficiency or unsuitability of packing or preparation of the
subject-matter insured (for the purpose of this Clause 4.3 "packing" shall be deemed to include
stowage in a container or liftvan but only when such stowage is carried out prior to attachment of this
insurance or by the Assured or their servants)

    4.4   loss damage or expense caused by inherent vice or nature of the subject-matter insured

    4.5   loss damage or expense proximately caused by delay, even though the delay be caused by a risk insured
against (except expenses payable under Clause 2 above)

    4.6   loss damage or expense arising from insolvency or financial default of the owners managers charterers
or operators of the vessel

    4.7   deliberate damage to or deliberate destruction of the subject-matter insured or any part thereof by the
wrongful act of any person or persons

    4.8   loss damage or expense arising from the use of any weapon of war employing atomic or nuclear fission
and/or fusion or other like reaction or radioactive force or matter.

5   5.1   In no case shall this insurance cover loss damage or expense arising from   Unseaworthiness
                                                                                           and Unfitness
    unseaworthiness of vessel or craft,   Exclusion
                                                                  Clause
    unfitness of vessel craft conveyance container or liftvan for the safe carriage of the subject-matter
insured,

    where the Assured or their servants are privy to such unseaworthiness or unfitness, at the time the
subject-matter insured is loaded therein.

    5.2   The Underwriters waive any breach of the implied warranties of seaworthiness of the ship and fitness of
the ship to carry the subject-matter insured to destination, unless the Assured or their servants are privy
to such unseaworthiness or unfitness.

6   In no case shall this insurance cover loss damage or expense caused by   War
                                                                                   Exclusion
    6.1   war civil war revolution rebellion insurrection, or civil strife arising therefrom, or any hostile act by or   Clause
against a belligerent power

    6.2   capture seizure arrest restraint or detainment, and the consequences thereof or any attempt thereat

    6.3   derelict mines torpedoes bombs or other derelict weapons of war.

7   In no case shall this insurance cover loss damage or expense   Strikes
                                                                         Exclusion
    7.1   caused by strikers, locked-out workmen, or persons taking part in labour disturbances, riots or civil   Clause
commotions

    7.2   resulting from strikes, lock-outs, labour disturbances, riots or civil commotions

    7.3   caused by any terrorist or any person acting from a political motive.

DURATION

8   8.1   This insurance attaches from the time the goods leave the warehouse or place of storage at the   Transit
place named herein for the commencement of the transit, continues during the ordinary course of   Clause
transit and terminates either

    8.1.1   on delivery to the Consignees' or other final warehouse or place of storage at the destination
named herein,

    8.1.2   on delivery to any other warehouse or place of storage, whether prior to or at the destination
named herein, which the Assured elect to use either

    8.1.2.1   for storage other than in the ordinary course of transit or

    8.1.2.2   for allocation or distribution,

        or

    8.1.3   on the expiry of 60 days after completion of discharge overside of the goods hereby insured
from the oversea vessel at the final port of discharge,

    whichever shall first occur.

Continued

8.2 If, after discharge overside from the oversea vessel at the final port of discharge, but prior to termination of this insurance, the goods are to be forwarded to a destination other than that to which they are insured hereunder, this insurance, whilst remaining subject to termination as provided for above, shall not extend beyond the commencement of transit to such other destination.

8.3 This insurance shall remain in force (subject to termination as provided for above and to the provisions of Clause 9 below) during delay beyond the control of the Assured, any deviation, forced discharge, reshipment or transhipment and during any variation of the adventure arising from the exercise of a liberty granted to shipowners or charterers under the contract of affreightment.

9 If owing to circumstances beyond the control of the Assured either the contract of carriage is terminated at a port or place other than the destination named therein or the transit is otherwise terminated before delivery of the goods as provided for in Clause 8 above, then this insurance shall also terminate *unless prompt notice is given to the Underwriters and continuation of cover is requested when the insurance shall remain in force, subject to an additional premium if required by the Underwriters*, either

Termination of Contract of Carriage Clause

9.1 until the goods are sold and delivered at such port or place, or, unless otherwise specially agreed, until the expiry of 60 days after arrival of the goods hereby insured at such port or place, whichever shall first occur,

or

9.2 if the goods are forwarded within the said period of 60 days (or any agreed extension thereof) to the destination named herein or to any other destination, until terminated in accordance with the provisions of Clause 8 above.

10 Where, after attachment of this insurance, the destination is changed by the Assured, *held covered at a premium and on conditions to be arranged subject to prompt notice being given to the Underwriters.*

Change of Voyage Clause

CLAIMS

11 11.1 In order to recover under this insurance the Assured must have an insurable interest in the subject-matter insured at the time of the loss.

Insurable Interest Clause

11.2 Subject to 11.1 above, the Assured shall be entitled to recover for insured loss occurring during the period covered by this insurance, notwithstanding that the loss occurred before the contract of insurance was concluded, unless the Assured were aware of the loss and the Underwriters were not.

12 Where, as a result of the operation of a risk covered by this insurance, the insured transit is terminated at a port or place other than that to which the subject-matter is covered under this insurance, the Underwriters will reimburse the Assured for any extra charges properly and reasonably incurred in unloading storing and forwarding the subject-matter to the destination to which it is insured hereunder.

Forwarding Charges Clause

This Clause 12, which does not apply to general average or salvage charges, shall be subject to the exclusions contained in Clauses 4, 5, 6 and 7 above, and shall not include charges arising from the fault negligence insolvency or financial default of the Assured or their servants.

13 No claim for Constructive Total Loss shall be recoverable hereunder unless the subject-matter insured is reasonably abandoned either on account of its actual total loss appearing to be unavoidable or because the cost of recovering, reconditioning and forwarding the subject-matter to the destination to which it is insured would exceed its value on arrival.

Constructive Total Loss Clause

14 14.1 If any Increased Value insurance is effected by the Assured on the cargo insured herein the agreed value of the cargo shall be deemed to be increased to the total amount insured under this insurance and all Increased Value insurances covering the loss, and liability under this insurance shall be in such proportion as the sum insured herein bears to such total amount insured.
In the event of claim the Assured shall provide the Underwriters with evidence of the amounts insured under all other insurances.

Increased Value Clause

14.2 **Where this insurance is on Increased Value the following clause shall apply:**
The agreed value of the cargo shall be deemed to be equal to the total amount insured under the primary insurance and all Increased Value insurances covering the loss and effected on the cargo by the Assured, and liability under this insurance shall be in such proportion as the sum insured herein bears to such total amount insured.
In the event of claim the Assured shall provide the Underwriters with evidence of the amounts insured under all other insurances.

BENEFIT OF INSURANCE

15 This insurance shall not inure to the benefit of the carrier or other bailee.

Not to Inure Clause

MINIMISING LOSSES

16 It is the duty of the Assured and their servants and agents in respect of loss recoverable hereunder

Duty of Assured Clause

16.1 to take such measures as may be reasonable for the purpose of averting or minimising such loss, and

16.2 to ensure that all rights against carriers, bailees or other third parties are properly preserved and exercised

and the Underwriters will, in addition to any loss recoverable hereunder, reimburse the Assured for any charges properly and reasonably incurred in pursuance of these duties.

17 Measures taken by the Assured or the Underwriters with the object of saving, protecting or recovering the subject-matter insured shall not be considered as a waiver or acceptance of abandonment or otherwise prejudice the rights of either party.

Waiver Clause

AVOIDANCE OF DELAY

18 It is a condition of this insurance that the Assured shall act with reasonable despatch in all circumstances within their control.

Reasonable Despatch Clause

LAW AND PRACTICE

19 This insurance is subject to English law and practice.

English Law and Practice Clause

NOTE:— *It is necessary for the Assured when they become aware of an event which is "held covered" under this insurance to give prompt notice to the Underwriters and the right to such cover is dependent upon compliance with this obligation.*

5   Institute Time Clauses — Hulls

1/10/83   **(FOR USE ONLY WITH THE NEW MARINE POLICY FORM)**

INSTITUTE TIME CLAUSES
HULLS

This insurance is subject to English law and practice

1	**NAVIGATION**		1

1 **NAVIGATION**   1

1.1   The Vessel is covered subject to the provisions of this insurance at all times and has leave to sail or 2
navigate with or without pilots, to go on trial trips and to assist and tow vessels or craft in distress, but it 3
is warranted that the Vessel shall not be towed, except as is customary or to the first safe port or place 4
when in need of assistance, or undertake towage or salvage services under a contract previously arranged 5
by the Assured and/or Owners and/or Managers and/or Charterers. This Clause 1.1 shall not exclude 6
customary towage in connection with loading and discharging. 7

1.2   In the event of the Vessel being employed in trading operations which entail cargo loading or discharging 8
at sea from or into another vessel (not being a harbour or inshore craft) no claim shall be recoverable 9
under this insurance for loss of or damage to the Vessel or liability to any other vessel arising from such 10
loading or discharging operations, including whilst approaching, lying alongside and leaving, unless 11
previous notice that the Vessel is to be employed in such operations has been given to the Underwriters 12
and any amended terms of cover and any additional premium required by them have been agreed. 13

1.3   In the event of the Vessel sailing (with or without cargo) with an intention of being (a) broken up, or (b) 14
sold for breaking up, any claim for loss of or damage to the Vessel occurring subsequent to such sailing 15
shall be limited to the market value of the Vessel as scrap at the time when the loss or damage is sustained, 16
unless previous notice has been given to the Underwriters and any amendments to the terms of cover, 17
insured value and premium required by them have been agreed. Nothing in this Clause 1.3 shall affect 18
claims under Clauses 8 and/or 11. 19

2   **CONTINUATION**   20

Should the Vessel at the expiration of this insurance be at sea or in distress or at a port of refuge or of call, she 21
shall, provided previous notice be given to the Underwriters, be held covered at a pro rata monthly premium to her 22
port of destination. 23

3   **BREACH OF WARRANTY**   24

Held covered in case of any breach of warranty as to cargo, trade, locality, towage, salvage services or date of 25
sailing, provided notice be given to the Underwriters immediately after receipt of advices and any amended terms 26
of cover and any additional premium required by them be agreed. 27

4   **TERMINATION**   28

This Clause 4 shall prevail notwithstanding any provision whether written typed or printed in this insurance 29
inconsistent therewith. 30

Unless the Underwriters agree to the contrary in writing, this insurance shall terminate automatically at the time of 31

4.1   change of the Classification Society of the Vessel, or change, suspension, discontinuance, withdrawal or 32
expiry of her Class therein, provided that if the Vessel is at sea such automatic termination shall be 33
deferred until arrival at her next port. However where such change, suspension, discontinuance or 34
withdrawal of her Class has resulted from loss or damage covered by Clause 6 of this insurance or which 35
would be covered by an insurance of the Vessel subject to current Institute War and Strikes Clauses Hulls- 36
Time such automatic termination shall only operate should the Vessel sail from her next port without the 37
prior approval of the Classification Society, 38

4.2   any change, voluntary or otherwise, in the ownership or flag, transfer to new management, or charter on 39
a bareboat basis, or requisition for title or use of the Vessel, provided that, if the Vessel has cargo on 40
board and has already sailed from her loading port or is at sea in ballast, such automatic termination shall 41
if required be deferred, whilst the Vessel continues her planned voyage, until arrival at final port of 42
discharge if with cargo or at port of destination if in ballast. However, in the event of requisition for title 43
or use without the prior execution of a written agreement by the Assured, such automatic termination 44
shall occur fifteen days after such requisition whether the Vessel is at sea or in port. 45

A pro rata daily net return of premium shall be made. 46

5   **ASSIGNMENT**   47

No assignment of or interest in this insurance or in any moneys which may be or become payable thereunder is to 48
be binding on or recognised by the Underwriters unless a dated notice of such assignment or interest signed by the 49
Assured, and by the assignor in the case of subsequent assignment, is endorsed on the Policy and the Policy with 50
such endorsement is produced before payment of any claim or return of premium thereunder. 51

6   **PERILS**   52

6.1   This insurance covers loss of or damage to the subject-matter insured caused by   53

6.1.1   perils of the seas rivers lakes or other navigable waters   54

6.1.2   fire, explosion   55

6.1.3   violent theft by persons from outside the Vessel   56

6.1.4   jettison   57

6.1.5   piracy   58

6.1.6   breakdown of or accident to nuclear installations or reactors   59

6.1.7   contact with aircraft or similar objects, or objects falling therefrom, land conveyance, dock or 60
harbour equipment or installation 61

6.1.8   earthquake volcanic eruption or lightning.   62

(Continued)

6.2	This insurance covers loss of or damage to the subject-matter insured caused by	63
6.2.1	accidents in loading discharging or shifting cargo or fuel	64
6.2.2	bursting of boilers breakage of shafts or any latent defect in the machinery or hull	65
6.2.3	negligence of Master Officers Crew or Pilots	66
6.2.4	negligence of repairers or charterers provided such repairers or charterers are not an Assured hereunder	67
6.2.5	barratry of Master Officers or Crew,	68
	provided such loss or damage has not resulted from want of due diligence by the Assured, Owners or Managers.	69 70
6.3	Master Officers Crew or Pilots not to be considered Owners within the meaning of this Clause 6 should they hold shares in the Vessel.	71 72

7 POLLUTION HAZARD 73

This insurance covers loss of or damage to the Vessel caused by any governmental authority acting under the powers vested in it to prevent or mitigate a pollution hazard or threat thereof, resulting directly from damage to the Vessel for which the Underwriters are liable under this insurance, provided such act of governmental authority has not resulted from want of due diligence by the Assured, the Owners, or Managers of the Vessel or any of them to prevent or mitigate such hazard or threat. Master, Officers, Crew or Pilots not to be considered Owners within the meaning of this Clause 7 should they hold shares in the Vessel. 74 75 76 77 78 79

8 3/4THS COLLISION LIABILITY 80

8.1	The Underwriters agree to indemnify the Assured for three-fourths of any sum or sums paid by the Assured to any other person or persons by reason of the Assured becoming legally liable by way of damages for	81 82 83
8.1.1	loss of or damage to any other vessel or property on any other vessel	84
8.1.2	delay to or loss of use of any such other vessel or property thereon	85
8.1.3	general average of, salvage of, or salvage under contract of, any such other vessel or property thereon,	86 87
	where such payment by the Assured is in consequence of the Vessel hereby insured coming into collision with any other vessel.	88 89
8.2	The indemnity provided by this Clause 8 shall be in addition to the indemnity provided by the other terms and conditions of this insurance and shall be subject to the following provisions:	90 91
8.2.1	Where the insured Vessel is in collision with another vessel and both vessels are to blame then, unless the liability of one or both vessels becomes limited by law, the indemnity under this Clause 8 shall be calculated on the principle of cross-liabilities as if the respective Owners had been compelled to pay to each other such proportion of each other's damages as may have been properly allowed in ascertaining the balance or sum payable by or to the Assured in consequence of the collision.	92 93 94 95 96
8.2.2	In no case shall the Underwriters' total liability under Clauses 8.1 and 8.2 exceed their proportionate part of three-fourths of the insured value of the Vessel hereby insured in respect of any one collision.	97 98
8.3	The Underwriters will also pay three-fourths of the legal costs incurred by the Assured or which the Assured may be compelled to pay in contesting liability or taking proceedings to limit liability, with the prior written consent of the Underwriters.	99 100 101

EXCLUSIONS 102

8.4	Provided always that this Clause 8 shall in no case extend to any sum which the Assured shall pay for or in respect of	103 104
8.4.1	removal or disposal of obstructions, wrecks, cargoes or any other thing whatsoever	105
8.4.2	any real or personal property or thing whatsoever except other vessels or property on other vessels	106
8.4.3	the cargo or other property on, or the engagements of, the insured Vessel	107
8.4.4	loss of life, personal injury or illness	108
8.4.5	pollution or contamination of any real or personal property or thing whatsoever (except other vessels with which the insured Vessel is in collision or property on any other vessels).	109 110

9 SISTERSHIP 111

Should the Vessel hereby insured come into collision with or receive salvage services from another vessel belonging wholly or in part to the same Owners or under the same management, the Assured shall have the same rights under this insurance as they would have were the other vessel the property of Owners not interested in the Vessel hereby insured; but in such cases the liability for the collision or the amount payable for the services rendered shall be referred to a sole arbitrator to be agreed upon between the Underwriters and the Assured. 112 113 114 115 116

10 NOTICE OF CLAIM AND TENDERS 117

10.1	In the event of accident whereby loss or damage may result in a claim under this insurance, notice shall be given to the Underwriters prior to survey and also, if the Vessel is abroad, to the nearest Lloyd's Agent so that a surveyor may be appointed to represent the Underwriters should they so desire.	118 119 120
10.2	The Underwriters shall be entitled to decide the port to which the Vessel shall proceed for docking or repair (the actual additional expense of the voyage arising from compliance with the Underwriters' requirements being refunded to the Assured) and shall have a right of veto concerning a place of repair or a repairing firm.	121 122 123 124
10.3	The Underwriters may also take tenders or may require further tenders to be taken for the repair of the Vessel. Where such a tender has been taken and a tender is accepted with the approval of the Underwriters, an allowance shall be made at the rate of 30% per annum on the insured value for time lost between the despatch of the invitations to tender required by Underwriters and the acceptance of a tender to the extent that such time is lost solely as the result of tenders having been taken and provided that the tender is accepted without delay after receipt of the Underwriters' approval.	125 126 127 128 129 130
	Due credit shall be given against the allowance as above for any amounts recovered in respect of fuel and stores and wages and maintenance of the Master Officers and Crew or any member thereof, including amounts allowed in general average, and for any amounts recovered from third parties in respect of damages for detention and/or loss of profit and/or running expenses, for the period covered by the tender allowance or any part thereof.	131 132 133 134 135
	Where a part of the cost of the repair of damage other than a fixed deductible is not recoverable from the Underwriters the allowance shall be reduced by a similar proportion.	136 137
10.4	In the event of failure to comply with the conditions of this Clause 10 a deduction of 15% shall be made from the amount of the ascertained claim.	138 139

(Continued)

11 GENERAL AVERAGE AND SALVAGE   140

11.1   This insurance covers the Vessel's proportion of salvage, salvage charges and/or general average, reduced   141
in respect of any under-insurance, but in case of general average sacrifice of the Vessel the Assured may   142
recover in respect of the whole loss without first enforcing their right of contribution from other parties.   143

11.2   Adjustment to be according to the law and practice obtaining at the place where the adventure ends, as if   144
the contract of affreightment contained no special terms upon the subject; but where the contract of   145
affreightment so provides the adjustment shall be according to the York-Antwerp Rules.   146

11.3   When the Vessel sails in ballast, not under charter, the provisions of the York-Antwerp Rules, 1974   147
(excluding Rules XX and XXI) shall be applicable, and the voyage for this purpose shall be deemed to   148
continue from the port or place of departure until the arrival of the Vessel at the first port or place   149
thereafter other than a port or place of refuge or a port or place of call for bunkering only. If at any such   150
intermediate port or place there is an abandonment of the adventure originally contemplated the voyage   151
shall thereupon be deemed to be terminated.   152

11.4   No claim under this Clause 11 shall in any case be allowed where the loss was not incurred to avoid or in   153
connection with the avoidance of a peril insured against.   154

12 DEDUCTIBLE   155

12.1   No claim arising from a peril insured against shall be payable under this insurance unless the aggregate of   156
all such claims arising out of each separate accident or occurrence (including claims under Clauses 8, 11   157

and 13) exceeds ....in which case this sum shall be   158
deducted. Nevertheless the expense of sighting the bottom after stranding, if reasonably incurred   159
specially for that purpose, shall be paid even if no damage be found. This Clause 12.1 shall not apply to a   160
claim for total or constructive total loss of the Vessel or, in the event of such a claim, to any associated   161
claim under Clause 13 arising from the same accident or occurrence.   162

12.2   Claims for damage by heavy weather occurring during a single sea passage between two successive ports   163
shall be treated as being due to one accident. In the case of such heavy weather extending over a period   164
not wholly covered by this insurance the deductible to be applied to the claim recoverable hereunder shall   165
be the proportion of the above deductible that the number of days of such heavy weather falling within   166
the period of this insurance bears to the number of days of heavy weather during the single sea passage.   167
The expression "heavy weather" in this Clause 12.2 shall be deemed to include contact with floating ice.   168

12.3   Excluding any interest comprised therein, recoveries against any claim which is subject to the above   169
deductible shall be credited to the Underwriters in full to the extent of the sum by which the aggregate of   170
the claim unreduced by any recoveries exceeds the above deductible.   171

12.4   Interest comprised in recoveries shall be apportioned between the Assured and the Underwriters, taking   172
into account the sums paid by the Underwriters and the dates when such payments were made, i   173
notwithstanding that by the addition of interest the Underwriters may receive a larger sum than they have   174
paid.   175

13 DUTY OF ASSURED (SUE AND LABOUR)   176

13.1   In case of any loss or misfortune it is the duty of the Assured and their servants and agents to take such   177
measures as may be reasonable for the purpose of averting or minimising a loss which would be   178
recoverable under this insurance.   179

13.2   Subject to the provisions below and to Clause 12 the Underwriters will contribute to charges properly and   180
reasonably incurred by the Assured their servants or agents for such measures. General average, salvage   181
charges (except as provided for in Clause 13.5) and collision defence or attack costs are not recoverable   182
under this Clause 13.   183

13.3   Measures taken by the Assured or the Underwriters with the object of saving, protecting or recovering the   184
subject-matter insured shall not be considered as a waiver or acceptance of abandonment or otherwise   185
prejudice the rights of either party.   186

13.4   When expenses are incurred pursuant to this Clause 13 the liability under this insurance shall not exceed   187
the proportion of such expenses that the amount insured hereunder bears to the value of the Vessel as   188
stated herein, or to the sound value of the Vessel at the time of the occurrence giving rise to the expenditure   189
if the sound value exceeds that value. Where the Underwriters have admitted a claim for total loss and   190
property insured by this insurance is saved, the foregoing provisions shall not apply unless the expenses of   191
suing and labouring exceed the value of such property saved and then shall apply only to the amount of   192
the expenses which is in excess of such value.   193

13.5   When a claim for total loss of the Vessel is admitted under this insurance and expenses have been   194
reasonably incurred in saving or attempting to save the Vessel and other property and there are no   195
proceeds, or the expenses exceed the proceeds, then this insurance shall bear its pro rata share of such   196
proportion of the expenses, or of the expenses in excess of the proceeds, as the case may be, as may   197
reasonably be regarded as having been incurred in respect of the Vessel; but if the Vessel be insured for   198
less than its sound value at the time of the occurrence giving rise to the expenditure, the amount   199
recoverable under this clause shall be reduced in proportion to the under-insurance.   200

13.6   The sum recoverable under this Clause 13 shall be in addition to the loss otherwise recoverable under this   201
insurance but shall in no circumstances exceed the amount insured under this insurance in respect of the   202
Vessel.   203

14 NEW FOR OLD   204
Claims payable without deduction new for old.   205

(Continued)

15 BOTTOM TREATMENT   206
In no case shall a claim be allowed in respect of scraping gritblasting and/or other surface preparation or painting   207
of the Vessel's bottom except that   208

15.1   gritblasting and/or other surface preparation of new bottom plates ashore and supplying and applying   209
any "shop" primer thereto,   210

15.2   gritblasting and/or other surface preparation of: 211
the butts or area of plating immediately adjacent to any renewed or refitted plating damaged during the   212
course of welding and/or repairs,   213
areas of plating damaged during the course of fairing, either in place or ashore,   214

15.3   supplying and applying the first coat of primer/anti-corrosive to those particular areas mentioned in 15.1   215
and 15.2 above,   216

shall be allowed as part of the reasonable cost of repairs in respect of bottom plating damaged by an insured peril.   217

16 WAGES AND MAINTENANCE   218
No claim shall be allowed, other than in general average, for wages and maintenance of the Master, Officers and   219
Crew, or any member thereof, except when incurred solely for the necessary removal of the Vessel from one port   220
to another for the repair of damage covered by the Underwriters, or for trial trips for such repairs, and then only   221
for such wages and maintenance as are incurred whilst the Vessel is under way.   222

17 AGENCY COMMISSION   223
In no case shall any sum be allowed under this insurance either by way of remuneration of the Assured for time   224
and trouble taken to obtain and supply information or documents or in respect of the commission or charges of   225
any manager, agent, managing or agency company or the like, appointed by or on behalf of the Assured to   226
perform such services.   227

18 UNREPAIRED DAMAGE   228
18.1   The measure of indemnity in respect of claims for unrepaired damage shall be the reasonable depreciation   229
in the market value of the Vessel at the time this insurance terminates arising from such unrepaired   230
damage, but not exceeding the reasonable cost of repairs.   231

18.2   In no case shall the Underwriters be liable for unrepaired damage in the event of a subsequent total loss   232
(whether or not covered under this insurance) sustained during the period covered by this insurance or   233
any extension thereof.   234

18.3   The Underwriters shall not be liable in respect of unrepaired damage for more than the insured value at   235
the time this insurance terminates.   236

19 CONSTRUCTIVE TOTAL LOSS   237
19.1   In ascertaining whether the Vessel is a constructive total loss, the insured value shall be taken as the   238
repaired value and nothing in respect of the damaged or break-up value of the Vessel or wreck shall be   239
taken into account.   240

19.2   No claim for constructive total loss based upon the cost of recovery and/or repair of the Vessel shall be   241
recoverable hereunder unless such cost would exceed the insured value. In making this determination,   242
only the cost relating to a single accident or sequence of damages arising from the same accident shall be   243
taken into account.   244

20 FREIGHT WAIVER   245
In the event of total or constructive total loss no claim to be made by the Underwriters for freight whether notice   246
of abandonment has been given or not.   247

21 DISBURSEMENTS WARRANTY   248
21.1   Additional insurances as follows are permitted: 249

21.1.1   *Disbursements, Managers' Commissions, Profits or Excess or Increased Value of Hull and*   250
Machinery. A sum not exceeding 25% of the value stated herein.   251

21.1.2   *Freight, Chartered Freight or Anticipated Freight, insured for time.* A sum not exceeding 25% of   252
the value as stated herein less any sum insured, however described, under 21.1.1.   253

21.1.3   *Freight or Hire, under contracts for voyage.* A sum not exceeding the gross freight or hire for the   254
current cargo passage and next succeeding cargo passage (such insurance to include, if required, a   255
preliminary and an intermediate ballast passage) plus the charges of insurance. In the case of a   256
voyage charter where payment is made on a lump sum basis, the sum permitted for insurance shall be   257
calculated on the estimated duration of the voyage, subject to the limitation of two cargo passages   258
as laid down herein. Any sum insured under 21.1.2 to be taken into account and only the excess   259
thereof may be insured, which excess shall be reduced as the freight or hire is advanced or earned by   260
the gross amount so advanced or earned.   261

21.1.4   *Anticipated Freight if the Vessel sails in ballast and not under Charter.* A sum not exceeding the   262
anticipated gross freight on next cargo passage, such sum to be reasonably estimated on the basis of   263
the current rate of freight at time of insurance plus the charges of insurance. Any sum insured under   264
21.1.2 to be taken into account and only the excess thereof may be insured.   265

21.1.5   *Time Charter Hire or Charter Hire for Series of Voyages.* A sum not exceeding 50% of the gross   266
hire which is to be earned under the charter in a period not exceeding 18 months. Any sum insured   267
under 21.1.2 to be taken into account and only the excess thereof may be insured, which excess shall   268
be reduced as the hire is advanced or earned under the charter by 50% of the gross amount so   269
advanced or earned but the sum insured need not be reduced while the total of the sums insured   270
under 21.1.2 and 21.1.5 does not exceed 50% of the gross hire still to be earned under the charter.   271
An insurance under this Section may begin on the signing of the charter.   272

21.1.6   *Premiums.* A sum not exceeding the actual premiums of all interests insured for a period not   273
exceeding 12 months (excluding premiums insured under the foregoing sections but including, if   274
required, the premium or estimated calls on any Club or War etc. Risk insurance) reducing pro rata   275
monthly.   276

21.1.7   *Returns of Premium.* A sum not exceeding the actual returns which are allowable under any   277
insurance but which would not be recoverable thereunder in the event of a total loss of the Vessel   278
whether by insured perils or otherwise.   279

21.1.8   *Insurance irrespective of amount against:*   280
Any risks excluded by Clauses 23, 24, 25 and 26 below.   281

21.2   Warranted that no insurance on any interests enumerated in the foregoing 21.1.1 to 21.1.7 in excess of the   282
amounts permitted therein and no other insurance which includes total loss of the Vessel P.P.I., F.I.A.,   283
or subject to any other like term, is or shall be effected to operate during the currency of this insurance by   284
or for account of the Assured, Owners, Managers or Mortgagees. Provided always that a breach of this   285
warranty shall not afford the Underwriters any defence to a claim by a Mortgagee who has accepted this   286
insurance without knowledge of such breach.   287

(Continued)

22 RETURNS FOR LAY-UP AND CANCELLATION   288

22.1   To return as follows: 289

22.1.1   Pro rata monthly net for each uncommenced month if this insurance be cancelled by agreement.   290

22.1.2   For each period of 30 consecutive days the Vessel may be laid up in a port or in a lay-up area   291
provided such port or lay-up area is approved by the Underwriters (with special liberties as   292
hereinafter allowed)   293

(a)....................................per cent net not under repair   294

(b)....................................per cent net under repair.   295

If the Vessel is under repair during part only of a period for which a return is claimable, the return   296
shall be calculated pro rata to the number of days under each respectively.   297

22.2   PROVIDED ALWAYS THAT   298

22.2.1   a total loss of the Vessel, whether by insured perils or otherwise, has not occurred during the period   299
covered by this insurance or any extension thereof   300

22.2.2   in no case shall a return be allowed when the Vessel is lying in exposed or unprotected waters, or in a   301
port or lay-up area not approved by the Underwriters but, provided the Underwriters agree that   302
such non-approved lay-up area is deemed to be within the vicinity of the approved port or lay-up   303
area, days during which the Vessel is laid up in such non-approved lay-up area may be added to days   304
in the approved port or lay-up area to calculate a period of 30 consecutive days and a return shall be   305
allowed for the proportion of such period during which the Vessel is actually laid up in the approved   306
port or lay-up area   307

22.2.3   loading or discharging operations or the presence of cargo on board shall not debar returns but no   308
return shall be allowed for any period during which the Vessel is being used for the storage of cargo   309
or for lightering purposes   310

22.2.4   in the event of any amendment of the annual rate, the above rates of return shall be adjusted   311
accordingly   312

22.2.5   in the event of any return recoverable under this Clause 22 being based on 30 consecutive days which   313
fall on successive insurances effected for the same Assured, this insurance shall only be liable for an   314
amount calculated at pro rata of the period rates 22.1.2(a) and/or (b) above for the number of days   315
which come within the period of this insurance and to which a return is actually applicable. Such   316
overlapping period shall run, at the option of the Assured, either from the first day on which the   317
Vessel is laid up or the first day of a period of 30 consecutive days as provided under 22.1.2(a) or (b),   318
or 22.2.2 above.   319

The following clauses shall be paramount and shall override anything contained in this insurance inconsistent   320
therewith.   321

23 WAR EXCLUSION   322
In no case shall this insurance cover loss damage liability or expense caused by   323

23.1   war civil war revolution rebellion insurrection, or civil strife arising therefrom, or any hostile act by or   324
against a belligerent power   325

23.2   capture seizure arrest restraint or detainment (barratry and piracy excepted), and the consequences   326
thereof or any attempt thereat   327

23.3   derelict mines torpedoes bombs or other derelict weapons of war.   328

24 STRIKES EXCLUSION   329
In no case shall this insurance cover loss damage liability or expense caused by   330

24.1   strikers, locked-out workmen, or persons taking part in labour disturbances, riots or civil   331
commotions   332

24.2   any terrorist or any person acting from a political motive.   333

25 MALICIOUS ACTS EXCLUSION   334
In no case shall this insurance cover loss damage liability or expense arising from   335

25.1   the detonation of an explosive   336

25.2   any weapon of war   337

and caused by any person acting maliciously or from a political motive.   338

26 NUCLEAR EXCLUSION   339
In no case shall this insurance cover loss damage liability or expense arising from any weapon of war employing   340
atomic or nuclear fission and/or fusion or other like reaction or radioactive force or matter.   341

CL. 280 *Sold by Witherby & Co. Ltd., London.*

Appendix H

A Federal Marine Insurance Act

Interest in Canada on a federal marine insurance act stems from the 1983 Supreme Court of Canada judgment in the case of *Terrasses Jewellers Inc.*[1] Both the Canadian Maritime Law Association (CMLA) and the Canadian Board of Marine Underwriters (CBMU) have since that decision formed sub-committees to investigate the possibility and desirability of such legislation. Both committees have considered the 1976 Report on Marine Insurance by the Committee on the Contract of Marine Insurance, from the Civil Code Revision Office, as the basis for the new legislation. The "1976 Quebec draft" as this report in known, modernizes the language of the 1906 Marine Insurance Act and rearranges the order of the sections. The draft was prepared as a recommendation for legislation to be adopted by the Province of Quebec. The CMLA has recommended that this draft be used as the basis for federal legislation. The CBMU recommends that the 1906 Act be adopted as the legislation for the entire Country.

---

1. *Zararoralna Skupnost Triglav (Insurance Community Triglav Ltd.) v. Terrasses Jewellers Inc. et al.*, [1983] 1 S.C.R. 283, 54 N.R. 321, [1983] I.L.R. 1-1627. See also *International Terminal Operators Ltd. v. Miida Electronics Inc.*, [1986] 1 S.C.R. 752, 68 N.R. 241 (*sub nom. Miida Electronics Inc. v. Mitsui O.S.K. Lines Ltd. and ITO-International Terminal Operators Ltd.*), 28 D.L.R. (4th) 641.

Index